FINAL WAR

ε g. white

"Teach me Thy way, O Lord,
and lead me in a plain path."

Inspiration Books
Phoenix, Arizona

An Inspiration Book

Cover design by John Enright

Final War
  (Parts taken from The Great Controversey)

First printing, March 1979, 100,000
Second printing, June 1979, 175,000
Third printing, July 1980, 155,000

Published by Inspiration Books
Post Office Box 8249
Phoenix, Arizona 85066

Contents

1. The Origin of Evil 1
2. Man's Worst Enemy 14
3. Work of Evil Angels 20
4. The Apostasy 27
5. Luther's Separation From Rome 39
6. Satan's Traps 63
7. The First Great Deception 76
7A. What is The Sanctuary? 94A
8. Spiritualism 95
9. Liberty Threatened 106
10. The Impending Conflict 124
11. The Scriptures A Safeguard 135
12. The Final Warning 145
13. The Time of Trouble 155
14. God's People Delivered 176
15. Desolation of The Earth 193
16. End of The War 202

PREFACE TO THE READER

The present is a time of overwhelming interest to all living. Thinking men and women of all classes have their attention fixed on the events that seem to be hastening the world forward in an ever-increasing momentum toward its rendezvous with destiny. Statesmen, rulers, church leaders, business men, men and women everywhere sense that something great and decisive is about to take place—that the world is on the verge of a stupendous crisis.

What is the meaning of these times? What comes tomorrow? Here at last is an authoritative answer that probes the persistent realities of this tense age. Now at last you will recognize the clear-cut issues involved. In bold strokes this volume reveals what has made the United States the greatest nation of all time, but you will be shocked when you discover the greatest threat to the Constitution. You will be taken behind the play and counterplay of world politics where you will view the final struggle for world supremacy.

The masterful volume you hold in your hand has been described as "the greatest book in the world outside the Bible for the twentieth century." This production will hold you spellbound from cover to cover as you are carried into the most thrilling drama of the past, the present, and the future. Here is the most excellent biography, a penetrating analysis of the most fascinating issues.

This could well be the most important book you have read! The lives of hundreds of thousands have been greatly enriched and affected by it already. It holds for you a most exciting and thrilling adventure.

Chapter 1

THE ORIGIN OF EVIL

To MANY MINDS, THE ORIGIN of sin and the reason for its existence are a source of great perplexity. They see the work of evil, with its terrible results of woe and desolation, and they question how all this can exist under the sovereignty of One who is infinite in wisdom, in power, and in love. Here is a mystery, of which they find no explanation. And in their uncertainty and doubt, they are blinded to truths plainly revealed in God's Word, and essential to salvation. There are those who, in their inquiries concerning the existence of sin, endeavor to search into that which God has never revealed; hence they find no solution of their difficulties; and such as are actuated by a disposition of doubt and cavil, seize upon this as an excuse for rejecting the words of Holy Writ. Others, however, fail of a satisfactory understanding of the great problem of evil, from the fact that tradition and misinterpretation have obscured the teaching of the Bible concerning the character of God, the nature of His government, and the principles of His dealing with sin.

It is impossible to so explain the origin of sin as to give a reason for its existence. Yet enough may be understood concerning both the origin and the final disposition of sin, to fully make manifest the justice and benevolence of God in His dealings with evil. Nothing is more plainly taught in Scripture than that God was in nowise responsible for the entrance of sin; that there was no arbitrary withdrawal of divine grace, no deficiency in the divine government, that gave occasion for the uprising of rebellion. Sin is an intruder, for whose presence no reason can be given.

1

It is mysterious, unaccountable; to excuse it, is to defend. it. Could excuse for it be found, or cause be shown for its existence, if would cease to be sin. Our only definition of sin is that given in the Word of God; it is "the transgression of the law;" it is the outworking of a principle at war with the great law of love which is the foundation of the divine government.

Before the entrance of evil, there was peace and joy throughout the universe. All was in perfect harmony with the Creator's will. Love for God was supreme, love for one another impartial. Christ the Word, the only begotten of God, was one with the eternal Father—one in nature, in character, and in purpose—the only being in all the universe that could enter into all the counsels and purposes of God. By Christ, the Father wrought in the creation of all heavenly beings. "For by Him were all things created, that are in Heaven, . . . whether they be thrones, or dominions, or principalities, or powers;" (*Col.* 1:16) and to Christ, equally with the Father, all Heaven gave allegiance.

The law of love being the foundation of the government of God, the happiness of all created beings depended upon their perfect accord with its great principles of righteousness. God desires from all His creatures the service of love—homage that springs from an intelligent appreciation of His character. He takes no pleasure in a forced allegiance, and to all He grants freedom of will, that they may render Him voluntary service.

But there was one that chose to pervert this freedom. Sin originated with him, who, next to Christ, had been most honored of God, and who stood highest in power and glory among the inhabitants of Heaven. Before his fall, Lucifer was first of the covering cherubs, holy and undefiled. "Thus saith the Lord God: Thou sealest up the sum full of wisdom and perfect in beauty. Thou hast been in Eden the garden of God; every precious stone was thy covering." "Thou art the anointed cherub that covereth; and I have set thee so; thou wast upon the holy mountain of God; thou hast walked up and down in the midst of the stones of fire. Thou wast perfect in thy ways from the day that thou was created, till iniquity wast found in thee." (*Eze*. 28:12-15, 17)

Lucifer might have remained in favor with God, beloved and honored by all the angelic host, exercising the noble powers to bless others and to glorify his Maker. But, says the prophet, "Thine heart was lifted up because of thy beauty, thou hast corrupted thy wisdom by reason of thy brightness." (*Ez*. 28:17; *Isa*. 14:13, 14) Little by little, Lucifer came to indulge a desire for self-exaltation. "Thou hast set thine heart as the heart of God." "Thou hast said: . . . I will exalt my throne above the stars of God; I will sit also upon the mount of the congregation." "I will ascend above the heights of the clouds; I will be like the Most High." (*Isa*. 14:13,14) Instead of seeking to make God supreme in the affections and allegiance of His creatures, it was Lucifer's endeavor to win their service and homage to himself. And, coveting the honor which the infinite Father had bestowed upon His Son, this prince of angels aspired to power which it was the prerogative of Christ alone to wield.

All Heaven had rejoiced to reflect the Creator's glory and to show forth His praise. And while God was thus honored, all had been peace and gladness. But a note of discord now marred the celestial harmonies. The service and exaltation of self, contrary to the Creator's plan, awakened forebodings of evil in minds to whom God's glory was supreme. The heavenly councils pleaded with Lucifer. The Son of God presented before him the greatness, the goodness, and the justice of the Creator, and the sacred, unchanging nature of His law. God Himself had established the order of Heaven; and in departing from it, Lucifer would dishonor his Maker, and bring ruin upon himself. But the warning, given in infinite love and mercy, only aroused a spirit of resistance. Lucifer allowed jealousy of Christ to prevail, and he became the more determined.

Pride in his own glory nourished his desire for supremacy. The high honors conferred upon Lucifer were not appreciated as the gift of God, and called forth no gratitude to the Creator. He gloried in his brightness and exaltation, and aspired to be equal with God. He was beloved and reverenced by the heavenly host. Angels delighted to execute his commands, and he was clothed with wisdom and glory above them all. Yet the Son of God was the acknowledged sovereign of Heaven, one in power and authority with the Father. In all the counsels of God, Christ was a participant, while Lucifer was not permitted thus to enter into the divine purposes. "Why," questioned this mighty angel, "should Christ have the supremacy? Why is He thus honored above Lucifer?"

Leaving his place in the immediate presence of God, Lucifer went forth to diffuse the spirit of discontent among the angels. Working with mysterious secrecy, and for a time concealing his real purpose under an appearance of reverence for God, he endeavored to excite dissatisfaction concerning the laws that governed heavenly beings, intimating that they imposed an unnecessary restraint. Since their natures were holy, he urged that the angels should obey the dictates of their own will. He sought to create sympathy for himself, by representing that God had dealt unjustly with him in bestowing supreme honor upon Christ. He claimed that in aspiring to greater power and honor he was not aiming at self-exaltation, but was seeking to secure liberty for all the inhabitants of Heaven, that by this means they might attain to a higher state of existence.

God, in His great mercy, bore long with Lucifer. He was not immediately degraded from his exalted station when he first indulged the spirit of discontent, nor even when he began to present his false claims before the loyal angels. Long was he retained in Heaven. Again and again he was offered pardon, on condition of repentance and submission. Such efforts as only infinite love and wisdom could devise, were made to convince him of his error. The spirit of discontent had never before been known in Heaven. Lucifer himself did not at first see whither he was drifting; he did not understand the real nature of his feelings. But as his dissatisfaction was proved to be without cause, Lucifer was convinced that he was in the wrong, that the divine claims were just, and that he ought to acknowledge them as such before all Heaven. Had he done this, he might have saved himself and many angels. He had not at this time fully cast off his allegiance to God. Though he had forsaken his position as covering cherub, yet if he had been willing to return to God, acknowledging the Creator's wisdom, and satisfied to fill the place appointed him in God's great plan, he would have been re-instated in his office. But pride forbade him to submit. He persistently defended his own course, maintained that he had no need of repentance, and fully committed himself, in the great controversy, against his Maker.

All the powers of his master-mind were now bent to the work of deception, to secure the sympathy of the angels that had been under his command. Even the fact that Christ had warned and counseled him, was perverted to serve his traitorous designs. To those whose loving trust bound them most closely to him, Satan had represented that he was wrongly judged, that his position was not respected, and that his liberty was to be abridged. From misrepresentation of the words of Christ, he passed to prevarication and direct falsehood, accusing the Son of God of a design to humiliate him before the inhabitants of Heaven. He sought also to make a false issue between himself and the loyal angels. All whom he could not subvert and bring fully to his side, he accused of indifference to the interests of heavenly beings. The very work which he himself was doing, he charged upon those who remained true to God. And to sustain his charge of God's injustice toward him, he resorted to misrepresentation of the words and acts of the Creator. It was his policy to perplex the angels with subtle arguments concerning the purposes of God. Everything that was simple he shrouded in mystery, and by artful perversion cast doubt upon the plainest statements of Jehovah. His high position, in such close connection with the divine administration, gave greater force to his representations, and many were induced to unite with him in rebellion against Heaven's authority.

God in His wisdom permitted Satan to carry forward his work, until the spirit of disaffection ripened into active revolt. It was necessary for his plans to be fully developed, that their true nature and tendency might be seen by all. Lucifer, as the anointed cherub, had been highly exalted; he was greatly loved by the heavenly beings, and his influence over them was strong. God's government included not only the inhabitants of Heaven, but of all the worlds that He had created; and Satan thought that if he could carry the angels of Heaven with him in rebellion, he could carry also the other worlds. He had artfully presented his side of the question, employing sophistry and fraud to secure his objects. His power to deceive was very great, and by disguising himself in a cloak of falsehood he had gained an advantage. Even the loyal agents could not fully discern his character, or see to what his work was leading.

Satan had been so highly honored, and all his acts were so clothed with mystery, that it was difficult to disclose to the angels the true nature of his work. Until fully developed, sin would not appear the evil thing it was. Heretofore it had had no place in the universe of God, and holy beings had no conception of its nature and malignity. They could not discern the terrible consequences that would result from setting aside the divine law. Satan had, at first, concealed his work under a specious profession of loyalty to God. He claimed to be seeking to promote the honor of God, the stability of his government, and the good of all the inhabitants of Heaven. While instilling discontent into the minds of the angels under him, he had artfully made it appear that he was seeking to remove dissatisfaction. When he urged that changes be made in the order and laws of God's government, it was under the pretense that these were necessary in order to preserve harmony in Heaven.

In his dealing with sin, God could employ only righteousness and truth. Satan could use what God could not —flattery and deceit. He had sought to falsify the word of God, and had misrepresented His plan of government before the angels, claiming that God was not just in laying laws and rules upon the inhabitants of Heaven; that in requiring submission and obedience from His creatures, He was seeking merely the exaltation of Himself. Therefore it must be demonstrated before the inhabitants of Heaven as well as of all the worlds, that God's government was just, His law perfect. Satan had made it appear that he himself was seeking to promote the good of the universe. The true character of the usurper, and his real object, must be understood by all. He must have time to manifest himself by his wicked works.

The discord which his own course had caused in Heaven, Satan charged upon the law and government of God. All evil he declared to be the result of the divine administration. He claimed that it was his own object to improve upon the statutes of Jehovah. Therefore it was necessary that he should demonstrate the nature of his claims, and show the working out of his proposed changes in the divine law. His own work must condemn him. Satan had claimed from the first that he was not in rebellion. The whole universe must see the deceiver unmasked.

Even when it was decided that he could no longer remain in Heaven, infinite wisdom did not destroy Satan. Since the service of love can alone be acceptable to God, the allegiance of His creatures must rest upon a conviction of His justice and benevolence. The inhabitants of Heaven and of other worlds, being unprepared to comprehend the nature or consequences of sin, could not then have seen the justice and mercy of God in the destruction of Satan. Had he been immediately blotted from existence, they would have served God from fear, rather than from love. The influence of the deceiver would not have been fully destroyed, nor would the spirit of rebellion have been utterly eradicated. Evil must be permitted to come to maturity. For the good of the entire universe through ceaseless ages, Satan must more fully develop his principles, that his charges against the divine government might be seen in their true light by all created beings, that the justice and mercy of God and the immutability of His law might forever be placed beyond all question.

Satan's rebellion was to be a lesson to the universe through all coming ages, a perpetual testimony to the nature and terrible results of sin. The working out of Satan's rule, its effects upon both men and angels, would show what must be the fruit of setting aside the divine authority. It would testify that with the existence of God's government and his Law is bound up the well-being of all the creatures He has made. Thus the history of his terrible experiment of rebellion was to be a perpetual safeguard to all holy intelligences, to prevent them from being deceived as to the nature of transgression, to save them from committing sin, and suffering its punishment.

To the very close of the controversy in Heaven, the great usurper continued to justify himself. When it was announced that with all his sympathizers he must be expelled from the abodes of bliss, then the rebel leader boldly avowed his contempt for the Creator's law. He reiterated his claim that angels needed no control, but should be left to follow their own will, which would ever guide them right. He denounced the divine statutes as a restriction of their liberty, and declared that it was his purpose to secure the abolition of law; that, freed from its restraint, the hosts of Heaven might enter upon a more exalted, more glorious state of existence.

With one accord, Satan and his host threw the blame of their rebellion wholly upon Christ, declaring that if they had not been reproved, they would never have rebelled. Thus stubborn and defiant in their disloyalty, seeking vainly to overthrow the government of God, yet blasphemously claiming to be themselves the innocent victims of oppressive power, the arch-rebel and all his sympathizers were at last banished from Heaven.

The same spirit that prompted rebellion in Heaven, still inspires rebellion on earth. Satan has continued with men the same policy which he pursued with the angels. His spirit now reigns in the children of disobedience. Like him they seek to break down the restraints of the law of God, and promise men liberty through transgression of its precepts. Reproof of sin still arouses the spirit of hatred and resistance. When God's messages of warning are brought home to the conscience, Satan leads men to justify themselves, and to seek the sympathy of others in their course of sin. Instead of correcting their errors, they excite indignation against the reprover, as if he were the sole cause of difficulty. From the days of righteous Abel to our own time, such is the spirit which has been displayed toward those who dare to condemn sin.

By the same misrepresentation of the character of God as he had practiced in Heaven, causing Him to be regarded as severe and tyrannical, Satan induced man to sin. And having succeeded thus far, he declared that God's unjust restrictions had led to man's fall, as they had led to his own rebellion.

But the Eternal One Himself proclaims His character: "The Lord God, merciful and gracious, long-suffering, and abundant in goodness and truth, keeping mercy for thousands, forgiving iniquity and transgression and sin, and that will by no means clear the guilty." (*Ex.* 34:6,7)

In the banishment of Satan from Heaven, God declared His justice, and maintained the honor of His throne. But when man had sinned through yielding to the deceptions of this apostate spirit, God gave an evidence of His love by yielding up His only begotten Son to die for the fallen race. In the atonement the character of God is revealed. The mighty argument of the cross demonstrates to the whole universe that the course of sin which Lucifer had chosen was in nowise chargeable upon the government of God.

In the contest between Christ and Satan, during the Saviour's earthy ministry, the character of the great deceiver was unmasked. Nothing could so effectually have uprooted Satan from the affections of the heavenly angels and the whole loyal universe as did his cruel warfare upon the world's Redeemer. The daring blasphemy of his demand that Christ should pay him homage, his presumptuous boldness in bearing Him to the mountain summit and the pinnacle of the temple, the malicious intent betrayed in urging him to cast Himself down from the dizzy height, the unsleeping malice that hunted Him from place to place, inspiring the hearts of priests and people to reject His love, and at the last to cry, "Crucify Him! crucify Him!"—all this excited the amazement and indignation of the universe.

It was Satan that prompted the world's rejection of Christ. The prince of evil exerted all his power and cunning to destroy Jesus; for he saw that the Saviour's mercy and love, His compassion and pitying tenderness, were representing to the world the character of God. Satan contested every claim put forth by the Son of God, and employed men as his agents to fill the Saviour's life with suffering and sorrow. The sophistry and falsehood by which he had sought to hinder the work of Jesus, the hatred manifested through the children of disobedience, his cruel accusations against Him whose life was one of unexampled goodness, all sprang from deep-seated revenge. The pent-up fires of envy and malice, hatred and revenge, burst forth on Calvary against the Son of God, while all Heaven gazed upon the scene in silent horror.

When the great sacrifice had been consummated, Christ ascended on high, refusing the adoration of angels until He had presented the request, "I will that they also, whom Thou hast given Me be with Me where I am." (*John* 17:24) Then with inexpressible love and power came forth the answer from the Father's throne, "Let all the angels of God worship him." (*Heb.* 1:6) Not a stain rested upon Jesus. His humiliation ended, His sacrifice completed, there was given unto Him a name that is above every name.

Now the guilt of Satan stood forth without excuse. He had revealed his true character as a liar and a murderer. It was seen that the very same spirit with which he ruled the children of men, who were under his power, he would have manifested had he been permitted to control the inhabitants of Heaven. He had claimed that the transgression of God's law would bring liberty and exaltation; but it was seen to result in bondage and degradation.

Satan's lying charges against the divine character and government appeared in their true light. He had accused God of seeking merely the exaltation of Himself in requiring submission and obedience from His creatures, and had declared that while the Creator exacted self-denial from all others, He Himself practiced no self-denial, and made no sacrifice. Now it was seen that for the salvation of a fallen and sinful race, the Ruler of the universe had made the greatest sacrifice which love could make; for "God was in Christ, reconciling the world unto Himself." (*2 Cor.* 5:19) It was seen, also, that while Lucifer had opened the door for the entrance of sin, by his desire for honor and supremacy, Christ had, in order to destroy sin, humbled Himself and become obedient unto death.

God had manifested His abhorrence of the principles of rebellion. All Heaven saw His justice revealed, both in the condemnation of Satan and in the redemption of man. Lucifer had declared that if the law of God was changeless, and its penalty could not be remitted, every transgressor must be forever debarred from the Creator's favor. He had claimed that the sinful race were placed beyond redemption, and were therefore his rightful prey. But the death of Christ was an argument in man's behalf that could not be overthrown. The penalty of the law fell upon Him who was equal with God, and man was free to accept the righteousness of Christ, and by a life of penitence and humiliation to triumph, as the Son of God had triumphed, over the power of Satan. Thus God is just, and yet the justifier of all who believe in Jesus.

But it was not merely to accomplish the redemption of man that Christ came to the earth to suffer and to die. He came to "magnify the law" and to "make it honorable." Not alone that the inhabitants of this world might regard the law as it should be regarded; but it was to demonstrate to all the worlds of the universe that God's law is unchangeable. Could its claims have been set aside, then the Son of God need not have yielded up His life to atone for its transgression. The death of Christ proves it immutable. And the sacrifice to which infinite love impelled the Father and the Son, that sinners might be redeemed, demonstrates to all the universe—what nothing less than this plan of atonement could have sufficed to do—that justice and mercy are the foundation of the law and government of God.

In the final execution of the Judgment it will be seen that no cause for sin exists. When the Judge of all the earth shall demand of Satan, "Why hast thou rebelled against Me, and robbed Me of the subjects of My kingdom?" the originator of evil can render no excuse. Every mouth will be stopped, and all the hosts of rebellion will be speechless.

The cross of Calvary, while it declares the law immutable, proclaims to the universe that the wages of sin is death. In the Saviour's expiring cry, "It is finished," the death-knell of Satan was rung. The great controversy which had been so long in progress was then decided, and the final eradication of evil was made certain. The Son of God passed through the portals of the tomb, that "through death He might destroy him that had the power of death, that is, the devil." (*Heb.* 2:14) Lucifer's desire for self-exaltation had led him to say, "I will exalt my throne above the stars of God. . . . I will be like the Most High." God declares, "I will bring thee to ashes upon the earth, . . . and never shall thou be any more." (*Isa.* 14:13, 14; *Eze.* 28:18, 19) When "the day cometh that shall burn as an oven," "all the proud, yea, and all that do wickedly, shall be stubble; and the day that cometh shall burn them up, saith the Lord of hosts, that it shall leave them neither root nor branch." (*Mal.* 4:1)

The whole universe will have become witnesses to the nature and results of sin. And its utter extermination, which in the beginning would have brought fear to angels and dishonor to God, will now vindicate His love and establish His honor before a universe of beings who delight to do His will, and in whose heart is His law. Never will evil again be manifest. Says the Word of God, "Affliction shall not rise up the second time." (*Nahum* 1:9) The law of God, which Satan reproached as the yoke of bondage, will be honored as the law of liberty. A tested and proved creation will never again be turned from allegiance to Him whose character has been fully manifested before them as fathomless love and infinite wisdom.

Chapter 2

MAN'S WORST ENEMY

"I WILL PUT ENMIMTY BETWEEN thee and the woman, and between thy seed and her seed; it shall bruise thy head, and thou shalt bruise his heel." (*Gen.* 3:15) The divine sentence pronounced against Satan after the fall of man, was also a prophecy, embracing all the ages to the close of time, and foreshadowing the great conflict to engage all the races of men who should live upon the earth.

God declares, "I will put enmity." This enmity is not naturally entertained. When man transgressed the divine law, his nature became evil, and he was in harmony, and not at variance, with Satan. There exists naturally no enmity between sinful man and the originator of sin. Both became evil through apostasy. The apostate is never at rest, except as he obtains sympathy and support by inducing others to follow his example. For this reason, fallen angels and wicked men unite in desperate companionship. Had not God specially interposed, Satan and man would have entered into an alliance against Heaven; and instead of cherishing enmity against Satan, the whole human family would have been united in opposition to God.

Satan tempted man to sin, as he had caused angels to rebel, that he might thus secure co-operation in his warfare against Heaven. There was no dissension between himself and the fallen angels as regards their hatred of Christ; while on all other points there was discord, they were firmly united in opposing the authority of the Ruler of the universe. But when Satan heard the declaration that enmity should exist between himself and the woman, and between his seed and her seed, he knew that his efforts to deprave human nature would be interrupted; that by some means man was to be enabled to resist his power.

Satan's enmity against the human race, is kindled, because, through Christ, they are the objects of God's love and mercy. He desires to thwart the divine plan for man's redemption, to cast dishonor upon God, by defacing and defiling His handiwork; he would cause grief in Heaven, and fill the earth with woe and desolation. And he points to all this evil as the result of God's work in creating man.

It is the grace that Christ implants in the soul which creates in man enmity against Satan. Without this converting grace and renewing power, man would continue the captive of Satan, a servant ever ready to do his bidding. But the new principle in the soul creates conflict where hitherto had been peace. The power which Christ imparts enables man to resist the tyrant and usurper. Whoever is seen to abhor sin instead of loving it, whoever resists and conquers those passions that have held sway within, displays the operation of a principle wholly from above.

The antagonism that exists between the spirit of Christ and the spirit of Satan was most strikingly displayed in the world's reception of Jesus. It was not so much because He appeared without worldly wealth, pomp, or grandeur, that the Jews were led to reject Him. They saw that He possessed power which would more than compensate for the lack of these outward advantages. But the purity and holiness of Christ called forth against Him the hatred of the ungodly. His life of self-denial and sinless devotion was a perpetual reproof to a proud, sensual people. It was this that evoked enmity against the Son of God. Satan and evil angels joined with evil men. All the energies of apostasy conspired against the champion of truth.

The same enmity is manifested toward Christ's followers as was manifested toward their Master. Whoever sees the repulsive character of sin, and, in strength from above, resists temptation, will assuredly arouse the wrath of Satan and his subjects. Hatred of the pure principles of truth, and reproach and persecution of its advocates, will exist as long as sin and sinners remain. The followers of Christ and the servants of Satan cannot harmonize. The offense of the cross has not ceased. "All that will live godly in Christ Jesus shall suffer persecution." (*2 Tim.* 3:12)

Satan's agents are constantly working under his direction to establish his authority and build up his kingdom in opposition to the government of God. To this end they seek to deceive Christ's followers, and allure them from their allegiance. Like their leader, they misconstrue and pervert the Scriptures to accomplish their object. As Satan endeavored to cast reproach upon God, so do his agents seek to malign God's people. The spirit which put Christ to death moves the wicked to destroy His followers. All this is foreshadowed in that first prophecy, "I will put enmity between thee and the woman, and between thy seed and her seed." And this will continue to the close of time.

Satan summons all his forces, and throws his whole power into the combat. Why is it that he meets with no greater resistance? Why are the soldiers of Christ so sleepy and indifferent?—Because they have so little real connection with Christ; because they are so destitute of His Spirit. Sin is not to them repulsive and abhorrent, as it was to their Master. They do not meet it, as did Christ, with decisive and determined resistance. They do not realize the exceeding evil and malignity of sin, and they are blinded both to the character and the power of the prince of darkness. There is little enmity against Satan and his works, because there is so great ignorance concerning his power and malice, and the vast extent of his warfare against Christ and His church. Multitudes are deluded here. They do not know that their enemy is a mighty general, who controls the minds of evil angels, and that with well-matured plans and skillful movements he is warring against Christ to prevent the salvation of souls. Among professed Christians, and even among ministers of the gospel, there is heard scarcely a reference to Satan, except perhaps an incidental mention in the pulpit. They overlook the evidences of his continual activity and success; they neglect the many warnings of his subtlety; they seem to ignore his very existence.

While men are ignorant of his devices, this vigilant foe is upon their track every moment. He is intruding his presence in every department of the household, in every street of our cities, in the churches, in the national councils, in the courts of justice, perplexing, deceiving, seducing, everywhere ruining the souls and bodies of men, women, and children, breaking up families, sowing hatred, emulation, strife, sedition, murder. And the Christian world seem to regard these things as though God had appointed them, and they must exist.

Satan is continually seeking to overcome the people of God by breaking down the barriers which separate them from the world. Ancient Israel were enticed into sin when they ventured into forbidden association with the heathen. In a similar manner are modern Israel led astray. "The god of this world hath blinded the minds of them which believe not, lest the light of the glorious gospel of Christ, Who is the image of God, should shine unto them." (2 *Cor*. 4:4) All who are not decided followers of Christ are servants of Satan. In the unregenerate heart there is love of sin, and a disposition to cherish and excuse it. In the renewed heart there is hatred of sin, and determined resistance against it. When Christians choose the society of the ungodly and unbelieving, they expose themselves to temptation. Satan conceals himself from view, and stealthily draws his deceptive covering over their eyes. They cannot see that such company is calculated to do them harm; and while all the time assimilating to the world in character, words, and actions, they are becoming more and more blinded.

Conformity to worldly customs converts the church to the world; it never converts the world to Christ. Familiarity with sin will inevitably cause it to appear less repulsive. He who chooses to associate with the servants of

Satan, will soon cease to fear their master. When in the way of duty we are brought into trial, as was Daniel in the king's court, we may be sure that God will protect us; but if we place ourselves under temptation, we shall fall sooner or later.

The tempter often works most successfully through those who are least suspected of being under his control. The possessors of talent and education are admired and honored, as if these qualities could atone for the absence of the fear of God, or entitle men to His favor. Talent and culture, considered in themselves, are gifts of God; but when these are made to supply the place of piety; when, instead of bringing the soul nearer to God, they lead away from Him, then they become a curse and a snare. The opinion prevails with many that all which appears like courtesy or refinement must, in some sense, pertain to Christ. Never was there a greater mistake. These qualities should grace the character of every Christian, for they would exert a powerful influence in favor of true religion; but they must be consecrated to God, or they also are a power for evil. Many a man of cultured intellect and pleasant manners who would not stoop to what is commonly regarded as an immoral act, is but a polished instrument in the hands of Satan. The insidious, deceptive character of his influence and example renders him a more dangerous enemy to the cause of Christ than are those who are ignorant and uncultured.

By earnest prayer and dependence upon God, Solomon obtained the wisdom which excited the wonder and admiration of the world. But when he turned from the Source of his strength, and went forward relying upon himself, he fell a prey to temptation. Then the marvelous powers bestowed on this wisest of kings, only rendered him a more effective agent of the adversary of souls.

While Satan is constantly seeking to blind their minds to the fact, let Christians never forget that they "wrestle not against flesh and blood, but against principalities, against powers, against the rulers of the darkness of this world against wicked spirits in high places." (*Eph.* 6:12, margin) The inspired warning is sounding down the centuries to our time: "Be sober, be vigilant; because your adversary the devil, as a roaring lion, walketh about, seeking whom he may devour." (*1 Pet.* 5:8) Put on the whole armor of God, that ye may be able to stand against the wiles of the devil." (*Eph.* 6:11)

From the days of Adam to our own time, our great enemy has been exercising his power to oppress and destroy. He is now preparing for his last campaign against the church. All who seek to follow Jesus will be brought into conflict with this relentless foe. The more nearly the Christian imitates the divine Pattern, the more surely will he make himself a mark for the attacks of Satan. All who are actively engaged in the cause of God, seeking to unveil the deceptions of the evil one and to present Christ before the people, will be able to join in the testimony of Paul, in which he speaks of serving the Lord with all humility of mind, with many tears and temptations.

Satan assailed Christ with his fiercest and most subtle temptations; but he was repulsed in every conflict. Those battles were fought in our behalf; those victories make it possible for us to conquer. Christ will give strength to all who seek it. No man without his own consent can be overcome by Satan. The tempter has no power to control the will or to force the soul to sin. He may distress, but he cannot contaminate. He can cause agony, but not defilement. The fact that Christ has conquered should inspire His followers with courage to fight manfully the battle against sin and Satan.

Chapter 3

WORK OF EVIL ANGELS

THE CONNECTION OF THE VISIBLE with the invisible world, the ministration of angels of God, and the agency of evil spirits, are plainly revealed in the Scriptures, and inseparably interwoven with human history. There is a growing tendency to disbelief in the existence of evil spirits, while the holy angels that "minister for them who shall be heirs of salvation," (*Heb.* 1:14) are regarded by many as the spirits of the dead. But the Scriptures not only teach the existence of angels, both good and evil, but present unquestionable proof that these are not the disembodied spirits of dead men.

Before the creation of man, angels were in existence; for when the foundations of the earth were laid, "the morning stars sang together, and all the sons of God shouted for joy." (*Job* 38:7) After the fall of man, angels were sent to guard the tree of life, and this before a human being had died. Angels are in nature superior to men, for the psalmist says that man was made "a little lower than the angels." (*Ps.* 8:5)

We are informed in Scripture as to the number, and the power and glory, of the heavenly beings, of their connection with the government of God, and also of their relation to the work of redemption. "The Lord hath prepared his throne in the heavens; and His kingdom ruleth over all." And, says the prophet, "I heard the voice of many angels round about the throne." In the presence-chamber of the King of kings they wait—"angels that excel in strength," "ministers of His, that do His pleasure," "hearkening unto the voice of His word," (*Ps.*

103:19-21; *Rev.* 5:11) Ten thousand times ten thousand and thousands of thousands, were the heavenly messengers beheld by the prophet Daniel. The apostle Paul declared them "an innumerable company." (*Dan.* 7:10; *Heb.* 12:22) As God's messengers they go forth, like "the appearance of a flash of lightning," (*Eze.* 1:14) so dazzling their glory, and so swift their flight. The angel that appeared at the Saviour's tomb, his countenance "like lightning, and his raiment white as snow," caused the keepers for fear of him to quake, and they "became as dead men." (*Matt.* 28:3, 4) When Sennacherib, the haughty Assyrian, reproached and blasphemed God, and threatened Israel with destruction, "it came to pass that night, that the angel of the Lord went out, and smote in the camp of the Assyrians an hundred fourscore and five thousand." There were "cut off all the mighty men of valor, and the leaders and captains," from the army of Sennacherib. "So he returned with shame of face to his own land." (*2 Kings* 19:35; *2 Chron.* 32:21)

Angels are sent on missions of mercy to the children of God. To Abraham, with promises of blessing; to the gates of Sodom, to rescue righteous Lot from its fiery doom; to Elijah, as he was about to perish from weariness and hunger in the desert; to Elisha, with chariots and horses of fire surrounding the little town where he was shut in by his foes; to Daniel, while seeking divine wisdom in the court of a heathen king, or abandoned to become the lions' prey; to Peter, doomed to death in Herod's dungeon; to the prisoners at Philippi; to Paul and his companions in the night of tempest on the sea; to open the mind of Cornelius to receive the gospel; to dispatch Peter, with the message of salvation to the Gentile stranger—thus holy angels have, in all ages, ministered to God's people.

A guardian angel is appointed to every follower of Christ. These heavenly watchers shield the righteous from the power of the wicked one. This Satan himself recognized when he said, "Doth Job fear God for naught? Hast not thou made a hedge about him, and about his house,

and about all that he hath on every side?" (*Job* 1:9, 10)
The agency by which God protects His people is
presented in the words of the psalmist, "The angel of the
Lord encampeth round about them that fear Him and delivereth them." (*Ps.* 34:7) Said the Saviour, speaking of
those that believe in Him. "Take heed that ye despise not
one of these little ones; for I say unto you, that in Heaven
their angels do always behold the face of My Father."
(*Matt.* 18:10) The angels appointed to minister to the
children of God have at all times access to His presence.

Thus God's people, exposed to the deceptive power
and unsleeping malice of the prince of darkness, and in
conflict with all the forces of evil, are assured of the unceasing guardianship of heavenly angels. Nor is such assurance given without need. If God has granted to His
children promise of grace and protection, it is because
there are mighty agencies of evil to be met—agencies numerous, determined, and untiring, of whose malignity and
power none can safely be ignorant or unheeding.

Evil spirits, in the beginning created sinless, were equal
in nature, power, and glory with the holy beings that are
now God's messengers. But fallen through sin, they are
leagued together for the dishonor of God and the destruction of men. United with Satan in his rebellion, and with
him cast out from Heaven, they have, through all succeeding ages, co-operated with him in his warfare against
the divine authority. We are told in Scripture of their con-
federacy and government, of their various orders, of their
intelligence and subtlety, and of their malicious designs
against the peace and happiness of men.

Old Testament history presents occasional mention of
their existence and agency; but it was during the time
when Christ was upon the earth that evil spirits manifested their power in the most striking manner. Christ had
come to enter upon the plan devised for man's redemption, and Satan determined to assert his right to control
the world. He had succeeded in establishing idolatry in
every part of the earth except the land of Palestine. To
the only land that had not fully yielded to the tempter's

sway, Christ came to shed upon the people the light of Heaven. Here two rival powers claimed supremacy. Jesus was stretching out His arms of love, inviting all who would to find pardon and peace in Him. The hosts of darkness saw that they did not possess unlimited control, and they understood that if Christ's mission should be successful, their rule was soon to end. Satan raged like a chained lion, and defiantly exhibited his power over the bodies as well as the souls of men.

The fact that men have been possessed with demons is clearly stated in the New Testament. The persons thus afflicted were not merely suffering with disease from natural causes. Christ had perfect understanding of that with which He was dealing, and He recognized the direct presence and agency of evil spirits.

A striking example of their number, power, and malignity, and also of the power and mercy of Christ, is given in the Scripture account of the healing of the demoniacs at Gadara. Those wretched maniacs, spurning all restraint, writhing, foaming, raging, were filling the air with their cries, doing violence to themselves, and endangering all who should approach them. Their bleeding and disfigured bodies and distracted minds presented a spectacle well-pleasing to the prince of darkness. One of the demons controlling the sufferers declared, "My name is Legion; for we are many." (*Mark*. 5:9) In the Roman army a legion consisted of from three to five thousand men. Satan's hosts also are marshaled in companies, and the single company to which these demons belonged numbered no less than a legion.

At the command of Jesus, the evil spirits departed from their victims, leaving them calmly sitting at the Saviour's feet, subdued, intelligent, and gentle. But the demons were permitted to sweep a herd of swine into the sea; and to the dwellers of Gadara the loss of these outweighed the blessings which Crhist had bestowed, and the divine Healer was entreated to depart. This was the result which Satan designed to secure. By casting the blame of their loss upon Jesus, he aroused the selfish fears of the people, and prevented them from listening to His words. Satan is constantly accusing Christians as the cause of loss, misfortune, and suffering, instead of allowing the reproach to fall where it belongs, upon himself and his agents.

But the purposes of Christ were not thwarted. He allowed the evil spirits to destroy the herd of swine as a rebuke to those Jews who were raising these unclean beasts for the sake of gain. Had not Christ restrained the demons, they would have plunged into the sea, not only the swine, but also their keepers and owners. The preservation of both the keepers and the owners was due alone to His power, mercifully exercised for their deliverance. Furthermore, this event was permitted to take place that the disciples might witness the cruel power of Satan upon both man and beast. The Saviour desired His followers to have a knowledge of the foe whom they were to meet, that they might not be deceived and overcome by his devices. It was also His will that the people of that region should behold His power to break the bondage of Satan and release his captives. And though Jesus Himself departed, the men so marvelously delivered remained to declare the mercy of their Benefactor.

Other instances of a similar nature are recorded in the Scriptures. The daughter of the Syro-Phenician woman was grievously vexed with a devil, whom Jesus cast out by His word. (*Mark*. 7:26-30) One "possessed with a devil, blind, and dumb," (*Matt*. 12:22) a youth who had a dumb spirit, that ofttimes "cast him into the fire, and into the waters, to destroy him," (*Mark* 9:17–27) the maniac, who, tormented by "a spirit of an unclean devil," disturbed the Sabbath quiet of the synagogue at Capernaum, were all healed by the compassionate Savior. In nearly every instance Christ addressed the demon as an intelligent entity, commanding him to come out of his victim and to torment him no more. The worshipers at Capernaum, beholding His mighty power, "were all amazed, and spake among themselves, saying, What a word is this! for with authority and power He commandeth the unclean spirits, and they come out." (*Luke* 4:33-36)

Those possessed with devils are usually represented as being in a condition of great suffering; yet there were exceptions to this rule. For the sake of obtaining supernatural power, some welcomed the Satanic influence. These of course had no conflict with the demons. Of this class were those who possessed the spirit of divination—Simon Magus, Elymas the sorcerer, and the damsel who followed Paul and Silas at Philippi.

None are in greater danger from the influence of evil spirits than are those who, notwithstanding the direct and ample testimony of the Scriptures, deny the existence and agency of the devil and his angels. So long as we are ignorant of their wiles, they have almost inconceivable advantage; many give heed to their suggestions while they suppose themselves to be following the dictates of their own wisdom. This is why, as we approach the close of time when Satan is to work with greatest power to deceive and destroy, he spreads everywhere the belief that he does not exist. It is his policy to conceal himself and his manner of working.

There is nothing that the great deceiver fears so much as that we shall become acquainted with his devices. The better to disguise his real character and purposes, he has caused himself to be so represented as to excite no stronger emotion than ridicule or contempt. He is well pleased to be painted as a ludicrous or loathsome object, misshapen, half animal and half human. He is pleased to hear his name used in sport and mockery by those who think themselves intelligent and well-informed.

It is because he has masked himself with consummate skill that the question is so widely asked, "Does such a being really exist?" It is an evidence of his success that theories giving the lie to the plainest testimony of the Scriptures are so generally received in the religious world. And it is because Satan can most readily control the minds of those who are unconscious of his influence that the Word of God gives us so many examples of his malignant work, unveiling before us his secret forces, and thus placing us on our guard against his assaults.

The power and malice of Satan and his host might justly alarm us, were it not that we may find shelter and deliverance in the superior power of our Redeemer. We carefully secure our houses with bolts and locks to protect our property and our lives from evil men; but we seldom think of the evil angels who are constantly seeking access to us, and against whose attacks we have, in our own strength, no method of defense. If permitted, they can distract our minds, disorder, torment our bodies, destroy our possessions and our lives. Their only delight is in misery and destruction. Fearful is the condition of those who resist the divine claims and yield to Satan's temptations until God gives them up to the control of evil spirits. But those who follow Christ are ever safe under His watch-care. Angels that excel in strength are sent from Heaven to protect them. The wicked one cannot break through the guard which God has stationed about His people.

Chapter 4

THE APOSTASY

THE APOSTLE PAUL in his second letter to the Thessalonians foretold the great apostasy which would result in the establishment of the papal power. He declared that the day of Christ should not come, "except there come a falling away first, and that man of sin be revealed, the son of perdition; who opposeth and exalteth himself above all that is called God, or that is worshiped; so that he as God sitteth in the temple of God, showing himself that he is God." (2 Thess. 2:3, 4, 7) And furthermore, the apostle warns his brethren that "the mystery of iniquity doth already work." (2 Thess. 2:3 4, 7) Even at that early date he saw, creeping into the church, errors that would prepare the way for the development of the papacy.

Little by little, at first in stealth and silence, and then more openly as it increased in strength and gained control of the minds of men, the mystery of iniquity carried forward its deceptive and blasphemous work. Almost imperceptibly the customs of heathenism found their way into the Christian church. The spirit of compromise and conformity was restrained for a time by the fierce persecutions which the church endured under paganism. But as persecution ceased, and Christianity entered the courts and palaces of kings, she laid aside the humble simplicity of Christ and His apostles for the pomp and pride of pagan priests and rulers; and in place of the requirements of God she substituted human theories and traditions. The nominal conversion of Constantine, in the early part of the fourth century, caused great rejoicing; and the world, cloaked with a form of righteousness, walked into the

27

church. Now the work of corruption rapidly progressed. Paganism, while appearing to be vanquished, became the conqueror. Her spirit controlled the church. Her doctrines, ceremonies, and superstitions were incorporated into the faith and worship of the professed followers of Christ.

This compromise between paganism and Christianity resulted in the development of the "man of sin" foretold in prophecy as opposing and exalting himself above God. That gigantic system of false religion is a masterpiece of Satan's power—a monument of his efforts to seat himself upon the throne to rule the earth according to his will.

Satan once endeavored to form a compromise with Christ. He came to the Son of God in the wilderness of temptation, and showing Him all the kingdoms of the world and the glory of them, offered to give all into His hands if He would but acknowledge the supremacy of the prince of darkness. Christ rebuked the presumptuous tempter, and forced him to depart. But Satan meets with greater success in representing the same temptations to man. To secure worldly gains and honors, the church was led to seek the favor and support of the great men of earth, and having thus rejected Christ, she was induced to yield allegiance to the representative of Satan, the bishop of Rome.

It is one of the leading doctrines of Romanism that the pope is the visible head of the universal church of Christ, invested with supreme authority over bishops and pastors in all parts of the world. More than this, the pope has arrogated the very titles of Diety. He styles himself "Lord God the Pope," assumes infallibility, and demands that all men pay him homage. Thus the same claim urged by Satan in the wilderness of temptation is still urged by him through the Church of Rome, and vast numbers are ready to yield him homage.

But those who fear and reverence God meet this Heaven-daring assumption as Christ met the solicitations, of the wily foe: "Thou shalt worship the Lord thy God, and Him only shalt thou serve." (*Luke* 4:8) God has never given a hint in His Word that He has appointed any man to be the head of the church. The doctrine of papal supremacy is directly opposed to the teachings of the Scriptures. The pope can have no power over Christ's church except by usurpation.

Romanists have persisted in bringing against Protestants the charge of heresy and willful separation from the true church. But these accusations apply rather to themselves. They are the ones who laid down the banner of Christ and departed from "the faith which was once delivered unto the saints." (*Jude* 3)

Satan well knew that the Holy Scriptures would enable men to discern his deceptions and withstand his power. It was by the Word that even the Saviour of the world had resisted his attacks. At every assault Christ presented the shield of eternal truth, saying, "It is written." To every suggestion of the adversary he opposed the wisdom and power of the Word. In order for Satan to maintain his sway over men and establish the authority of the papal usurper, he must keep them in ignorance of the Scriptures. The Bible would exalt God and place finite men in their true position; therefore its sacred truths must be concealed and suppressed. This logic was adopted by the Roman Church. For hundreds of years the circulation of the Bible was prohibited. The people were forbidden to read it or to have it in their houses, and unprincipled priests and prelates interpreted its teachings to sustain their pretensions. Thus the pope came to be almost universally acknowledged as the vicegerent of God on earth, endowed with authority over Church and State.

The detector of error having been removed, Satan worked according to his will. Prophecy had declared that the papacy was to "think to change times and laws." (*Dan.* 7:25) This work it was not slow to attempt. To afford converts from heathenism a substitute for the worship of idols, and thus to promote their nominal acceptance of Christianity, the adoration of images and relics was gradually introduced into the Christian worship. The decree of a general council (Second Council of Nice, A.D. 787.) finally established this system of idolatry. To complete the sacrilegious work, Rome presumed to expunge from the law of God the second commandment, forbidding image worship, and to divide the tenth commandment in order to preserve the number.

The spirit of concession to paganism opened the way for a still further disregard of Heaven's authority. Satan tampered with the fourth commandment also and essayed to set aside the ancient Sabbath, the day which God had blessed and sanctified, *(Gen.* 2:2, 3) and in its stead to exalt the festival observed by the heathen as "the venerable day of the sun." This change was not at first attempted openly. In the first centuries the true Sabbath had been kept by all Christians. They were jealous for the honor of God, and, believing that His law is immutable, they zealously guarded the sacredness of its precepts. But with great subtlety Satan worked through his agents to bring about his object. That the attention of the people might be called to the Sunday, it was made a festival in honor of the resurrection of Christ. Religious services were held upon it; yet it was regarded as a day of recreation, the Sabbath being still sacredly observed.

To prepare the way for the work which he designed to accomplish, Satan had led the Jews, before the advent of Christ, to load down the Sabbath with the most rigorous exactions, making its observance a burden. Now, taking advantage of the false light in which he had thus caused it to be regarded, he cast contempt upon it as a Jewish institution. While Christians continued to observe the Sunday as a joyous festival, he led them, in order to show their hatred of Judaism, to make the Sabbath a fast, a day of sadness and gloom.

In the early part of the fourth century, the emperor Constantine issued a decree making Sunday a public festival throughout the Roman Empire. The day of the sun was reverenced by his pagan subjects and was honored by Christians; it was the emperor's policy to unite the conflicting interests of heathenism and Christianity. He was urged to do this by the bishops of the church, who, inspired by ambition, and thirst for power, perceived that if the same day was observed by both Christians and the heathen, it would promote the nominal acceptance of Christianity by pagans, and thus advance the power and the glory of the church. But while Christians were gradually led to regard Sunday as possessing a degree of sacredness, they still held the true Sabbath as the holy of the Lord and observed it in obedience to the fourth commandment.

The arch-deceiver had not completed his work. He was resolved to gather the Christian world under his banner and to exercise his power through his vicegerent, the proud pontiff who claimed to be the respresentative of Christ. Through half-converted pagans, ambitious prelates, and world-loving churchmen, he accomplished his purpose. Vast councils were held from time to time in which the dignitaries of the church were convened from all the world. In nearly every council the Sabbath which God had instituted was pressed down a little lower, while the Sunday was correspondingly exalted. Thus the pagan festival came finally to be honored as a divine institution, while the Bible Sabbath was pronounced a relic of Judaism, and its observers were declared to be accursed.

The great apostate had succeeded in exalting himself "above all that is called God, or that is worshipped." (*2 Thess.* 2:4) He had dared to change the only precept of the divine law that unmistakably points all mankind to the true and living God. In the fourth commandment God is revealed as the Creator of the heavens and the earth, and is thereby distinguished from all false gods. It was as a memorial of the work of creation that the seventh day was sanctified as a rest-day for man. It was designed to keep the living God ever before the minds of men as the source of being and the object of reverence and worship. Satan strives to turn men from their allegiance to God and from rendering obedience to His law; therefore he directs his efforts especially against that commandment which points to God as the Creator.

Protestants now urge that the resurrection of Christ on

Sunday made it the Christian Sabbath. But Scripture evidence is lacking. No such honor was given to the day by Christ or His apostles. The observance of Sunday as a Christian institution had its origin in that "mystery of lawlessness," (2 *Thess.* 2:7, revised version) which even in Paul's day had begun its work. Where and when did the Lord adopt this child of the papacy? What valid reason can be given for a change which the Scriptures do not sanction?

In the sixth century the papacy had become firmly established. Its seat of power was fixed in the imperial city, and the bishop of Rome was declared to be the head over the entire church. Paganism had given place to the papacy. The dragon had given to the beast "his power, and his seat, and great authority." (*Rev.* 13:2) And now began the 1260 years of papal oppression foretold in the prophecies of Daniel and the Revelation. (*Dan.* 7:25; *Rev.* 13:5.7) Christians were forced to choose, either to yield their integrity and accept the papal ceremonies and worship, or to wear away their lives in dungeons or suffer death by the rack, the fagot, or the headsman's ax. Now were fulfilled the words of Jesus, "Ye shall be betrayed both by parents, and brethren, and kinsfolks, and friends; and some of you shall they cause to be put to death. And ye shall be hated of all men for My name's sake." (*Luke* 21:16, 17) Persecution opened upon the faithful with greater fury than ever before, and the world became a vast battle-field. For hundreds of years the church of Christ found refuge in seclusion and obscurity. Thus says the prophet: "The woman fled into the wilderness, where she hath a place prepared of God, that they should feed her there a thousand two hundred and threescore days." (*Rev.* 12:6)

The accession of the Roman Church to power marked the beginning of the Dark Ages. As her power increased, the darkness deepened. Faith was transferred from Christ, the true foundation, to the pope of Rome. Instead of trusting in the Son of God for forgiveness of sins and for eternal salvation, the people looked to the pope and to the priests and prelates to whom he delegated authority. They were taught that the pope was their earthly mediator, and that none could approach God except through him, and, further, that he stood in the place of God to them and was therefore to be implicitly obeyed. A deviation from his requirements was sufficient cause for the severest punishment to be visited upon the bodies and souls of the offenders. Thus the minds of the poeple were turned away from God to fallible, erring, and cruel men; nay more, to the prince of darkness himself, who exercised his power through them. Sin was disguised in a garb of sanctity. When the Scriptures are suppressed, and man comes to regard himself as supreme, we need look only for fraud, deception, and debasing iniquity. With the elevation of human laws and traditions, was manifest the corruption that ever results from setting aside the law of God.

Those were days of peril for the church of Christ. The faithful standard-bearers were few indeed. Though the truth was not left without witnesses, yet at times it seemed that error and superstition would wholly prevail, and true religion would be banished from the earth. The gospel was lost sight of, but the forms of religion were multiplied, and the people were burdened with rigorous exactions.

They were taught not only to look to the pope as their mediator, but to trust to works of their own to atone for sin. Long pilgrimages, acts of penance, the worship of relics, the erection of churches, shrines, and altars, the payment of large sums to the church—these and many similar acts were enjoined to appease the wrath of God or to secure His favor; as if God were like men, to be angered at trifles, or pacified by gifts or acts of penance!

Notwithstanding that vice prevailed, even among the leaders of the Roman Church, her influence seemed steadily to increase. About the close of the eighth century papists put forth the claim that in the first ages of the church the bishops of Rome had possessed the same spiritual power which they now assumed. To establish this claim, some means must be employed to give it a show of authority; and this was readily suggested by the father of lies. Ancient writings were forged by monks. Decrees of councils before unheard of were discovered, establishing the universal supremacy of the pope from the earliest times. And a church that had rejected the truth greedily accepted these deceptions.

The few faithful builders upon the true foundation (*1 Cor.* 3:10,11) were perplexed and hindered, as the rubbish of false doctrine obstructed the work. Like the builders upon the wall of Jerusalem in Nehemiah's day, some were ready to say, "The strength of the bearers of burdens is decayed, and there is much rubbish, so that we are not able to build." (*Neh.* 4:10) Wearied with the constant struggle against persecution, fraud, iniquity, and every other obstacle that Satan could devise to hinder their progress, some who had been faithful builders became disheartened; and for the sake of peace and security for their property and their lives they turned away from the true foundation. Others, undaunted by the opposition of their enemies, fearlessly declared, "Be not ye afraid of them; remember the Lord, which is great and terrible, (*Neh.* 4:14) and they proceeded with the work, every one with his sword girded by the side. (*Eph.* 6:17)

The same spirit of hatred and opposition to the truth has inspired the enemies of God in every age, and the same vigilance and fidelity have been required in His servants. The words of Christ to the first disciples are applicable to His followers to the close of time: "What I say unto you I say unto all, Watch." (*Mark* 13:37)

The darkness seemed to grow more dense. Image worship became more general. Candles were burned before images, and prayers were offered to them. The most absurd and superstitious customs prevailed. The minds of men were so completely controlled by superstition that reason itself seemed to have lost her sway. While priests and bishops were themselves pleasure-loving, sensual, and corrupt, it could only be expected that the people who looked to them for guidance would be sunken in ignorance and vice.

Another step in papal assumption was taken, when, in the eleventh century, Pope Gregory VII proclaimed the perfection of the Roman Church. Among the propositions which he put forth was one declaring that the church had never erred, nor would it ever err, according to the Scriptures. But the Scripture proofs did not accompany the assertion. The proud pontiff next claimed the power to depose emperors and declared that no sentence which he pronounced could be reversed by any one, but that it was his prerogative to reverse the decisions of all others.

A striking illustration of the tyrannical character of this advocate of infallibility was given in his treatment of the German emperor, Henry IV. For presuming to disregard the pope's authority, this monarch was declared to be excommunicated and dethroned. Terrified by the desertion and threats of his own princes, who were encouraged in rebellion against him by the papal mandate, Henry felt the necessity of making his peace with Rome. In company with his wife and a faithful servant he crossed the Alps in midwinter, that he might humble himself before the pope. Upon reaching the castle whither Gregory had withdrawn, he was conducted without his guards into an outer court, and there, in the severe cold of winter, with uncovered head and naked feet, and in a miserable dress, he awaited the pope's permission to come into his presence. Not until he had continued three days fasting and making confession did the pontiff condescend to grant him pardon. Even then it was only upon condition that the emperor should await the sanction of the pope before resuming the insignia or exercising the power of royalty. And Gregory, elated with his triumph, boasted that it was his duty "to pull down the pride of kings."

How striking the contrast between the overbearing pride of this haughty pontiff and the meekness and gentleness of Christ, who represents Himself as pleading at the door of the heart for admittance that He may come in to bring pardon and peace and who taught His disciples, "Whosoever will be chief among you, let him be your servant." (*Matt.* 20:27)

The advancing centuries witnessed a constant increase of error in the doctrines put forth from Rome. Even before the establishment of the papacy the teachings of heathen philosophers had received attention and exerted an influence in the church. Many who professed conversion still clung to the tenets of their pagan philosophy, and not only continued its study themselves, but urged it upon others as a means of extending their influence among the heathen. Serious errors were thus introduced into the Christian faith. Prominent among these was the belief in man's natural immortality and his consciousness in death. This doctrine laid the foundation upon which Rome established the invocation of saints and the adoration of the virgin Mary. From this sprung also the heresy of eternal torment for the finally impenitent, which was early incorporated into the papal faith.

Then the way was prepared for the introduction of still another invention of paganism, which Rome named purgatory, and employed to terrify the credulous and superstitious multitudes. By this heresy is affirmed the existence of a place of torment in which the souls of such as have not merited eternal damnation are to suffer punishment for their sins, and from which, when freed from impurity, they are admitted to Heaven.

Still another fabrication was needed to enable Rome to profit by the fears and the vices of her adherents. This was supplied by the doctrine of indulgences. Full remission of sins, past, present, and future, and release from all the pains and penalties incurred, were promised to all who would enlist in the pontiff's wars to extend his temporal dominion, to punish his enemies, or to exterminate those who dared deny his spiritual supremacy. The people were also taught that by the payment of money to the church they might free themselves from sin, and also release the souls of their deceased friends who were confined in the tormenting flames. By such means did Rome fill her coffers, and sustain the magnificence, luxury, and vice of the pretended representatives of Him who had not where to lay His head.

The scriptural ordinance of the Lord's supper had been supplanted by the idolatrous sacrifice of the mass. Papist priests pretended, by their senseless mummery, to convert the simple bread and wine into the actual body and blood of Christ. With blasphemous presumption, they openly claimed the power of "creating God, the Creator of all things." All Christians were required, on pain of death, to avow their faith in this horrible, Heaven-insulting heresy. Multitudes who refused were given to the flames.

In the thirteenth century was established that most terrible of all the engines of the papacy,—the Inquisition. The prince of darkness wrought with the leaders of the papal hierarchy. In their secret councils Satan and his angels controlled the minds of evil men, while unseen in the midst stood an angel of God, taking the fearful record of their iniquitous decrees and writing the history of deeds too horrible to appear to human eyes. "Babylon the great" was "drunken with the blood of the saints." The mangled forms of millions of martyrs cried to God for vengeance upon that apostate power.

Popery had become the world's despot. Kings and emperors bowed to the decrees of the Roman pontiff. The destinies of men, both for time and for eternity, seemed under his control. For hundreds of years the doctrines of Rome had been extensively and implicitly received, its rites reverently performed, its festivals generally observed. Its clergy were honored and liberally sustained. Never since has the Roman Church attained to greater dignity, magnificence, or power.

The noontide of the papacy was the world's moral midnight. The Holy Scriptures were almost unknown, not only to the people, but to the priests. Like the Pharisees of old, the papal leaders hated the light which would reveal their sins. God's law, the standard of righteousness, having been removed, they exercised power without limit, and practiced vice without restraint. Fraud, avarice, and profligacy prevailed. Men shrank from no crime by which they could gain wealth or position. The palaces of popes and prelates were scenes of the vilest debauchery. Some of the reigning pontiffs were guilty of crimes so revolting that secular rulers endeavored to depose these dignitaries of the church as monsters too vile to be tolerated. For centuries Europe had made no progress in learning, arts, or civilization. A moral and intellectual paralysis had fallen upon Christendom.

The condition of the world under the Roman power presented a fearful and striking fulfillment of the words of the prophet Hosea: "My people are destroyed for lack of knowledge; because thou hast rejected knowledge, I will also reject thee; . . . seeing thou has forgotten the law of thy God, I will also forget thy children." "There is no truth nor mercy, nor knowledge of God in the land. By swearing, and lying, and killing, and stealing, and committing adultery, they break out, and blood toucheth blood." (*Hosea* 4:6, 1, 2) Such were the results of banishing the Word of God.

Chapter 5

LUTHER'S SEPARATION FROM ROME

FOREMOST AMONG THOSE WHO were called to lead the church from the darkness of popery into the light of a purer faith stood Martin Luther. Zealous, ardent, and devoted, knowing no fear but the fear of God, and acknowledging no foundation for religious faith but the Holy Scriptures, Luther was the man for his time; through him, God accomplished a great work for the reformation of the church and the enlightenment of the world.

Like the first heralds of the gospel, Luther sprang from the ranks of poverty. His early years were spent in the humble home of a German peasant. By daily toil as a miner his father earned the means for his education. He intended him for a lawyer; but God purposed to make him a builder in the great temple that was rising so slowly through the centuries. Hardship, privation, and severe discipline were the school in which Infinite Wisdom prepared Luther for the important mission of his life.

Luther's father was a man of strong and active mind, and great force of character, honest, resolute, and straightforward. He was true to his convictions of duty, let the consequences be what they might. His sterling good sense led him to regard the monastic system with distrust. He was highly displeased when Luther, without his consent, entered a monastery; and it was two years before the father was reconciled to his son, and even then his opinions remained the same.

Luther's parents bestowed great care upon the education and training of their children. They endeavored to instruct them in the knowledge of God and the practice of

Christian virtues. The father's prayer often ascended in the hearing of his son, that the child might remember the name of the Lord, and one day aid in the advancement of His truth. Every advantage for moral or intellectual culture which their life of toil permitted them to enjoy was eagerly improved by these parents. Their efforts were earnest and persevering to prepare their children for a life of piety and usefulness. With their firmness and strength of character they sometimes exercised too great severity; but the reformer himself, though conscious that in some respects they had erred, found in their discipline more to approve than to condemn.

At school, where he was sent at an early age, Luther was treated with harshness and even violence. So great was the poverty of his parents that upon going from home to school in another town he was for a time obligated to obtain his food by singing from door to door, and he often suffered from hunger. The gloomy, superstitious ideas of religion then prevailing filled him with fear. He would lie down at night with a sorrowful heart, looking forward with trembling to the dark future, and in constant terror at the thought of God as a stern, unrelenting judge, a cruel tyrant, rather than a kind heavenly Father. Yet under so many and so great discouragements, Luther pressed resolutely forward toward the high standard of moral and intellectual excellence which attracted his soul.

He thirsted for knowledge, and the earnest and practical character of his mind led him to desire the solid and useful rather than the showy and superficial. When at the age of eighteen he entered the University of Erfurt, his situation was more favorable and his prospects brighter than in his earlier years. His parents having by thrift and industry acquired a competence, they were able to render him all needed assistance. And the influence of judicious friends had somewhat lessened the gloomy effects of his former training. He applied himself to the study of the best authors, diligently treasuring their most weighty thoughts and making the wisdom of the wise his own. Even under the harsh discipline of his former instructors he had early given promise of distinction; and with favorable influences his mind rapidly developed. A retentive memory, a lively imagination, strong reasoning powers, and untiring application, soon placed him in the foremost rank among his associates. Intellectual discipline ripened his understanding and aroused an activity of mind and a keenness of perception that were preparing him for the conflicts of his life.

The fear of the Lord dwelt in the heart of Luther, enabling him to maintain his steadfastness of purpose, and leading him to deep humility before God. He had an abiding sense of his dependence upon divine aid, and he did not fail to begin each day with prayer, while his heart was continally breathing a petition for guidance and support. "To pray well," he often said, "is the better half of study."

While one day examining the books in the library of the university, Luther discovered a Latin Bible. Such a book he had never before seen. He was ignorant even of its existence. He had heard portions of the Gospels and Epistles, which were read to the people at public worship, and he supposed that these were the entire Bible. Now, for the first time, he looked upon the whole of God's Word. With mingled awe and wonder he turned the sacred pages; with quickened pulse and throbbing heart he read for himself the words of life, pausing now and then to exclaim, "Oh, if God would give me such a book for my own!" Angels of Heaven were by his side, and rays of light from the throne of God revealed the treasures of truth to his understanding. He had ever feared to offend God, but now the deep conviction of his condition as a sinner took hold upon him as never before.

An earnest desire to be free from sin and to find peace with God, led him at last to enter a cloister and devote himself to a monastic life. Here he was required to perform the lowest drudgery and to beg from house to house. He was at an age when respect and appreciation are most eagerly craved, and these menial offices were deeply mortifying to his natural feelings; but he patiently endured this humiliation, believing that it was necessary because of his sins.

Every moment that could be spared from his daily duties he employed in study, robbing himself of sleep, and grudging even the time spent at his scanty meals. Above everything else he delighted in the study of God's Word. He had found a Bible chained to the convent wall, and to this he often repaired. As his convictions of sin deepened, he sought by his own works to obtain pardon and peace. He led a most rigorous life, endeavoring by fasting, vigils and scourgings, to subdue the evils of his nature, from which the monastic life had brought no release. He shrank from no sacrifice by which he might attain to that purity of heart, which would enable him to stand approved before God. "I was indeed a pious monk," he afterward said, "and followed the rules of my order more strictly than I can express. If ever monk could attain Heaven by his monkish works, I should certainly have been entitled to it. If I had continued much longer, I should have carried my mortifications even to death." As the result of this painful discipline, he lost strength, and suffered from fainting spasms, from the effects of which he never fully recovered. But with all his efforts his burdened soul found no relief. He was at last driven to the verge of despair.

When it appeared to Luther that all was lost, God raised up a friend and helper for him. The pious Staupitz opened the Word of God to Luther's mind and bade him look away from himself, cease the contemplation of infinite punishment for the violation of God's law, and look to Jesus, his sin-pardoning Saviour. "Instead of torturing yourself on account of your sins, cast yourself into the arms of your Redeemer. Trust in Him, in the righteousness of His life, in the atonement of His death. Listen to the Son of God. He became man to give you the assurance of divine favor. Love Him who has first loved you." Thus spoke this messenger of mercy. His words made a deep impression upon Luther's mind. After many a struggle with long-cherished errors, he was enabled to grasp the truth, and peace came to his troubled soul.

Luther was ordained a priest and was called from the cloister to a professorship in the University of Wittenberg. Here he applied himself to the study of the Scriptures in the original tongues. He began to lecture upon the Bible; and the book of Psalms, the Gospels, and the Epistles were opened to the understanding of crowds of delighted listeners. Staupitz, his friend and superior, urged him to ascend the pulpit and preach the Word of God. Luther hesitated, feeling himself unworthy to speak to the people in Christ's stead. It was only after a long struggle that he yielded to the solicitations of his friends. Already he was mighty in the Scriptures, and the grace of God rested upon him. His eloquence captivated his hearers, the clearness and power with which he presented the truth convinced their understanding, and his fervor touched their hearts.

Luther was still a true son of the papal church, and had no thought that he would ever be anything else. In the providence of God he was led to visit Rome. He pursued his journey on foot, lodging at the monasteries on the way. At a convent in Italy he was filled with wonder at the wealth, magnificence, and luxury that he witnessed. Endowed with a princely revenue, the monks dwelt in splendid apartments, attired themselves in the richest and most costly robes, and feasted at a sumptuous table. With painful misgivings Luther contrasted this scene with the self-denial and hardship of his own life. His mind was becoming perplexed.

At last he beheld in the distance the seven-hilled city. With deep emotion he prostrated himself upon the earth, exclaiming, "Holy Rome, I salute thee!" He entered the city, visited the churches, listened to the marvelous tales repeated by priests and monks, and performed all the ceremonies required. Everywhere he looked upon scenes that filled him with astonishment and horror. He saw that iniquity existed among all classes of the clergy. He heard indecent jokes from prelates, and was filled with horror at their awful profanity, even during mass. As he mingled with the monks and citizens, he met dissipation, debauchery. Turn where he would, in the place of sanctity he found profanation. "It is incredible," he wrote, "what sins and atrocities are committed in Rome; they must be seen and heard to be believed. So that it is usual to say, 'If there be a hell, Rome is built above it. It is an abyss whence all sins proceed.' "

By a recent decretal, an indulgence had been promised by the pope to all who should ascend upon their knees "Pilate's staircase," said to have been descended by our Saviour on leaving the Roman judgment-hall and to have been miraculously conveyed from Jerusalem to Rome. Luther was one day devoutly climbing these steps when suddenly a voice like thunder seemed to say to him, "The just shall live by faith." (*Rom.* 1.17) He sprang to his feet and hastened from the place in shame and horror. That text never lost its power upon his soul. From that time he saw more clearly than ever before the fallacy of trusting to human works for salvation and the necessity of constant faith in the merits of Christ. His eyes had been opened and were never again to be closed to the delusions of the papacy. When he turned his face from Rome, he had turned away also in heart, and from that time the separation grew wider, until he severed all connection with the papal church.

After his return from Rome Luther received at the University of Wittenberg the degree of doctor of divinity. Now he was at liberty to devote himself, as never before, to the Scriptures that he loved. He had taken a solemn vow to study carefully and to preach with fidelity the Word of God, not the sayings and doctrines of the popes, all the days of his life. He was no longer the mere monk or professor, but the authorized herald of the Bible. He had been called as a shepherd to feed the flock of God that were hungering and thirsting for the truth. He firmly declared that Christians should receive no other doctrines than those which rest on the authority of the Sacred Scriptures. These words struck at the very foundation of papal supremacy. They contained the vital principle of the Reformation.

Luther saw the danger of exalting human theories above the Word of God. He fearlessly attacked the speculative infidelity of the schoolmen, and opposed the philosophy and theology which had so long held a controlling influence upon the people. He denounced such studies as not only worthless but pernicious and sought to turn the minds of his hearers from the sophistries of philosophers and theologians to the eternal truths set forth by prophets and apostles.

Precious was the message which he bore to the eager crowds that hung upon his words. Never before had such teachings fallen upon their ears. The glad tidings of a Saviour's love, the assurance of pardon and peace through his atoning blood, rejoiced their hearts, and inspired within them an immortal hope. At Wittenberg a light was kindled whose rays should extend to the uttermost parts of the earth and which was to increase in brightness to the close of time.

But light and darkness cannot harmonize. Between truth and error there is an irrepressible conflict. To uphold and defend the one is to attack and overthrow the other. Our Saviour Himself declared, "I came not to send peace, but a sword." (*Matt.* 10:34) Said Luther, a few years after the opening of the Reformation, "God does not conduct, but drives me forward. I am not master of my own actions. I would gladly live in repose, but I am thrown into the midst of tumults and revolutions." He was now about to be urged into the contest.

The Roman Church had made merchandise of the grace of God. The tables of the money-changers (*Matt.* 21:12) were set up beside her altars, and the air resounded with the shouts of buyers and sellers. Under the plea of raising funds for the erection of St. Peter's church at Rome, indulgences for sin were publicly offered for sale by the authority of the pope. By the price of crime a temple was to be built up for God's worship, the corner-stone laid with the wages of iniquity. But the very means adopted for Rome's aggrandizement provoked the deadliest blow to her power and greatness. It was this that aroused the most determined and successful of the enemies of popery and led to the battle which shook the papal throne and jostled the triple crown upon the pontiff's head.

The official appointed to conduct the sale of indulgences in Germany—Tetzel by name—had been convicted of the basest offenses against society and against the law of God; but having escaped the punishment due to his crimes, he was employed to further the mercenary and unscrupulous projects of the pope. With great effrontery he repeated the most glaring falsehoods and related marvelous tales to deceive an ignorant, credulous, and superstitious people. Had they possessed the Word of God, they would not have been thus deceived. It was to keep them under the control of the papacy, in order to swell the power and wealth of her ambitious leaders, that the Bible had been withheld from them.

As Tetzel entered a town, a messenger went before him, announcing, "The grace of God and of the holy father is at your gates." And the people welcomed the blasphemous pretender as if he were God Himself come down from Heaven to them. The infamous traffic was set up in the church, and Tetzel, ascending the pulpit, extolled indulgences as the most precious gift of God. He declared that by virtue of his certificates of pardon all the sins which the purchaser should afterward desire to commit would be forgiven him, and that "even repentance was not indispensable." More than this, he assured his hearers that the indulgences had power to save not only the living but the dead; that the very moment the money should clink against the bottom of his chest, the soul in whose behalf it had been paid would escape from purgatory and make its way to Heaven.

When Simon Magus offered to purchase of the apostles the power to work miracles, Peter answered him, "Thy money perish with thee, because thou hast thought that the gift of God may be purchased with money." (*Acts*

8:20) But Tetzel's offer was grasped by eager thousands. Gold and silver flowed into his treasury. A salvation that could be bought with money was more easily obtained than that which requires repentance, faith, and diligent effort to resist and overcome sin.

The doctrine of indulgences had been opposed by men of learning and piety in the Roman Church, and there were many who had no faith in pretensions so contrary to both reason and revelation. No prelate dared lift his voice against this iniquitous traffic, but the minds of men were becoming disturbed and uneasy, and many eagerly inquired if God would not work through some instrumentality for the purification of His church.

Luther, though still a papist of the straitest sort, was filled with horror at the blasphemous assumptions of the indulgence-mongers. Many of his own congregation had purchased certificates of pardon, and they soon began to come to their pastor, confessing their various sins, and expecting absolution, not because they were penitent and wished to reform, but on the ground of the indulgence. Luther refused them absolution and warned them that unless they should repent and reform their lives, they must perish in their sins. In great perplexity they repaired to Tetzel with the complaint that their confessor had refused his certificates; and some boldly demanded that their money be returned to them. The friar was filled with rage. He uttered the most terrible curses, caused fires to be lighted in the public squares, and declared that he had orders from the pope "to burn the heretics who dared oppose his most holy indulgences."

Luther now entered boldly upon his work as a champion of the truth. His voice was heard from the pulpit in earnest, solemn warning. He set before the people the offensive character of sin and taught them that it is impossible for man, by his own works, to lessen its guilt or evade its punishment. Nothing but repentance toward God and faith in Christ can save the sinner. The grace of Christ cannot be purchased; it is a free gift. He counseled the people not to buy the indulgences, but to look in faith to a crucified Redeemer. He related his own painful experience in vainly seeking by humiliation and penance to secure salvation and assured his hearers that it was by looking away from himself and believing in Christ that he found peace and joy.

As Tetzel continued his traffic and his impious pretensions, Luther determined upon a more effectual protest against these crying abuses. An occasion soon offered. The castle church of Wittenberg possessed many relics, which on certain holy days were exhibited to the people, and full remission of sins was granted to all who then visited the church and made confession. Accordingly on these days the people in great numbers resorted thither. One of the most important of these occasions, the festival of "All-Saints," was approaching. On the preceding day, Luther, joining the crowds that were already making their way to the church, posted on its door a paper containing ninety-five propositions against the doctrine of indulgences. He declared his willingness to defend these theses next day at the university against all who should see fit to attack them.

His propositions attracted universal attention. They were read and re-read and repeated in every direction. Great excitement was created in the university and in the whole city. By these theses it was shown that the power to grant the pardon of sin and to remit its penalty had never been committed to the pope or to any other man. The whole scheme was a farce, an artifice to extort money by playing upon the superstitions of the people, a device of Satan to destroy the souls of all who should trust to its lying pretensions. It was also clearly shown that the gospel of Christ is the most valuable treasure of the church, and that the grace of God, therein revealed, is freely bestowed upon all who seek it by repentance and faith.

Luther's theses challenged discussion; but no one dared accept the challenge. The questions which he proposed had in a few days spread through all Germany, and in a few weeks they had sounded throughout Christendom.

Many devoted Romanists, who had seen and lamented the terrible iniquity prevailing in the church, but had not known how to arrest its progress, read the propositions with great joy, recognizing in them the voice of God. They felt that the Lord had graciously set His hand to arrest the rapidly swelling tide of corruption that was issuing from the see of Rome. Princes and magistrates secretly rejoiced that a check was to be put upon the arrogant power which denied the right of appeal from its decisions.

But the sin-loving and superstitious multitudes were terrified as the sophistries that had soothed their fears were swept away. Crafty ecclesiastics, interrupted in their work of sanctioning crime, and seeing their gains endangered, were enraged, and rallied to uphold their pretentions. The reformer had bitter accusers to meet. Some charged him with acting hastily and from impulse. Others accused him of presumption, declaring that he was not directed of God, but was acting from pride and forwardness. "Who does not know," he responded, "that one can seldom advance a new idea without having some appearance of pride, and without being accused of exciting quarrels? Why were Christ and all the martyrs put to death?—Because they appeared proud despisers of the wisdom of the times in which they lived, and because they brought forward new truths without having first consulted the oracles of the old opinions."

Again he declared: "What I am doing will not be effected by the prudence of man, but by the counsel of God. If the work be of God, who shall stop it? If it be not, who shall forward it? Not my will, not theirs, not ours, but Thy will, holy Father who art in Heaven!"

Though Luther had been moved by the Spirit of God to begin his work, he was not to carry it forward without severe conflicts. The reproaches of his enemies, their misrepresentation of his purposes, and their unjust and malicious reflections upon his character and motives, came in upon him like an overwhelming flood; and they were not without effect. He had felt confident that the leaders of

the people, both in the church and in the schools, would
gladly unite with him in efforts for reform. Words of encouragement from those in high position had inspired him
with joy and hope. Already in anticipation he had seen a
brighter day dawning for the Church. But encouragement
had changed to reproach and condemnation. Many dignitaries, both of Church and State, were convicted of the
truthfulness of his theses; but they soon saw that the
acceptance of these truths would involve great changes.
To enlighten and reform the people would be virtually to
undermine the authority of Rome, to stop thousands of
streams now flowing into her treasury, and thus greatly
curtail the extravagance and luxury of the papal leaders.
Furthermore, to teach the people to think and act as responsible beings, looking to Christ alone for salvation,
would overthrow the pontiff's throne, and eventually
destroy their own authority. For this reason they refused
the knowledge tendered them of God, and arrayed themselves against Christ and the truth by their opposition to
the man whom He had sent to enlighten them.

Luther trembled as he looked upon himself—one man
opposed to the mightiest powers on earth. He sometimes
doubted whether he had indeed been led of God to set
himself against the authority of the church. "Who was I,"
he writes, "to oppose the majesty of the pope, before
whom the kings of the earth and the whole world
trembled? No one can know what I suffered in those
first two years, and into what dejection and even despair I
was often plunged." But he was not left to become utterly
disheartened. When human support failed, he looked to
God alone and learned that he could lean in perfect
safety upon that all-powerful arm.

To a friend of the Reformation Luther wrote: "We
cannot attain to the understanding of Scripture either by
study or by strength of intellect. Therefore your first duty
must be to begin with prayer. Entreat the Lord to deign
to grant you, in His rich mercy, rightly to understand His
Word. There is no other interpreter of the Word but the
Author of that Word himself. Even as He has said, 'They

shall all be taught of God.' Hope nothing from your study and the strength of your intellect; but simply put your trust in God, and in the guidance of His Spirit. Believe one who has made trial of this matter." Here is a lesson of vital importance to those who feel that God has called them to present to others the solemn truths for this time. These truths will stir the enmity of Satan, and of men who love the fables that he has devised. In the conflict with the powers of evil, there is need of something more than strength of intellect and human wisdom.

When enemies appealed to custom and tradition, or to the assertions and authority of the pope, Luther met them with the Bible, and the Bible only. Here were arguments which they could not answer; therefore the slaves of formalism and superstition clamored for his blood, as the Jews had clamored for the blood of Christ. "He is a heretic," cried the Roman zealots; "it is a sin to allow him to live an hour longer! Away with him at once to the scaffold!" But Luther did not fall a prey to their fury. God had a work for him to do, and angels of Heaven were sent to protect him. Many, however, who had received from Luther the precious light, were made the objects of Satan's wrath, and for the truth's sake fearlessly suffered torture and death.

Luther's teachings attracted the attention of thoughtful minds throughout all Germany. From his sermons and writings issued beams of light which awakened and illuminated thousands. A living faith was taking the place of the dead formalism in which the church had so long been held. The people were daily losing confidence in the superstitions of Romanism. The barriers of prejudice were giving way. The Word of God, by which Luther tested every doctrine and every claim, was like a two-edged sword, cutting its way to the hearts of the people. Everywhere there was awakening a desire for spiritual progress. Everywhere was such a hungering and thirsting after righteousness as had not been known for ages. The eyes of the people, so long directed to human rites and earthly mediators, were now turning, in penitence and faith, to Christ and Him crucified.

This widespread interest aroused still further the fears of the papal authorities. Luther received a summons to appear at Rome to answer to the charge of heresy. The command filled his friends with terror. They knew full well the danger that threatened him in that corrupt city, already drunk with the blood of the martyrs of Jesus. They protested against his going to Rome and requested that he receive his examination in Germany.

This arrangement was finally effected, and the pope's legate was appointed to hear the case. In the instructions communicated by the pontiff to this official it was stated that Luther had already been declared a heretic. The legate was therefore charged to "prosecute and reduce him to submission without delay." If he should remain steadfast, and the legate should fail to gain possession of his person, he was empowered to "proscribe him in all places in Germany, to put away, curse, and excommunicate all who were attached to him." And further, the pope directed his legate, in order entirely to root out the pestilent heresy, to excommunicate all, of whatever dignity in Church or State, except the emperor, who should neglect to seize Luther and his adherents and deliver them up to the vengeance of Rome.

Here is displayed the true spirit of popery. Not a trace of Christian principle, or even of common justice, is to be seen in the whole document. Luther was at a great distance from Rome; he had had no opportunity to explain or defend his position; yet before his case had been investigated, he was summarily pronounced a heretic, and, in the same day, exhorted, accused, judged, and condemned; and all this by the self-styled holy father, the only supreme, infallible auhority in Church or State!

At this time, when Luther so much needed the sympathy and counsel to a true friend, God's providence sent Melancthon to Wittenberg. Young in years, modest and diffident in his manners, Melancthon's sound judgment, extensive knowledge, and winning eloquence, combined with the purity and uprightness of his character, won universal admiration and esteem. The brilliancy of his talents was not more marked than his gentleness of disposition. He soon became an earnest disciple of the gospel, and Luther's most trusted friend and valued supporter; his gentleness, caution, and exactness serving as a complement to Luther's courage and energy. Their union in the work added strength to the Reformation, and was a source of great encouragement to Luther.

Augsburg had been fixed upon as the place of trial, and the reformer set out on foot to perform the journey thither. Serious fears were entertained in his behalf. Threats had been made openly that he would be seized and murdered on the way, and his friends begged him not to venture. They even entreated him to leave Wittenberg for a time, and find safety with those who would gladly protect him. But he would not leave the position where God had placed him. He must continue faithfully to maintain the truth, notwithstanding the storms that were beating upon him. His language was: "I am like Jeremiah, a man of strife and contention; but the more they increase their threatenings, the more they multiply my joy. . . . They have already torn to pieces my honor and my good name. All I have left is my wretched body; let them have it; they will then shorten my life by a few hours. But as to my soul, they shall not have that. He who resolves to bear the word of Christ to the world must expect death at every hour."

The tidings of Luther's arrival at Augsburg gave great satisfaction to the papal legate. The troublesome heretic who was exciting the attention of the whole world seemed now in the power of Rome, and the legate determined that he should not escape. The reformer had failed to provide himself with a safe-conduct. His friends urged him not to appear before the legate without one, and they themselves undertook to procure it from the emperor. The legate intended to force Luther, if possible, to retreat, or, failing in this, to cause him to be conveyed to Rome, to share the fate of Huss and Jerome. Therefore through

his agents he endeavored to induce Luther to appear
without a safe-conduct, trusting himself to his mercy. This
the reformer firmly declined to do. Not until he had received the document pledging him the emperor's protection, did he appear in the presence of the papal
ambassador.

As a matter of policy, the Romanists had decided to attempt to win Luther by an appearance of gentleness. The
legate, in his interviews with him, professed great friend-
liness; but he demanded that Luther submit implicitly to
the authority of the church, and yield every point, without
argument or question. He had not rightly estimated the
character of the man with whom he had to deal. Luther,
in reply, expressed his regard for the church, his desire
for the truth, his readiness to answer all objections to
what he had taught, and to submit his doctrines to the decision of certain leading universities. But at the same time
he protested against the cardinal's course in requiring him
to retract without having proved him in error.

The only response was, "Recant, recant." The reformer
showed that his position was sustained by the Scriptures,
and firmly declared that he could not renounce the truth.
The legate, unable to reply to Luther's arguments, overwhelmed him with a storm of reproaches, gibes, and flattery, interspersed with quotations from tradition and the
sayings of the Fathers, granting the reformer no opportunity to speak. Seeing that the conference, thus continued, would be utterly futile, Luther finally obtained a
reluctant permission to present his answer in writing.

"In so doing," said he, writing to a friend, "the
oppressed find double gain; first, what is written may be
submitted to the judgment of others; and second, one has
a better chance of working on the fears, if not on the conscience, of an arrogant and babbling despot, who would
otherwise overpower by his imperious language." At the
next interview, Luther presented a clear, concise, and for-
cible exposition of his views, fully supported by many
quotations from Scripture. This paper, after reading
aloud, he handed to the cardinal, who, however, cast it

contemptuously aside, declaring it to be a mass of idle words and irrelevant quotations. Luther, fully roused, now met the haughty prelate on his own ground, the traditions and teachings of the church, and utterly overthrew his assumptions.

When the prelate saw that Luther's reasoning was unanswerable, he lost all self-control, and in a rage cried out: "Retract, or I will send you to Rome, there to appear before the judges commissioned to take cognizance of your case. I will excommunicate you and all your partisans, and all who shall at any time countenance you, and will cast them out of the church." And he finally declared, in a haughty and angry tone, "Retract, or return no more."

The reformer promptly withdrew with his friends, thus declaring plainly that no retraction was to be expected from him. This was not what the cardinal had purposed. He had flattered himself that by violence he could awe Luther to submission. Now, left alone with his supporters, he looked from one to another, in utter chagrin at the unexpected failure of his schemes.

Luther's efforts on this occasion were not without good results. The large assembly present had opportunity to compare the two men, and to judge for themselves of the spirit manifested by them, as well as of the strength and truthfulness of their positions. How marked the contrast! The reformer, simple, humble, firm, stood up in the strength of God, having truth on his side; the pope's representative, self-important, overbearing, haughty, and unreasonable, was without a single argument from the Scriptures, yet vehemently crying, "Retract, or be sent to Rome for punishment."

Notwithstanding Luther had secured a safe-conduct, the Romanists were plotting to seize and imprison him. His friends urged that it was useless for him to prolong his stay, he should return to Wittenberg without delay, and that the utmost caution should be observed in order to conceal his intentions. He accordingly left Augsburg before daybreak, on horseback, accompanied only by a guide furnished him by the magistrate. With many forebodings he secretly made his way through the dark and silent streets of the city. Enemies, vigilant and cruel, were plotting his destruction. Would he escape the snares prepared for him? Those were moments of anxiety and earnest prayer. He reached a small gate in the wall of the city. It was opened for him, and with his guide he passed through without hindrance. Once safely outside, the fugitives hastened their flight, and before the legate learned of Luther's departure, he was beyond the reach of his persecutors. Satan and his emissaries were defeated. The man whom they had thought in their power was gone, escaped as a bird from the snare of the fowler.

At the news of Luther's escape, the legate was overwhelmed with surprise and anger. He had expected to receive great honor for his wisdom and firmness in dealing with this disturber of the church; but his hope was disappointed. He gave expression to his wrath in a letter to Frederick, the Elector of Saxony, bitterly denouncing Luther, and demanding that Frederick send the reformer to Rome or banish him from Saxony.

In defense, Luther urged that the legate or the pope show him his errors from the Scriptures, and pledged himself in the most solemn manner to renounce his doctrines if they could be shown to contradict the Word of God. And he expressed his gratitude to God that he had been counted worthy to suffer in so holy a cause.

The elector had, as yet, little knowledge of the reformed doctrines, but he was deeply impressed by the candor, force, and clearness of Luther's words; and, until the reformer should be proved to be in error, Frederick resolved to stand as his protector. In reply to the legate's demand he wrote: "Since Doctor Martin has appeared before you at Augsburg, you should be satisfied. We did not expect that you would endeavor to make him retract without having convinced him of his errors. None of the learned men in our principality have informed us that Martin's doctrine is impious, antichristian, or heretical.

We must refuse, therefore, either to send Luther to Rome or to expel him from our States."

The elector saw that there was a general breaking down on the moral restraints of society. A great work of reform was needed. The complicated and expensive arrangements to restrain and punish crime would be unnecessary if men but acknowledged and obeyed the requirements of God and the dictates of an enlightened conscience. He saw that Luther was laboring to secure this object, and he secretly rejoiced that a better influence was making itself felt in the church.

He saw also that as a professor in the university Luther was eminently successful. Only a year had passed since the reformer posted his theses on the castle church, yet there was already a great falling off in the number of pilgrims that visited the church at the festival of All-Saints. Rome had been deprived of worshipers and offerings, but their place was filled by another class, who now came to Wittenberg—not pilgrims to adore her relicts, but students to fill her halls of learning. The writings of Luther had kindled everywhere a new interest in the Holy Scriptures, and not only from all parts of Germany, but from other lands, students flocked to the university. Young men, coming in sight of Wittenberg for the first time, would "raise their hands to heaven, and bless God for having caused the light of truth to shine forth from Wittenberg, as in former ages from Mount Zion, that it might penetrate to the most distant lands."

Luther was as yet but partially converted from the errors of Romanism. But as he compared the Holy Oracles with the papal decrees and constitutions, he was filled with wonder. "I am reading," he wrote, "the decretals of the popes, and . . . I know not whether the pope is antichrist himself, or whether he is his apostle; so misrepresented and even crucified does Christ appear in them." Yet at this time Luther was still a supporter of the Roman Church, and had no thought that he would ever separate from her communion.

The reformer's writings and his doctrine were extending

to every nation in Christendom. The work spread to Switzerland and Holland. Copies of his writings found their way to France and Spain. In England his teachings were received as the word of life. To Belguim and Italy also the truth had extended. Thousands were awakening from their death-like stupor to the joy and hope of a life of faith.

Rome became more and more exasperated by the attacks of Luther, and it was declared by some of his fanatical opponents, even by doctors in Catholic universities, that he who should kill the rebellious monk would be without sin. One day a stranger, with a pistol hidden under his cloak, approached the reformer, and inquired why he went thus alone. "I am in the hands of God," answered Luther. "He is my help and my shield. What can man do unto me?" Upon hearing these words, the stranger turned pale, and fled away, as from the presence of the angels of Heaven.

Rome was bent upon the destruction of Luther; but God was his defense. His doctrines were heard everywhere, in convents, in cottages, in the castles of the nobles, in the universities, in the palaces of kings; and noble men were rising on every hand to sustain his efforts.

It was about this time that Luther, reading the works of Huss, found that the great truth of justification by faith, which he himself was seeking to uphold and teach, had been held by the Bohemian reformer. "We have all," said Luther, "Paul, Augustine, and myself, been Hussites without knowing it. God will surely visit it upon the world," he continued, "that the truth was preached to it a century ago, and burned."

In an appeal to the emperor and nobility of Germany in behalf of the Reformation of Christianity, Luther wrote concerning the pope: "It is monstrous to see him who is called the vicar of Christ, displaying a magnificence unrivaled by that of any emperor. Is this to represent the poor and lowly Jesus or the humble St. Peter? The pope, say they, is the lord of the world! But Christ, whose vicar he boasts of being, said, 'My kingdom is not of this world.' Can the dominions of a vicar extend beyond those of his superior?"

He wrote thus of the universities: "I fear much that the universities will be found to be great gates leading down to hell, unless they take diligent care to explain the Holy Scriptures, and to engrave them in the hearts of our youth. I advise no one to place his child where the Holy Scriptures are not regarded as the rule of life. Every institution where the Word of God is not diligently studied, must become corrupt."

This appeal was rapidly circulated throughout Germany and exerted a powerful influence upon the people. The whole nation was stirred, and multitudes were roused to rally around the standard of reform. Luther's opponents, burning with a desire for revenge, urged the pope to take decisive measures against him. It was decreed that his doctrines should be immediately condemned. Sixty days were granted the reformer and his adherents after which, if they did not recant, they were all to be excommunicated.

That was a terrible crisis for the Reformation. For centuries Rome's sentence of excommunication had struck terror to powerful monarchs; it had filled mighty empires with woe and desolation. Those upon whom its condemnation fell, were universally regarded with dread and horror; they were cut off from intercourse with their fellows, and treated as outlaws, to be hunted to extermination. Luther was not blind to the tempest about to burst upon him; but he stood firm, trusting in Christ to be his support and shield. With a martyr's faith and courage he wrote: "What is about to happen I know not, and I care not to know. Wherever the blow may reach me, I fear not. Not so much as a leaf falls without the will of our Father; how much rather will He care for us! It is a light matter to die for the Word, since this Word, that was made flesh for us, hath Himself died. If we die with Him, we shall live with Him; and passing through that which He has passed through before us, we shall be where He is, and dwell with Him forever."

When the papal bull reached Luther, he said: "I despise it, and resist it, as impious and false. . . . It is *Christ* Himself who is condemned therein. I glory in the prospect of suffering for the best of causes. Already I feel greater liberty; for I know now that the pope is antichrist, and that his throne is that of Satan himself."

Yet the mandate of Rome was not without effect. Prison, torture, and sword were weapons potent to enforce obedience. The weak and superstitious trembled before the decree of the pope, and while there was general sympathy for Luther, many felt that life was too dear to be risked in the cause of reform. Everything seemed to indicate that the reformer's work was about to close.

But Luther was fearless still. Rome had hurled her anathemas against him, and the world looked on, nothing doubting that he would perish or be forced to yield. But with terrible power he flung back upon herself the sentence of condemnation, and publicly declared his determination to abandon her forever. In the presence of a crowd of students, doctors, and citizens of all ranks, Luther burned the pope's bull, with the canon laws, the decretals, and certain writings sustaining the papal power. "My enemies have been able by burning my books," he said, "to injure the cause of truth in the minds of some, and to destroy souls: for this reason I consume their books in return. A serious struggle has just commenced. Hitherto I have been playing with the pope; now I wage open war. I began this work in God's name; it will be ended without me, and by His might."

To the reproaches of his enemies, who taunted him with the weakness of his cause, Luther answered: "Who knows if God has not chosen and called me to perform this needed work, and if these babblers ought not to fear that by despising me, they despise God himself? They say I am alone; no, for Jehovah is with me. In their sense, Moses was alone at the departure from Egypt; Elijah was alone in the reign of King Ahab; Isaiah was alone in Jerusalem; Ezekiel was alone in Babylon. Hear this, O Rome: God never selected as a prophet either the high priest or any great personage; but rather, He chose low and despised men, once even the sheperd Amos. In every age the saints have been compelled to rebuke kings, princes, recreant priests, and wise men at the peril of their lives. I do not say that I also am a prophet; but I do say that they ought to fear precisely because I am alone, while on the side of the oppressor are numbers, caste, wealth, and mocking letters. Yes, I am alone; but I stand serene, because side by side with me is the Word of God; and with all their boasted numbers, this, the greatest of powers, is not with them."

Yet it was not without a terrible struggle with himself that Luther decided upon a final separation from the church. It was about this time that he wrote: "I feel more and more every day how difficult it is to lay aside the scruples which one has imbibed in childhood. Oh, how much pain it cost me, though I had the Scriptures on my side, to justify it to myself that I should dare to make a stand alone against the pope, and hold him forth as antichrist! What have the tribulations of my heart not been! How many times have I asked myself with bitterness that question which was so frequent on the lips of the papists: 'Art thou alone wise? Can every one else be mistaken? How will it be, if, after all, it is thyself who art wrong, and who art involving in thy error so many souls, who will then be eternally damned?' 'Twas so I fought with myself and with Satan, till Christ, by His infallible Word, fortified my heart against these doubts."

The pope had theatened Luther with excommunication if he did not recant, and the threat was now fulfilled. A new bull appeared, declaring the reformer's final separation from the Roman Church, denouncing him as accursed of Heaven, and including the same condemnation all who should receive his doctrines. The great contest had been fully entered upon.

Opposition is the lot of all whom God employs to present truths specially applicable to their time. There was a present truth in the days of Luther, a truth at that time of special importance; there is a present truth for the

church to-day. He who does all things according to the
counsel of His will has been pleased to place men under
various circumstances and to enjoin upon them duties
peculiar to the time in which they live and the conditions
under which they are placed. If they would prize the light
given them, broader views of truth would be opened before them. But truth is no more desired by the majority
to-day than it was by the papists who opposed Luther.
There is the same disposition to accept the theories and
traditions of men instead of the Word of God as in former
ages. Those who present the truth for this time should not
expect to be received with greater favor than were earlier
reformers. The great controversy between truth and error,
between Christ and Satan, is to increase in intensity to the
close of this world's history.

Said Jesus to His disciples: "If ye were of the world,
the world would love his own; but because ye are not of
the world, but I have chosen you out of the world, therefore the world hateth you. Remember the word that I said
unto you, The servant is no greater than his Lord. If
they have persecuted Me, they will also persecute you; if
they have kept My saying, they will keep yours also."
(*John* 15:19, 20) And on the other hand our Lord declared plainly: "Woe unto you, when all men shall speak
well of you! for so did their fathers to the false
prophets." (*Luke* 6:26) The spirit of the world is no
more in harmony with the Spirit of Christ to-day than in
earlier times; and those who preach the Word of God in
its purity will be received with no greater favor now than
then. The forms of opposition to the truth may change,
the enmity may be less open because it is more subtle; but
the same antagonism still exists, and will be manifested to
the end of time.

Chapter 6

SATAN'S TRAPS

THE GREAT CONTROVERSY BETWEEN Christ and Satan, that has been carried forward for nearly six thousand years, is soon to close; and the wicked one redoubles his efforts to defeat the work of Christ in man's behalf, and to fasten souls in his snares. To hold the people in darkness and impenitence till the Saviour's mediation is ended and there is no longer a sacrifice for sin, is the one object which he seeks to accomplish.

When there is no special effort made to resist his power, when indifference prevails in the church and the world, Satan is not concerned; for he is in no danger of losing those whom he is leading captive at his will. But when the attention is called to eternal things, and souls are inquiring, "What must I do to be saved?" he is on the ground, seeking to match his power against the power of Christ, and to counteract the influence of the Holy Spirit.

The Scriptures declare that upon one occasion, when the angels of God came to present themselves before the Lord, Satan came also among them, (Job 1:6) not to bow before the Eternal King, but to further his own malicious designs against the righteous. With the same object he is in attendance when men assemble for the worship of God. Though hidden from sight, he is working with all diligence to control the minds of the worshipers. Like a skillful general, he lays his plans beforehand. As he sees the messenger of God searching the Scriptures, he takes note of the subject to be presented to the people. Then he employs all his cunning and shrewdness to so control circumstances that the message may not reach those whom

63

he is deceiving on that very point. The one who most needs the warning will be urged into some business transaction which requires his presence, or will by some other means be prevented from hearing the words that might prove to him a savor of life unto life.

Again, Satan sees the Lord's servants burdened because of the spiritual darkness that enshrouds the people. He hears their earnest prayers for divine grace and power to break the spell of indifference, carelessness, and idolence. Then with renewed zeal he plies his arts. He tempts men to the indulgence of appetite or to some other form of self-gratification, and thus benumbs their sensibilities, so that they fail to hear the very things which they most need to learn.

Satan well knows that all whom he can lead to neglect prayer and the searching of the Scriptures will be overcome by his attacks. Therefore he invents every possible device to engross the mind. There has ever been a class professing godliness, who, instead of following on to know the truth, make it their religion to seek some fault of character or error of faith in those with whom they do not agree. Such are Satan's right-hand helpers. Accusers of the brethren are not few; and they are always active when God is at work, and His servants are rendering Him true homage. They will put a false coloring upon the words and acts of those who love and obey the truth. They will represent the most earnest, zealous, self-denying servants of Christ as deceived or deceivers. It is their work to misrepresent the motives of every true and noble deed, to circulate insinuations, and arouse suspicion in the minds of the inexperienced. In every conceivable manner they will seek to cause that which is pure and righteous to be regarded as foul and deceptive.

But none need be deceived concerning them. It may be readily seen whose children they are, whose example they follow, and whose work they do. "Ye shall know them by their fruits." (*Matt.* 7:16) Their course resembles that of Satan, the envenomed slanderer, "the accuser of our brethren." (*Rev.* 12:10)

The great deceiver has many agents ready to present any and every kind of error to ensnare souls, heresies prepared to suit the varied tastes and capacities of those whom he would ruin. It is his plan to bring into the church insincere, unregenerate elements that will encourage doubt and unbelief, and hinder all who desire to see the work of God advance, and to advance with it. Many who have no real faith in God or in His work assent to some principles of truth and pass as Christians; and thus they are enabled to introduce their errors as scriptural doctrines.

The position that it is of no consequence what men believe is one of Satan's most successful deceptions. He knows that the truth, received in the love of it, sanctifies the soul of the receiver; therefore he is constantly seeking to substitute false theories, fables, another gospel. From the beginning, the servants of God have contended against false teachers, not merely as vicious men, but as inculcators of falsehoods that were fatal to the soul. Elijah, Jeremiah, Paul, firmly and fearlessly opposed those who were turning men from the Word of God. That liberality which regards a correct religious faith as unimportant, found no favor with these holy defenders of the truth.

The vague and fanciful interpretations of Scripture and the many conflicting theories concerning religious faith that are found in the Christian world are the work of our great adversary to so confuse minds that they shall not discern the truth. And the discord and division which exist among the churches of Christendom are in a great measure due to the prevailing custom of wresting the Scriptures to support a favorite theory. Instead of carefully studying God's Word with humility of heart to obtain a knowledge of His will, many seek only to discover something odd or original.

In order to sustain erroneous doctrines or unchristian practices, some will seize upon passages of Scripture separated from the context, perhaps quoting half of a single verse as proving their point, when the remaining portion would show the meaning to be quite the opposite. With the cunning of the serpent they entrench themselves behind disconnected utterances construed to suit their carnal desires. Thus do many willfully pervert the Word of God. Others, who have an active imagination, seize upon the figures and symbols of Holy Writ, interpret to suit their fancy with little regard to the testimony of Scripture as its own interpreter, and then they present their vagaries as the teachings of the Bible.

Whenever the study of the Scriptures is entered upon without a prayerful, humble, teachable spirit, the plainest and simplest as well as the most difficult passages will be wrested from their true meaning. The papal leaders select such portions of Scripture as best serve their purpose, interpret to suit themselves, and then present these to the people, while they deny them the privilege of studying the Bible, and understanding its sacred truths for themselves. The whole Bible should be given to the people just as it reads. It would be better for them not to have Bible instruction at all than to have the teaching of the Scriptures thus grossly misrepresented.

The Bible was designed to be a guide to all who wish to become acquainted with the will of their Maker. God gave to men the sure word of prophecy; angels and even Christ Himself came to make known to Daniel and John the things that must shortly come to pass. Those important matters that concern our salvation were not left involved in mystery. They were not revealed in such a way as to perplex and mislead the honest seeker after truth. Said the Lord by the prophet Habakkuk, "Write the vision, and make it plain, . . . that he may run that readeth it." (*Hab.* 2:2) The Word of God is plain to all who study it with a prayerful heart. Every truly honest soul will come to the light of truth. "Light is sown for the righteous." *Ps.* 97:11) And no church can advance in holiness unless its members are earnestly seeking for truth as for hid treasure.

By the cry, Liberality, men are blinded to the devices of their adversary, while he is all the time working steadily for the accomplishment of his object. As he succeeds in supplanting the Bible by human speculations, the law of God is set aside, and the churches are under the bondage of sin while they claim to be free.

To many, scientific research has become a curse. God has permitted a flood of light to be poured upon the world in discoveries in science and art; but even the greatest minds, if not guided by the Word of God in their research, become bewildered in their attempts to investigate the relations of science and revelation.

Human knowledge of both material and spiritual things is partial and imperfect; therefore many are unable to harmonize their views of science with Scripture statements. Many accept mere theories and speculations as scientific facts, and they think that God's word is to be tested by the teachings of "science falsely so called." The Creator and His works are beyond their comprehension: and because they cannot explain these by natural laws, Bible history is regarded as unreliable. Those who doubt the reliability of the records of the Old and New Testaments too often go a step farther, and doubt the existence of God, and attribute infinite power to nature. Having let go their anchor, they are left to beat about upon the rocks of infidelity.

Thus many err from the faith, and are seduced by the devil. Men have endeavored to be wiser than their Creator; human philosophy has attempted to search out and explain mysteries which will never be revealed through the eternal ages. If men would but search and understand what God has made known of Himself and His purposes, they would obtain such a view of the glory, majesty, and power of Jehovah, that they would realize their own littleness, and would be content with that which has been revealed for themselves and their children.

It is a masterpiece of Satan's deceptions to keep the minds of men searching and conjecturing in regard to that which God has not made known and which He does not intend that we shall understand. It was thus that Lucifer lost his place in Heaven. He became dissatisfied because all the secrets of God's purposes were not confided to him, and he entirely disregarded that which was revealed concerning his own work in the lofty position assigned him. By arousing the same discontent in the angels under his command, he caused their fall. Now he seeks to imbue the minds of men with the same spirit, and to lead them also to disregard the direct commands of God.

Those who are unwilling to accept the plain, cutting truths of the Bible are continually seeking for pleasing fables that will quiet the conscience. The less spiritual, self-denying, and humiliating the doctrines presented, the greater the favor with which they are received. These persons degrade the intellectual powers to serve their carnal desires. Too wise in their own conceit to search the Scriptures with contrition of soul and earnest prayer for divine guidance, they have no shield from delusion. Satan is ready to supply the heart's desire, and he palms off his deceptions in the place of truth. It was thus that the papacy gained its power over the minds of men; and by rejection of the truth because it involves a cross, Protestants are following the same path. All who neglect the Word of God to study convenience and policy, that they may not be at variance with the world, will be left to receive damnable heresy for religious truth. Every conceivable form of error will be accepted by those who willfully reject the truth. He who looks with horror upon one deception will readily receive another. The apostle Paul, speaking of a class who "received not the love of the truth, that they might be saved," declares, "For this cause God shall send them strong delusion, that they should believe a lie, that they all might be damned who believed not the truth, but had pleasure in unrighteousness." (2 *Thess.* 2:10-12) With such a warning before us it behooves us to be on our guard as to what doctrines we receive.

Among the most successful agencies of the great deceiver are the delusive teachings and lying wonders of Spiritualism. Disguised as an angel of light, he spreads his nets where least suspected. If men would but study the Book of God with earnest prayer that they might understand it, they would not be left in darkness or receive false doctrines. But as they reject the truth, they fall a prey to deception.

Another dangerous error is the doctrine that denies the divinity of Christ, claiming that He had no existence before His advent to this world. This theory is received with favor by a large class who profess to believe the Bible; yet it directy contradicts the plainest statements of our Saviour concerning His relationship with the Father, His divine character, and His pre-existence. It cannot be entertained without the most unwarranted wresting of the Scriptures. It not only lowers man's conceptions of the work of redemption, but undermines faith in the Bible as a revelation from God. While this renders it the more dangerous, it makes it also harder to meet. If men reject the testimony of the inspired Scriptures concerning the divinity of Christ, it is in vain to argue the point with them, for no argument, however conclusive, could convince them. "The natural man receiveth not the things of the Spirit of God; for they are foolishness unto him; neither can he know them, because they are spiritually discerned." (*1 Cor.* 2:14) None who hold this error can have a true conception of the character or the mission of Christ or of the great plan of God for man's redemption.

Still another subtle and mischievous error is the fast-spreading belief that Satan has no existence as a personal being; that the name is used in Scripture merely to represent men's evil thoughts and desires.

The teaching so widely echoed from popular pulpits, that the second advent of Christ is His coming to each individual at death, is a device to divert the minds of men from His personal coming in the clouds of heaven. For years Satan has thus been saying, "Behold, He is in the secret chambers;" (*Matt.* 24: 23-26) and many souls have been lost by accepting this deception.

Again, worldly wisdom teaches that prayer is not essential. Men of science claim that there can be no real answer to prayer; that this would be a violation of law, a miracle, and that miracles have no existence. The universe, say they, is governed by fixed laws, and God Himself does nothing contrary to these laws. Thus they represent God as bound by His own laws; as if the operation of divine laws could exclude divine freedom. Such teaching is opposed to the testimony of the Scriptures. Were not miracles wrought by Christ and His apostles? The same compassionate Saviour lives to-day, and He is as willing to listen to the prayer of faith as when He walked visibly among men. The natural co-operates with the supernatural. It is a part of God's plan to grant us, in answer to the prayer of faith, that which He would not bestow did we not thus ask.

Innumerable are the erroneous doctrines and fanciful ideas that are obtaining among the churches of Christendom. It is impossible to estimate the evil results of removing one of the landmarks fixed by the Word of God. Few who venture to do this stop with the rejection of a single truth. The majority continue to set aside one after another of the principles of truth, until they become actual infidels.

The errors of popular theology have driven many a soul to skepticism who might otherwise have been a believer in the Scriptures. It is impossible for him to accept doctrines which outrage his sense of justice, mercy, and benevolence; and since these are represented as the teaching of the Bible, he refuses to receive it as the Word of God.

And this is the object which Satan seeks to accomplish. There is nothing that he desires more than to destroy confidence in God and in His Word. Satan stands at the head of the great army of doubters, and he works to the utmost of his power to beguile souls into his ranks. It is becoming fashionable to doubt. There is a large class by whom the Word of God is looked upon with distrust for the same reason as was its Author—becuase it reproves and condemns sin. Those who are unwilling to obey its requirements endeavor to overthrow its authority. They read the Bible, or listen to its teachings as presented from the sacred desk, merely to find fault with the Scriptures or with the sermon. Not a few become infidels in order to justify or excuse themselves in neglect of duty. Others adopt skeptical principles from pride and indolence. Too ease-loving to distinguish themselves by accomplishing anything worthy of honor, which requires effort and self-denial, they aim to secure a reputation for superior wisdom by criticising the Bible. There is much which the finite mind, unenlightened by divine wisdom, is powerless to comprehend; and thus they find occasion to criticise. There are many who seem to feel that it is a virtue to stand on the side of unbelief, skepticism, and infidelity. But underneath an appearance of candor, it will be found that such persons are actuated by self-confidence and pride. Many delight in finding something in the Scriptures to puzzle the minds of others. Some at first criticise and reason on the wrong side from a mere love of controversy. They do not realize that they are thus entangling themselves in the snare of the fowler. But having openly expressed unbelief, they feel that they must maintain their position. Thus they unite with the ungodly, and close to themselves the gates of Paradise.

God has given in His Word sufficient evidence of its divine character. The great truths which concern our redemption are clearly presented. By the aid of the Holy Spirit, which is promised to all who seek it in sincerity, every man may understand these truths for himself. God has granted to men a strong foundation upon which to rest their faith.

Yet the finite minds of men are inadequate fully to comprehend the plans and purposes of the Infinite One. We can never by searching find out God. We must not attempt to lift with presumptuous hand the curtain behind which He veils His majesty. The apostle exclaims, "How unsearchable are His judgments, and His ways past finding out!" (*Rom.* 11:33) We can so far comprehend His dealings with us and the motives by which He is actuated that we may discern boundless love and mercy united to infinite power. Our Father in Heaven orders everything in wisdom and righteousness, and we are not to be dissatisfied and distrustful, but to bow in reverent submission. He will reveal to us as much of His purposes as it is for our good to know, and beyond that we must trust the Hand that is omnipotent, the Heart that is full of love.

While God has given ample evidence for faith, He will never remove all excuse for unbelief. All who look for hooks to hang their doubts upon, will find them. And those who refuse to accept and obey God's Word until every objection has been removed and there is no longer an opportunity for doubt, will never come to the light.

Distrust of God is the natural outgrowth of the unrenewed heart, which is at enmity with Him. But faith is inspired by the Holy Spirit, and it will flourish only as it is cherished. No man can become strong in faith without a determined effort. Unbelief strengthens as it is encouraged; and if men, instead of dwelling upon the evidences which God has given to sustain their faith, will permit themselves to question and cavil, they will find their doubts constantly becoming more confirmed.

But those who doubt God's promises, and distrust the assurance of His grace, are dishonoring Him; and their influence, instead of drawing others to Christ, tends to repel them from Him. They are unproductive trees, that spread their dark branches far and wide, shutting away the sunlight from other plants, and causing them to droop and die under the chilling shadow. The life-work of these persons will appear as a never-ceasing witness against them. They are sowing seeds of doubt and skepticism that will yield an unfailing harvest.

There is but one course for those to pursue who honestly desire to be freed from doubts. Instead of questioning and caviling concerning that which they do not understand, let them give heed to the light which already shines upon them, and they will receive greater light. Let them do every duty which has been made plain to their understanding, and they will be enabled to understand and perform those of which they are now in doubt.

Satan can present a counterfeit so closely resembling the truth that it deceives those who are willing to be deceived, who desire to shun the self-denial and sacrifice demanded by the truth; but it is impossible for him to hold under his power one soul who honestly desires, at whatever cost, to know the truth. Christ is the truth, and the "light which lighteth every man that cometh into the world." (*John* 1:9) The Spirit of truth has been sent, to guide men into all truth. And upon the authority of the Son of God it is declared, "Seek, and ye shall find." "If any man will do His will, he shall know of the doctrine." (*Matt* 7:7; *John* 7:17)

The followers of Christ know little of the plots which Satan and his hosts are forming against them. But He who sitteth in the heavens will overrule all these devices for the accomplishment of His deep designs. The Lord permits His people to be subjected to the fiery ordeal of temptation, not because He takes pleasure in their distress and affliction, but because this process is essential to their final victory. He could not, consistently with His own glory, shield them from temptation; for the very object of the trial is to prepare them to resist all the allurements of evil.

Neither wicked men nor devils can hinder the work of God or shut out His presence from His people, if they will, with subdued, contrite hearts, confess and put away their sins, and in faith claim His promises. Every temptation, every opposing influence, whether open or secret, may be successfully resisted, "not by might, nor by power, but by My Spirit, saith the Lord of hosts." (*Zech.* 4:6)

"The eyes of the Lord are over the righteous, and His ears are open unto their prayers. . . . And who is he that will harm you, if ye be followers of that which is good?" (*Pet.* 3:12, 13) When Balaam, allured by the promise of rich rewards, practiced enchantment against Israel, and by sacrifices to the Lord, sought to invoke a curse upon His people, the Spirit of God forbade the evil which he longed to pronounce, and Balaam was forced to exclaim, "How shall I curse, whom God hath not cursed? or how shall I defy, whom the Lord hath not defied?" "Let me die the death of the righteous, and let my last end be like his!" When sacrifice had again been offered, the ungodly prophet declared: "Behold, I have received commandment to bless; and He hath blessed; and I cannot reverse it. He hath not beheld iniquity in Jacob, neither hath He seen perverseness in Isarael; the Lord God is with him, and the shout of a King is among them." "Surely there is no enchantment against Jacob, neither is there any divination against Israel: according to this time it shall be said of Jacob and of Israel, What hath God wrought!" (*Num.* 23:8, 10, 12, 20, 21, 23, 24:9) Yet a third altar was erected and again Balaam essayed to secure a curse. But from the unwilling lips of the prophet, the Spirit of God declared the prosperity of His chosen, and rebuked the folly and malice of their foes: "Blessed is he that blesseth thee, and cursed is he that curseth thee." (*Num.* 23:8, 10, 20, 21, 23; 24:9) .

The people of Israel were at this time loyal to God; and so long as they continued in obedience to His law, no power in earth or hell could prevail against them. But the curse which Balaam had not been permitted to pronounce against God's people, he finally succeeded in bringing upon them by seducing them into sin. When they transgressed God's commandments, then they separated themselves from Him and they were left to feel the power of the destroyer.

Satan is well aware that the weakest soul who abides in Christ is more than a match for the hosts of darkness, and that, should he reveal himself openly, he would be met and resisted. Therefore he seeks to draw away the soldiers of the cross from their strong fortification, while he lies in ambush with his forces, ready to destroy all who venture upon his ground. Only in humble reliance upon God and obedience to all His commandments, can we be secure. No man is safe for a day or an hour without prayer. Especially should we entreat the Lord for wisdom to understand His Word. Here are revealed the wiles of the tempter and the means by which he may be successfully resisted. Satan is an expert in quoting Scripture, placing his own interpretation upon passages by which he hopes to cause us to stumble. We should study the Bible with humility of heart, never losing sight of our dependence upon God. While we must constantly guard against the devices of Satan, we should pray in faith continually, "Lead us not into temptation."

Chapter 7

THE FIRST GREAT DECEPTION

WITH THE EARLIEST HISTORY of man, Satan began his efforts to deceive our race. He who had incited rebellion in Heaven desired to bring the inhabitants of the earth to unite with him in his warfare against the government of God. Adam and Eve had been perfectly happy in obedience to the law of God, and this fact was a constant testimony against the claim which Satan had urged in Heaven, that God's law was oppressive and opposed to the good of His creatures. And, furthermore, Satan's envy was excited as he looked upon the beautiful home prepared for the sinless pair. He determined to cause their fall, that, having separated them from God, and brought them under his own power, he might gain possession of the earth, and here establish his kingdom in opposition to the Most High.

Had Satan revealed himself in his real character, he would have been repulsed at once, for Adam and Eve had been warned against this dangerous foe; but he worked in the dark, concealing his purpose that he might more effectually accomplish his object. Employing as his medium the serpent, then a creature of fascinating appearance, he addressed himself to Eve, "Hath God said, ye shall not eat of every tree of the garden?" (*Gen.* 3:1) Had Eve refrained from entering into argument with the tempter, she would have been safe; but she ventured to parley with him and fell a victim to his wiles. It is thus that many are still overcome. They doubt and argue concerning the requirements of God, and instead of obeying the divine commands, they accept human theories which but disguise the devices of Satan.

"The woman said unto the serpent, We may eat of the fruit of the trees of the garden, but of the fruit of the tree which is in the midst of the garden God hath said, Ye shall not eat of it, neither shall ye touch it, lest ye die. And the serpent said unto the woman, Ye shall not surely die; for God doth know that in the day ye eat thereof, then your eyes shall be opened, and ye shall be as gods, knowing good and evil." (*Gen.* 3:2-5) He declared that they would become like God, possessing greater wisdom than before, and being capable of a higher state of existence. Eve yielded to temptation; and through her influence, Adam was led into sin. They accepted the words of the serpent, that God did not mean what He said; they distrusted their Creator, and imagined that He was restricting their liberty, and that they might obtain great wisdom and exaltation by transgressing His law.

But what did Adam, after his sin, find to be the meaning of the words, "In the day that thou eatest thereof thou shalt surely die?" Did he find them to mean, as Satan had led him to believe, that he was to be ushered into a more exalted state of existence? Then indeed there was great good to be gained by transgression, and Satan was proved to be a benefactor of the race. But Adam did not find this to be the meaning of the divine sentence. God declared that as a penalty for his sin, man should return to the ground whence he was taken: "Dust thou art, and unto dust shalt thou return." (*Gen.* 3:19) The words of Satan, "Your eyes shall be opened," proved to be true in this sense only: After Adam and Eve had disobeyed God, their eyes were opened to discern their folly; they did know evil, and they tasted the bitter fruit of transgression.

In the midst of Eden grew the tree of life, whose fruit had the power of perpetuating life. Had Adam remained obedient to God, he would have continued to enjoy free access to this tree, and would have lived forever. But when he sinned, he was cut off from partaking of the tree of life, and he became subject to death. The divine sentence, "Dust thou art, and unto dust shalt thou return," points to the utter extinction of life.

Immortality, promised to man on condition of obedience, had been forfeited by transgression. Adam could not transmit to his posterity that which he did not possess; and there could have been no hope for the fallen race, had not God, by the sacrifice of His Son, brought immortality within their reach. While "death passed upon all men, for that all have sinned," Christ "hath brought life and immortality to light through the gospel." (*Rom.* 5:12 *Tim.* 1:10) And only through Christ can immortality be obtained. Said Jesus, "He that believeth on the Son hath everlasting life; and he that believeth not the Son shall not see life." (*John* 3:36) Every man may come in possession of this priceless blessing if he will comply with the conditions. All "who by patient continuance in well-doing seek for glory and honor and immortality," will receive eternal life (*Rom.* 2:7)

The only one who promised Adam life in disobedience was the great deceiver. And the declaration of the serpent to Eve in Eden, "Ye shall not surely die," was the first sermon ever preached upon the immortality of the soul. Yet this declaration, resting solely upon the authority of Satan, is echoed from the pulpits of Christendom, and is received by the majortiy of mankind as readily as it was received by our first parents. The divine sentence, "The soul that sinneth, it shall die," (*Eze.* 18:20) is made to mean, The soul that sinneth, it shall not die, but live eternally. We cannot but wonder at the strange infatuation which renders men so credulous concerning the words of Satan, and so unbelieving in regard to the words of God.

Had man, after his fall, been allowed free access to the tree of life, he would have lived forever, and thus sin would have been immortalized. But cherubim and a flaming sword kept "the way of the tree of life," (*Gen.* 3:24) and not one of the family of Adam has been permitted to pass that barrier. and partake of the life-giving fruit. Therefore there is not an immortal sinner.

But after the fall, Satan bade his angels make a special

effort to inculcate the belief in man's natural immortality; and having induced the people to receive this error, they were to lead them on to conclude that the sinner would live in eternal misery. Now the prince of darkness, working through his agents, represents God as a revengeful tyrant, declaring that He plunges into hell all those who do not please Him and causes them ever to feel his wrath; and that while they suffer unutterable anguish, and writhe in the eternal flames, their Creator looks down upon them with satisfaction.

Thus the arch-fiend clothes with his own attributes the Creator and Benefactor of mankind. Cruelty is Satanic. God is love; and all that He created was pure, holy, and lovely, until sin was brought in by the first great rebel. Satan himself is the enemy who tempts man to sin, and then destroys him if he can; and when he has made sure of his victim, then he exults in the ruin he has wrought. If permitted, he would sweep the entire race into his net. Were it not for the interposition of divine power, not one son or daughter of Adam would escape.

He is seeking to overcome men to-day, as he overcame our first parents, by shaking their confidence in their Creator, and leading them to doubt the wisdom of His government and the justice of His laws. Satan and his emissaries represent God as even worse than themselves, in order to justify their own malignity and rebellion. The great deceiver endeavors to shift his own horrible cruelty of character upon our heavenly Father, that he may cause himself to appear as one greatly wronged by his expulsion from Heaven because he would not submit to so unjust a governor. He presents before the world the liberty which they may enjoy under his mild sway, in contrast with the bondage imposed by the stern decrees of Jehovah. Thus he succeeds in luring souls away from their allegiance to God.

How repugnant to every emotion of love and mercy, and even to our sense of justice, is the doctrine that the wicked dead are tormented with fire and brimstone in an eternally burning hell; that for the sins of a brief, earthly life they are to suffer torture as long as God shall live. Yet this doctrine has been widely taught, and is still embodied in many of the creeds of Christendom. Said a learned doctor of divinity: "The sight of hell-torments will exalt the happiness of the saints forever. When they see others who are of the same nature and born under the same circumstances, plunged in such misery, and they so distinguished, it will make them sensible of how happy they are." Another used these words: "While the decree of reprobation is eternally executing on the vessels of wrath, the smoke of their torment will be eternally ascending in view of the vessels of mercy, who, instead of taking the part of these miserable objects, will say, Amen, Alleluia! praise ye the Lord!"

Where, in the pages of God's Word, is such teaching to be found? Will the redeemed in Heaven be lost to all emotions of pity and compassion, and even to feelings of common humanity? Are these to be exchanged for the indifference of the stoic, or the cruelty of the savage?—No, no; such is not the teaching of the Book of God. Those who present the views expressed in the quotations given above may be learned and even honest men; but they are deluded by the sophistry of Satan. He leads them to misconstrue strong expressions of Scripture, giving to the language the coloring of bitterness and malignity which pertains to himself, but not to our Creator. "As I live, saith the Lord God, I have no pleasure in the death of the wicked; but that the wicked turn from his way and live; turn ye, turn ye from your evil ways; for why will ye die?" (*Eze.* 33:11)

What would be gained to God should we admit that He delights in witnessing unceasing tortures; that He is regaled with the groans and shrieks and imprecations of the suffering creatures whom He holds in the flames of hell? Can these horrid sounds be music in the ear of Infinite Love? It is urged that the infliction of endless misery upon the wicked would show God's hatred of sin as an evil which is ruinous to the peace and order of the universe. Oh, dreadful blasphemy! As if God's hatred of sin is the reason why He perpetuates sin. For, according to the teachings of these theologians, continued torture without hope of mercy maddens its wretched victims, and as they pour out their rage in curses and blasphemy, they are forever augmenting their load of guilt. God's glory is not enhanced by thus perpetuating continually increasing sin through ceaseless ages.

It is beyond the power of the human mind to estimate the evil which has been wrought by the heresy of eternal torment. The religion of the Bible, full of love and goodness, and abounding in compassion, is darkened by superstition and clothed with terror. When we consider in what false colors Satan has painted the character of God, can we wonder that our merciful Creator is feared, dreaded, and even hated? The appalling views of God which have spread over the world from the teachings of the pulpit have made thousands, yes, millions, of skeptics and infidels.

The theory of eternal torment is one of the false doctrines that constitute the wine of the abominations of Babylon, of which she makes all nations drink. (*Rev.* 14:8; 17:2) That ministers of Christ should have accepted this heresy and proclaimed it from the sacred desk, is indeed a mystery. They received it from Rome, as they received the false sabbath. True, it has been taught by great and good men; but the light on this subject had not come to them as it has come to us. They were responsible only for the light which shone in their time; we are accountable for that which shines in our day. If we turn from the testimony of God's Word, and accept false doctrines because our fathers taught them, we fall under the condemnation pronounced upon Babylon; we are drinking of the wine of her abominations.

A large class to whom the doctrine of eternal torment is revolting, are driven to the opposite error. They see that the Scriptures represent God as a being of love and compassion, and they cannot believe that He will consign His creatures to the fires of an eternally burning hell. But, holding that the soul is naturally immortal, they see no alternative but to conclude that all mankind will finally be saved. Many regard the threatenings of the Bible as designed merely to frighten men into obedience, and not to be literally fulfilled. Thus the sinner can live in selfish pleasure, disregarding the requirements of God, and yet expect to be finally received into His favor. Such a doctrine, presuming upon God's mercy, but ignoring His justice, pleases the carnal heart, and emboldens the wicked in their iniquity.

To show how believers in universal salvation wrest the Scriptures to sustain their soul-destroying dogmas, it is needful only to cite their own utterances. At the funeral of an irreligious young man, who had been killed instantly by an accident, a Universalist minister selected as his text the Scripture statement concerning David, "He was comforted concerning Amnon, seeing he was dead." (2 *Sam.* 13:39)

"I am frequently asked," said the speaker, "what will be the fate of those who leave the world in sin, die, perhaps in a state of inebriation, die with the scarlet stains of crime unwashed from their robes, or die as this young man died, having never made a profession or enjoyed an experience of religion. We are content with the Scriptures; their answer shall solve the awful problem. Amnon was exceedingly sinful; he was unrepentant, he was made drunk, and while drunk was killed. David was a prophet of God; he must have known whether it would be ill or well for Amnon in the world to come. What were the expressions of his heart?—'The soul of King David longed to go forth unto Absalom; for he was comforted concerning Amnon, seeing he was dead.'

"And what is the inference to be deduced from this language? Is it not that endless suffering formed no part of his religious belief?—So we conceive; and here we discover a triumphant argument in support of the more pleasing, more enlightened, more benevolent hypothesis of ultimate universal purity and peace. He was comforted, seeing his son was dead. And why so?—Because by the eye of prophecy he could look forward into the glorious future, and see that son far removed from all temptations, released from the bondage and purified from the corruptions of sin, and after being made sufficiently holy and enlightened, admitted to the assembly of ascended and rejoicing spirits. His only comfort was, that in being removed from the present state of sin and suffering, his beloved son had gone where the loftiest breathings of the Holy Spirit would be shed upon his darkened soul; where his mind would be unfolded to the wisdom of Heaven and the sweet raptures of immortal love, and thus prepared with a sanctified nature to enjoy the rest and society of the heavenly inheritance.

"In these thoughts we would be understood to believe that the salvation of Heaven depends upon nothing which we can do in this life; neither upon a present change of heart, nor upon present belief, or a present profession of religion."

Thus does the professed minister of Christ reiterate the falsehood uttered by the serpent in Eden—"Ye shall not surely die." "In the day ye eat thereof, then your eyes shall be opened, and ye shall be as gods." He declares that the vilest of sinners—the murderer, the thief, and the adulterer—will after death be prepared to enter into immortal bliss.

And from what does this perverter of the Scriptures draw his conclusions?—From a single sentence expressing David's submission to the dispensation of Providence. His soul "longed to go forth unto Absalom; for he was comforted concerning Amnon, seeing he was dead." The poignancy of his grief having been softened by time, his thoughts turned from the dead to the living son, self-banished through fear of the just punishment of his crime. And this is the evidence that the incestuous, drunken Amnon was at death immediately transported to the abodes of bliss, there to be purified and prepared for the companionship of sinless angels! A pleasing fable indeed, well suited to gratify the carnal heart! This is Satan's own doctrine, and it does his work effectually. Should we be surprised that, with such instruction, wickedness abounds?

The course pursued by this one false teacher illustrates that of many others. A few words of Scripture are separated from the context, which would, in many cases, show their meaning to be exactly opposite to the interpretation put upon them; and such disjointed passages are perverted and used in proof of doctrines that have no foundation in the Word of God. The testimony cited as evidence that the drunken Amnon is in Heaven, is a mere inference, directly contradicted by the plain and positive statement of the Scriptures, that no drunkard shall inherit the kingdom of God. (*1 Cor.* 6:10) It is thus that doubters, unbelievers, and skeptics turn the truth into a lie. And multitudes have been deceived by their sophistry, and rocked to sleep in the cradle of carnal security.

If it were true that the souls of all men passed directly to Heaven at the hour of dissolution, then we might well covet death rather than life. Many have been led by this belief to put an end to their existence. When overwhelmed with trouble, perplexity, and disappointment, it seems an easy thing to break the brittle thread of life, and soar away into the bliss of the eternal world.

God has given in His Word decisive evidence that He will punish the transgressors of His law. Those who flatter themselves that He is too merciful to execute justice upon the sinner, have only to look to the cross of Calvary. The death of the spotless Son of God testifies that "the wages of sin is death," that every violation of God's law must receive its just retribution. Christ the sinless became sin for man. He bore the guilt of transgression, and the hiding of His Father's face, until His heart was broken and His life crushed out. All this sacrifice was made that sinners might be redeemed. In no other way could man be freed from the penalty of sin. And every soul that refuses to become a partaker of the atonement provided at such a cost, must bear, in his own person, the guilt and punishment of transgression.

Let us consider what the Bible teaches further concerning the ungodly and unrepentant, whom the Universalist places in Heaven as holy, happy angels.

"I will give unto him that is athirst of the fountain of the water of life freely." (*Rev.* 21:6, 7) This promise is only to those that thirst. None but those who feel their need of the water of life, and seek it at the loss of all things else, will be supplied. "He that overcometh shall inherit all things; and I will be his God, and he shall be My son." (*Rev.* 21:6, 7) Here, also, conditions are specified. In order to inherit all things, we must resist and overcome sin.

The Lord declares by the prophet Isaiah, "Say ye to the righteous, that it shall be well with him. Woe unto the wicked! it shall be ill with him; for the reward of his hands shall be given him." (*Isa.* 3: 10, 11) "Though a sinner do evil a hundred times," says the wise man, "and his days be prolonged, yet surely I know that it shall be well with them that fear God, which fear before Him but it shall not be well with the wicked." (*Eccl.* 8:12, 13) And Paul testifies that the sinner is treasuring up unto himself "wrath against the day of wrath and revelation of the righteous judgment of God, Who will render to every man according to his deeds, tribulation and anguish upon every soul of man that doeth evil." (*Rom.* 2:5,6, 9)

"No fornicator, nor unclean person, nor covetous man, who is an idolater, hath any inheritance in the kingdom of Christ and God." (*Eph.* 5:5 Revised Version) "Follow peace with all men, and holiness, without which no man shall see the Lord." (*Heb.* 12:14) "Blessed are they that do His commandments, that they may have right to the tree of life, and may enter in through the gates into the city. For without are dogs, and sorcerers, and whoremongers, and murderers, and idolaters, and whosoever loveth and maketh a lie." (*Rev.* 22:14, 15)

God has given to men a declaration of His character and of His method of dealing with sin. "The Lord God, merciful and gracious, long suffering, and abundant in goodness and truth, keeping mercy for thousands, forgiving iniquity and transgression and sin, and that will by no means clear the guilty." (*Ex.* 34:6, 7) "All the wicked will He destroy." "The transgressors shall be destroyed together; the end of the wicked shall be cut off." (*Ps.* 145: 20; 37:38) The power and authority of the divine government will be employed to put down rebellion; yet all the manifestations of retributive justice will be perfectly consistent with the character of God as a merciful, long-suffering, benevolent being.

God does not force the will or judgment of any. He takes no pleasure in a slavish obedience. He desires that the creatures of His hands shall love Him because He is worthy of love. He would have them obey Him because they have an intelligent appreciation of His wisdom, justice, and benevolence. And all who have a just conception of these qualities will love Him because they are drawn toward Him in admiration of His attributes.

The principles of kindness, mercy, and love, taught and exemplified by our Saviour, are a transcript of the will and character of God. Christ declared that He taught nothing except that which He had received from His Father. The principles of the divine government are in perfect harmony with the Saviour's precept, "Love your enemies." God executes justice upon the wicked, for the good of the universe, and even for the good of those upon whom His judgments are visited. He would make them happy if He could do so in accordance with the laws of His government and the justice of His character. He surrounds them with the tokens of His love, He grants them a knowledge of His law, and follows them with the offers of His mercy; but they despise His love, make void His law, and reject His mercy. While constantly receiving His gifts, they dishonor the Giver; they hate God because they know that He abhors their sins. The Lord bears long with their perversity; but the decisive hour will come at last, when their destiny is to be decided. Will He then chain these rebels to His side? Will He force them to do His will?

Those who have chosen Satan as their leader, and have been controlled by his power, are not prepared to enter the presence of God. Pride, deception, licentiousness, cruelty, have become fixed in their characters. Can they enter Heaven, to dwell forever with those whom they despised and hated on earth? Truth will never be agreeable to a liar; meekness will not satisfy self-esteem and pride; purity is not acceptable to the corrupt; disinterested love does not appear attractive to the selfish. What source of enjoyment could Heaven offer to those who are wholly absorbed in earthly and selfish interests?

Could those whose lives have been spent in rebellion against God be suddenly transported to Heaven and witness the high, the holy state of perfection that ever exists there—every soul filled with love; every countenance beaming with joy; enrapturing music in melodious strains rising in honor of God and the Lamb; and ceaseless streams of light flowing upon the redeemed from the face of Him who sitteth upon the throne—could those whose hearts are filled with hatred of God, of truth and holiness, mingle with the heavenly throng and join their songs of praise? Could they endure the glory of God and the Lamb?—No, no; years of probation were granted them that they might form characters for Heaven; but they have never trained the mind to love purity; they have never learned the language of Heaven, and now it is too late. A life of rebellion against God has unfitted them for Heaven. Its purity, holiness, and peace would be torture to them; the glory of God would be a consuming fire. They would long to flee from that holy place. They would welcome destruction, that they might be hidden from the face of Him who died to redeem them. The destiny of the wicked is fixed by their own choice. Their exclusion from Heaven is voluntary with themselves, and just and merciful on the part of God.

Like the waters of the flood, the fires of the great day declare God's verdict that the wicked are incurable. They have no disposition to submit to divine authority. Their will has been exercised in revolt; and when life is ended, it is too late to turn the current of their thoughts in the opposite direction—too late to turn from transgression to obedience, from hatred to love.

In sparing the life of Cain the murderer, God gave the world an example of what would be the result of permitting the sinner to live, to continue a course of unbridled iniquity. Through the influence of Cain's teaching and example, multitudes of his descendants were led into sin, until "the wickedness of man was great in the earth, and every imagination of the thoughts of his heart was only evil continually." "The earth also was corrupt before God, and the earth was filled with violence." (*Gen.* 6:5, 11)

In mercy to the world God blotted out its wicked inhabitants in Noah's time. In mercy He destroyed the corrupt dwellers in Sodom. Through the deceptive power of Satan the workers of iniquity obtain sympathy and admiration, and are thus constantly leading others to rebellion. It was so in Cain's and in Noah's day, and in the time of Abraham and Lot; it is so in our time. It is in mercy to the universe that God will finally destroy the rejecters of His grace.

"The wages of sin is death; but the gift of God is eternal life through Jesus Christ our Lord." (*Rom.* 6:23) While life is the inheritance of the righteous, death is the portion of the wicked. Moses declared to Israel. "I have set before thee this day life and good, and death and evil." (*Deut.* 30:15) The death referred to in these scriptures is not that pronounced upon Adam, for all mankind suffer the penalty of his transgression. It is the "second death" that is placed in contrast with everlasting life.

In consequence of Adam's sin, death passed upon the whole human race. All alike go down into the grave. And through the provisions of the plan of salvation, all are to be brought forth from their graves. "There shall be a resurrection of the dead, both of the just and unjust!" (*Acts* 24:15) "for as in Adam all die, even so in Christ shall all be made alive." (*1 Cor.* 15:22) But a distinction is made between the two classes that are brought forth. "All that are in the graves shall hear His voice, and shall come forth; they that have done good, unto the resurrection of life; and they that have done evil, unto the resurrection of damnation." (*John* 5:28, 29) They who have been "accounted worthy" of the resurrection of life are "blessed and holy. On such the second death hath no power." (*Rev.* 20:6) But those who have not, through repentance and faith, secured pardon, must receive the penalty of transgression—"the wages of sin." They suffer punishment varying in duration and intensity, "according to their works," but finally ending in the second death. Since it is impossible for God, consistently with His justice and mercy, to save the sinner in his sins, He deprives him of the existence which his transgressions have forfeited, and of which he has proved himself unworthy. Says an inspired writer, "Yet a little while, and the wicked shall not be; yea, thou shalt diligently consider his place, and it shall not be." And another declares, "They shall be as though they had not been." (*Ps.* 37:10; *Obad.* 16) Covered with infamy, they sink into hopeless eternal oblivion.

Thus will be made an end of sin, with all the woe and ruin which have resulted from it. Says the psalmist: "Thou has destroyed the wicked, thou hast put out their name forever and ever. O thou enemy, destructions are come to a perpetual end." (*Ps.* 9:5, 6) John, in the Revelation, looking forward to the eternal state, hears a universal anthem of praise, undisturbed by one note of discord. Every creature in Heaven and earth was heard ascribing glory to God. (*Rev.* 5:13) There will then be no lost souls to blaspheme God, as they writhe in never-ending torment; no wretched beings in hell will mingle their shrieks with the songs of the saved.

Upon the fundamental error of natural immortality rests the doctrine of consciousness in death, a doctrine, like eternal torment, opposed to the teachings of the Scriptures, to the dictates of reason, and to our feelings of humanity. According to the popular belief, the redeemed in Heaven are acquainted with all that takes place on the earth, and especially with the lives of the friends whom they have left behind. But how could it be a source of happiness to the dead to know the troubles of the living, to witness the sins committed by their own loved ones, and to see them enduring all the sorrows, disappointments, and anguish of life? How much of Heaven's bliss would be enjoyed by those who were hovering over their friends on earth? And how utterly revolting is the belief that as soon as the breath leaves the body, the soul of the impenitent is consigned to the flames of hell! To what depths of anguish must those be plunged who see their friends passing to the grave unprepared, to enter upon an eternity of woe and sin! Many have been driven to insanity by this harrowing thought.

What say the Scriptures concerning these things? David declares that man is not conscious in death. "His breath goeth forth, he returneth to his earth; in that very day his thoughts perish." (*Ps.* 146:4) Solomon bears the same testimony: "The living know that they shall die; but the dead know not anything. Their love, and their hatred, and their envy, is now perished; neither have they any more a portion forever in anything that is done under the sun. There is no work, nor device, nor knowledge, nor wisdom, in the grave, whither thou goest." (*Eccl.* 9:5, 6, 10)

When in answer to his prayer, Hezekiah's life was prolonged fifteen years, the grateful king rendered to God a tribute of praise for His great mercy. In this song he tells the reason why he thus rejoices: "The grave cannot praise Thee, death cannot celebrate Thee; they that go down into the pit cannot hope for Thy truth. The living, the living, he shall praise Thee as I do this day." (*Isa.* 38:18, 19) Popular theology represents the righteous dead as in Heaven, entered into bliss, and praising God with an immortal tongue; but Hezekiah could see no such glorious prospect in death. With his words agrees the testimony of the psalmist: "In death there is no remembrance of Thee in the grave who shall give Thee thanks?" "The dead praise not the Lord, neither any that go down into silence." (*Ps.* 6:5; 115:17)

Peter, on the day of Pentecost, declared that the patriarch David "is both dead and buried, and his sepulcher is with us unto this day. For David is not ascended into the heavens." (*Acts* 2:29, 34) The fact that David remains in the grave until the resurrection, proves that the righteous do not go to Heaven at death. It is only through the resurrection, and by virtue of the fact that Christ has risen, that David can at last sit at the right hand of God.

And said Paul: "If the dead rise not, then is not Christ raised. And if Christ be not raised, your faith is vain; ye are yet in your sins. Then they also which are fallen asleep in Christ are perished." (*1 Cor.* 15:16-18) If for four thousand years the righteous had gone directly to Heaven at death, how could Paul have said that if there is no resurrection, "they which are fallen asleep in Christ are perished?" No resurrection would be necessary.

The martyr Tyndale, defending the doctrine that the dead sleep, declared to his papist opponent: "Ye, in putting them [departed souls] in Heaven, hell, and purgatory, destroy the argument wherewith Christ and Paul prove the resurrection. If the souls be in Heaven, tell me why they be not in as good case as the angels be? And then what cause is there of the resurrection?"

It is an undeniable fact that the hope of immortal blessedness at death has led to widespread neglect of the Bible doctrine of the resurrection. This tendency was remarked by Dr. Adam Clarke, who, early in the present century said: "The doctrine of the resurrection appears to have been thought of much more consequence among the primitive Christians than it is *now!* How is this? The apostles were continually insisting on it, and exciting the followers of God to diligence, obedience, and cheerfulness through it. And their successors in the present day seldom mention it! So apostles preached, and so primitive Christians believed; so we preach, and so our hearers believe. There is not a doctrine in the gospel on which more stress is laid; and there is not a doctrine in the present system of preaching which is treated with more neglect!"

This has continued until the glorious truth of the resurrection has been almost wholly obscured, and lost sight of by the Christian world. Thus a leading religious writer, commenting on the words of Paul in 1 Thess. 4:13-18, says, "For all practical purposes of comfort the doctrine of the blessed immortality of the righteous takes the place for us of any doubtful doctrine of the Lord's second coming. At our death the Lord comes for us. That is what we are to wait and watch for. The dead are already passed into glory. They do not wait for the trump for their judgment and blessedness."

But when about to leave His disciples, Jesus did not tell them that they would soon come to Him. "I go to prepare a place for you," He said. "And if I go and prepare a place for you, I will come again, and receive you unto Myself." (*John* 14:2, 3) And Paul tells us, further, that "the Lord Himself shall descend from Heaven with a shout, with the voice of the archangel, and with the trump of God; and the dead in Christ shall rise first. Then we which are alive and remain shall be caught up together with them in the clouds, to meet the Lord in the air; and so shall we ever be with the Lord." And he adds, "Comfort one another with these words." (*1 Thess.* 4:16-18) How wide the contrast between these words of comfort and those of the Universalist minister previously quoted. The latter consoled the bereaved friends with the assurance, that, however sinful the dead might have been, when he breathed out his life here he was to be received among the angels. Paul points his brethren to the future coming of the Lord, when the fetters of the tomb shall be broken, and the "dead in Christ" shall be raised to eternal life.

Before any can enter the mansions of the blest, their cases must be investigated, and their characters and their deeds must pass in review before God. All are to be judged according to the things written in the books, and to be rewarded as their works have been. This Judgment does not take place at death. Mark the words of Paul: "He hath appointed a day, in the which He will judge the world in righteousness by that Man whom He hath ordained; whereof He hath given assurance unto all men, in that He hath raised Him from the dead." (*Acts* 17:31)

Here the apostle plainly stated that a specified time, then future, had been fixed upon the Judgment of the world.

Jude refers to the same period: "The angels which kept not their first estate, but left their own habitation, He hath reserved in everlasting chains under darkness unto the Judgment of the great day." And again he quotes the words of Enoch: "Behold, the Lord cometh with ten thousands of His saints, to execute judgment upon all." (*Jude* 6, 14, 15) John declares that he "saw the dead, small and great, stand before God; and the books were opened, and the dead were judged out of those things which were written in the books." (*Rev.* 20:12)

But if the dead are already enjoying the bliss of Heaven or writhing in the flames of hell, what need of a future Judgment? The teachings of God's Word on these important points are neither obscure nor contradictory; they may be understood by common minds. But what candid mind can see either wisdom or justice in the current theory? Will the righteous, after the investigation of their cases at the Judgment, receive the commendation, "Well done, good and faithful servant," *enter thou* into the joy of thy Lord," (*Matt.* 25:21, 41) when they have been dwelling in His presence, perhaps for long ages? Are the wicked summoned from the place of torment to receive the sentence from the Judge of all the earth, "Depart from Me, ye cursed, into everlasting fire?" Oh, solemn mockery! shameful impeachment of the wisdom and justice of God!

The theory of the immortality of the soul was one of those false doctrines that Rome, borrowing from paganism, incorporated into the religion of Christendom. Martin Luther classed it with "the numberless prodigies of the Roman dunghill of decretals." Commenting on the words of Solomon in Ecclesiastes, that the dead know not anything, the reformer says: "Another proof that the dead are insensible. Solomon thinks therefore, that the dead are altogether asleep, and think of nothing. They lie, not reckoning days or years, but when awakened, will seem to themselves to have slept scarcely a moment."

Nowhere in the Sacred Scriptures is found the statement that the righteous go to their reward or the wicked
to their punishment at death. The patriarchs and prophets
have left no such assurance. Christ and His apostles have
given no hint of it. The Bible clearly teaches that the dead
do not go immediately to Heaven. They are represented
as sleeping until the ressurection. (*1 Thess.* 4:14; *Job*
14:10-12) In the very day when the silver cord is loosed
and the golden bowl broken, (*Eccl.* 12:6) man's thoughts
perish. They that go down to the grave are in silence.
They know no more of anything that is done under the
sun. (*Job* 14:21) Blessed rest for the weary righteous!
Time, be it long or short, is but a moment to them.
They sleep, they are awakened by the trump of God to a
glorious immortality. "For the trumpet shall sound, and
the dead shall be raised incorruptible. . . . So when this
corruptible shall have put on incorruption, and this mortal
shall have put on immortality, then shall be brought to
pass the saying that is written, Death is swallowed up in
victory." (*1 Cor.* 15:52-55) As they are called forth from
their deep slumber, they began to think just where they
ceased. The last sensation was the pang of death, the last
thought that they were falling beneath the power of the
grave. When they arise from the tomb, their first glad
thought will be echoed in the triumphal shout, "Oh death,
where is thy sting? O grave, where is thy victory?" (*1 Cor.*
15:52-55)

Chapter 7A

WHAT IS THE SANCTUARY?

THE SCRIPTURE WHICH ABOVE all others has been both the foundation and central pillar of the Advent faith was the declaration, "Unto two thousand and three hundred days; then shall the sanctuary be cleansed." (*Dan.* 8:14) These had been familiar words to all believers in the Lord's soon coming. By the lips of thousands was this prophecy repeated as the watchword of their faith. All felt that upon the events therein foretold depended their brightest expectations and most cherished hopes. These prophetic days had been shown to terminate in the autumn of 1844. In common with the rest of the Christian world, Adventists then held that the earth, or some portion of it, was the sanctuary. They understood that the cleansing of the sanctuary was the purification of the earth by the fires of the last great day, and this would take place at the second advent. Hence the conclusion that Christ would return to the earth in 1844.

But the appointed time had passed, and the Lord had not appeared. The believers knew that God's Word could not fail; their interpretation of the prophecy must be at fault; but where was the mistake? Many rashly cut the knot of difficulty by denying that the 2300 days ended in 1844. No reason could be given for this, except that Christ had not come at the time they expected him. They argued that if the prophetic days had ended in 1844, Christ would then have returned to cleanse the sanctuary by the purification of the earth by fire; and that since he had not come, the days could not have ended.

To accept this conclusion was to renounce the former reckoning of the prophetic periods. The 2300 days had been found to begin when the commandment of Artaxerxes for the restoration and building of Jerusalem went into effect, in the autumn of B.C. 457. Taking this as the starting-point, there was perfect harmony in the application of all the events foretold in the explanation of that period in Dan. 9:25-27. Sixty-nine weeks, the first 483 of the 2300 days, were to reach to the Messiah, the Anointed One; and Christ's baptism and anointing by the Holy Spirit, A.D. 27, exactly fulfilled the specification. In the midst of the seventieth week, Messiah was to be cut off. Three and a half years after His baptism, Christ was crucified, in the spring of A.D. 31. The seventy weeks, or 490 years, were to pertain especially to the Jews. At the expiration of this period, the nation sealed its rejection of Christ by the persecution of His disciples, and the apostles turned to the Gentiles, A.D. 34. The first 490 years of the 2300 having then ended, 1810 years would remain. From A.D. 34, 1810 years extended to 1844. "Then," said the angel, "shall the sanctuary be cleansed." All the preceding specifications of the prophecy had been unquestionably fulfilled at the time appointed. With this reckoning, all was clear and harmonious, except that it was not seen that any event answering to the cleansing of the sanctuary had taken place in 1844. To deny that the days ended at that time was to involve the whole question in confusion, and to renounce positions, which had been established by unmistakable fulfillments of prophecy.

But God had led His people in the great Advent movement; His power and glory had attended the work, and He would not permit it to end in darkness and disappointment, to be reproached as a false and fanatical excitement. He would not leave His word involved in doubt and uncertainty. Though many abandoned their former reckoning of the prophetic periods, and denied the correctness of the movement based thereon, others, were unwilling to renounce points of faith and experience that were sustained by the Scriptures and by the witness of the Spirit of God. They believed that they had adopted sound principles of interpretation in their study of the prophecies, and that it was their duty to hold fast the truths already gained, and to continue the same course of Biblical research. With earnest prayer they reviewed their position, and studied the Scriptures to discover their mistake. As they could see no error in their reckoning of the prophetic periods, they were led to examine more closely the subject of the sanctuary.

In their investigation they learned that there is no Scripture evidence sustaining the popular view that the earth is the sanctuary; but they found in the Bible a full explanation of the subject of the sanctuary, its nature, location, and services; the testimony of the sacred writers being so clear and ample as to place the matter beyond all question. The apostle Paul, in the Epistle to the Hebrews, says: "Then verily the first covenant had also ordinances of divine service and a worldly sanctuary. For there was a tabernacle made; the first, wherein was the candlestick, and the table, and the show-bread; which is called the sanctuary. And after the second veil, the tabernacle which is called the holiest of all; which had the golden censer, and the ark of the covenant overlaid round about with gold, wherein was the golden pot that had manna, and Aaron's rod that budded, and the tables of the covenant; and over it the cherubim of glory shadowing the mercy-seat." (*Heb.* 9:1-5)

The sanctuary to which Paul here refers was the tabernacle built by Moses at the command of God, as the earthly dwelling-place of the Most High. "Let them make Me a sanctuary, that I may dwell among them." (*Ex.* 25:8) was the direction given to Moses while in the mount with God. The Israelites were journeying through the wilderness, and the tabernacle was so constructed that it could be removed from place to place; yet it was a structure of great magnificence. Its walls consisted of upright boards heavily plated with gold, and set in sockets of silver, while the roof was formed of a series of curtains, or coverings, the outer of skins, the innermost of fine linen beautifully wrought with figures of cherubim. Besides the outer court, which contained the altar of burnt-offering, the tabernacle itself consisted of two apartments called the holy and the most holy place, separated by a rich and beautiful curtain, or veil; a similar veil closed the entrance to the first apartment.

In the holy place was the candlestick, on the south, with its seven lamps giving light to the sanctuary both by day and by night; on the north stood the table of showbread; and before the veil separating the holy from the most holy was the golden altar of incense, from which the cloud of fragrance, with the prayers of Israel, was daily ascending before God.

In the most holy place stood the ark, a chest of precious wood overlaid with gold, the depository of the two tables of stone upon which God had inscribed the law of ten commandments. Above the ark, and forming the cover to the sacred chest, was the mercy-seat, a magnificent piece of workmanship, surmounted by two cherubim, one at each end, and all wrought of solid gold. In this apartment the divine presence was manifested in the cloud of glory between the cherubim.

After the settlement of the Hebrews in Canaan, the tabernacle was replaced by the temple of Solomon, which, though a permanent structure and upon a larger scale, observed the same proportions, and was similarly furnished. In this form the sanctuary existed—except while it lay in ruins in Daniel's time—until its destruction by the Romans, A.D. 70.

This is the only sanctuary that ever existed on the earth, of which the Bible gives any information. This was declared by Paul to be the sanctuary of the first covenant. But has the new covenant no sanctuary?

Turning again to the book of Hebrews, the seekers for truth found that the existence of a second, or new-covenant sanctuary was implied in the words of Paul already quoted: "Then verily the first covenant had *also* ordinances of divine service, and a worldly sanctuary." And the use of the word *also* intimates that Paul has before made mention of this sanctuary. Turning back to the beginning of the previous chapter they read: "Now of the things which we have spoken this is the sum: We have such a high priest, who is set on the right hand of the throne of the Majesty in the heavens; a minister of the sanctuary, and of the true tabernacle, which the Lord pitched, and not man." (*Heb.* 8:1, 2)

Here is revealed the sanctuary of the new covenant. The sanctuary of the first covenant was pitched by man, built by Moses; this is pitched by the Lord, not by man. In that sanctuary the earthly priests performed their service; in this, Christ, our great high priest, ministers at God's right hand. One sanctuary was on earth, the other is in Heaven.

Further, the tabernacle built by Moses was made after a pattern. The Lord directed him, "According to all that I show thee, after the pattern of the tabernacle, and the pattern of all the instruments thereof, even so shall ye make it." And again the charge was given, "Look that thou make them after their pattern, which was showed thee in the mount." (*Ex.* 25:9, 40) And Paul says, that the first tabernacle "was a figure for the time then present, in which were offered both gifts and sacrifices;" that its holy places were "patterns of things in the heavens;" that the priests who offered gifts according to the law, served, "unto the example and shadow of heavenly things," and that "Christ is not entered into the holy places made with hands, which are the figures of the true, but into Heaven itself, now to appear in the presence of Gor for us." (*Heb.* 9:9, 23; 8:5; 9:24)

The sanctuary in Heaven, in which Jesus ministers in

our behalf, is the great original, of which the sanctuary built by Moses was a copy. God placed His Spirit upon the builders of the earthly sanctuary. The artistic skill displayed in its construction was a manifestation of divine wisdom. The walls had the appearance of massive gold, reflecting in every direction the light of the seven lamps of the golden candlestick. The table of show-bread and the altar of incense glittered like burnished gold. The gorgeous curtain which formed the ceiling, inwrought with figures of angels in blue and purple and scarlet, added to the beauty of the scene. And beyond the second veil was the holy shekinah, the visible manifestation of God's glory, before which none but the high priest could enter and live. The matchless splendor of the earthly tabernacle reflected to human vision the glories of that heavenly temple where Christ our forerunner ministers for us before the throne of God. The abiding-place of the King of kings, where thousand thousands minister unto Him, and ten thousand times ten thousand stand before Him; (*Dan.* 7:10) that temple, filled with the glory of the eternal throne, where seraphim, its shining guardians, veil their faces in adoration, could find, in the most magnificent structure ever reared by human hands, but a faint reflection of its vastness and glory. Yet important truths concerning the heavenly sanctuary and the great work there carried forward for man's redemption, were taught by the earthly sanctuary and its services.

The holy places of the sanctuary in Heaven are represented by the two apartments in the sanctuary on earth. As in vision the apostle John was granted a view of the temple of God in Heaven, he beheld there "seven lamps of fire burning before the throne." (*Rev.* 4:5) He saw an angel "having a golden censer; and there was given unto him much incense, that he should offer it with the prayers of all saints upon the golden altar which was before the throne." (*Rev.* 8:3) Here the prophet was permitted to behold the first apartment of the sanctuary in Heaven; and he saw there the "seven lamps of fire" and the "golden altar" represented by the golden candlestick and the altar of incense in the sanctuary on earth. Again, "the temple of God was opened," (*Rev.* 11:19) and he looked within the inner veil, upon the holy of holies. Here he beheld "the ark of His testament," represented by the sacred chest constructed by Moses to contain the law of God.

Thus those who were studying the subject found indisputable proof of the existence of a sanctuary in Heaven. Moses made the earthly sanctuary after a pattern which was shown him. Paul delcares that that pattern was the true sanctuary which is in Heaven. And John testifies that he saw it in Heaven.

In the temple in Heaven, the dwelling-place of God, His throne is established in righteousness and judgment. In the most holy place is His law, the great rule of right by which all mankind are tested. The ark that enshrines the tables of the law is covered with the mercy-seat, before which Christ pleads His blood in the sinner's behalf. Thus is represented the union of justice and mercy in the plan of human redemption. This union infinite wisdom alone could devise, and infinite power accomplish; it is a union that fills all Heaven with wonder and adoration. The cherubim of the earthly sanctuary, looking reverently down upon the mercy-seat, represent the interest with which the heavenly host comtemplate the work of redemption. This is the mystery of mercy into which angels desire to look,—that God can be just while He justifies the repenting sinner, and renews His intercourse with the fallen race; that Christ could stoop to raise unnumbered multitudes from the abyss of ruin, and clothe them with the spotless garments of His own righteousness, to unite with angles who have never fallen, and to dwell forever in the presence of God.

The work of Christ as man's intercessor is presented in that beautiful prophecy of Zechariah concerning Him "whose name is The Branch." Says the prophet: "He shall build the temple of the Lord; and He shall bear the glory, and shall sit and rule upon His [the Father's] throne; and He shall be a priest upon His throne; and the *counsel of peace* shall be between them both." (*Zech.* 6:13)

"He shall build the temple of the Lord." By His sacrifice and mediation, Christ is both the foundation and the builder of the church of God. The apostle Paul points to Him as "the chief corner-stone; in whom all the building fitly framed together groweth unto a holy temple in the Lord; in whom ye also," he says, "are builded together for a habitation of God through the Spirit." (*Eph.* 2:20-22)

"And He shall bear the glory." To Christ belongs the glory of redemption for the fallen race. Through the eternal ages, the song of the ransomed ones will be, "Unto Him that loved us, and washed us from our sins in His own blood, . . . to Him be glory and dominion forever and ever." (*Rev.* 1:5, 6)

He "shall sit and rule upon His throne; and He shall be a priest upon His throne." Not now "upon the throne of his glory;" the kingdom of glory has not yet been ushered in. Not until His work as a mediator shall be ended, will God "give unto Him the throne of his father David," a kingdom of which "there shall be no end." (*Luke* 1:32, 33) As a priest, Christ is now set down with the Father in His throne. (*Rev.* 3:21) Upon the throne with the eternal, self-existent One, is He Who "hath borne our griefs, and carried our sorrows," Who "was in all points tempted like as we are, yet without sin," that He might be "able to succor them that are tempted." "If any man sin, we have an Advocate with the Father." (*Isa.* 53:4; *Heb.* 4:15; 2:18; *1 John* 2:1) His intercession is that of a pierced and broken body, of a spotless life. The wounded hands, the pierced side, the marred feet, plead for fallen man, whose redemption was purchased at such infinite cost.

"And the counsel of peace shall be between them both." The love of the Father, no less than of the Son, is the fountain of salvation for the lost race. Said Jesus to

His disciples, before He went away, "I say not unto you, that I will pray the Father for you; for the Father Himself loveth you." (*John* 16:26, 27) God was "in Christ, reconciling the world unto Himself." (*2 Cor.* 5:19) And in the ministration in the sanctuary above, "the counsel of peace shall be between Them both." "God *so loved* the world, that He gave His only begotten Son, that whosoever believeth in Him should not perish, but have everlasting life." (*John* 3:16)

The question, What is the sanctuary? is clearly answered in the Scriptures. The term sanctuary, as used in the Bible, refers, first, to the tabernacle built by Moses, as a pattern of heavenly things; and, secondly, to the "true tabernacle" in Heaven, to which the earthly sanctuary pointed. At the death of Christ the typical service ended. The "true tabernacle" in Heaven is the sanctuary of the new covenant. And as the prophecy of Dan. 8:14 is fulfilled in this dispensation, the sanctuary to which it refers must be the sanctuary of the new covenant. At the termination of the 2300 days, in 1844, there had been no sanctuary on earth for many centuries. Thus the prophecy, "Unto two thousand three hundred days; then shall the sanctuary be cleansed," unquestionably points to the sanctuary in Heaven.

But the most important question remains to be answered: What is the cleansing of the sanctuary? That there was such a service in connection with the earthly sanctuary, is stated in the Old-Testament Scriptures. But can there be anything in Heaven to be cleansed? In Hebrews 9 the cleansing of both the earthly and the heavenly sanctuary is plainly taught. "Almost all things are by the law purged with blood; and without shedding of blood is no remission. It was therefore necessary that the patterns of things in the heavens should be purified with these [the blood of animals]; but the heavenly things themselves with better sacrifices than these," (*Heb.* 9:22, 23) even the precious blood of Christ.

The cleansing, both in the typical and in the real service, must be accomplished with blood; in the former, with the blood of animals; in the latter, with the blood of Christ. Paul states, as the reason why this cleaning must be performed with blood, that without shedding of blood is no *remission*. Remission, or putting away of sin, is the work to be accomplished. But how could there be sin connected with the sanctuary, either in Heaven or upon the earth? This may be learned by reference to the symbolic service; for the priests who officiated on earth, served "unto the example and shadow of heavenly things." (*Heb.* 8:5)

The ministration of the earthly sanctuary consisted of two divisions; the priests ministered daily in the holy place, while once a year the high priest performed a special work of atonement in the most holy, for the cleansing of the sanctuary. Day by day the repentant sinner brought his offering to the door of the tabernacle, and placing his hand upon the victim's head, confessed his sins, thus in figure transferring them from himself to the innocent sacrifice. The animal was then slain. "Without shedding of blood," says the apostle, there is no remission of sin. "The life of the flesh, is in the blood." (*Lev.* 17:11) The broken law of God demanded the life of the transgressor. The blood, representing the forfeited life of the sinner, whose guilt the victim bore, was carried by the priest into the holy place and sprinkled before the veil, behind which was the ark containing the law that the sinner had transgressed. By this ceremony the sin was, through the blood transferred in figure to the sanctuary. In some cases the blood was not taken into the holy place; but the flesh was then to be eaten by the priest, as Moses directed the sons of Aaron, saying, "God hath given it you to bear the iniquity of the congregation." (*Lev.* 10:17) Both ceremonies alike symbolized the transfer of the sin from the penitent to the sanctuary.

Such was the work that went on, day by day, throughout the year. The sins of Israel were thus transferred to the sanctuary, and a special work became necessary for their removal. God commanded that an atonement be made for each of the sacred apartments. "He shall make an atonement for the holy place, because of the uncleanness of the children of Israel, and because of their transgressions in all their sins; and so shall he do for the tabernacle of the congregation, that remaineth among them in the midst of their uncleanness." An atonement was also to be made for the altar, to "cleanse it, and hallow it from the uncleanness of the children of Israel." (*Lev.* 16:16, 19)

Once a year on the great day of atonement, the priest entered the most holy place for the cleansing of the sanctuary. The work there performed completed the yearly round of ministration. On the day of atonement, two kids of the goats were brought to the door of the tabernacle, and lots were cast upon them, "one lot for the Lord, and the other lot for the scape-goat." (*Lev.* 16:8, 21, 22) The goat upon which fell the lot for the Lord was to be slain as a sin-offering for the people. And the priest was to bring his blod within the veil, and sprinkle it upon the mercy-seat, and before the mercy-seat. The blood was also to be sprinkled upon the altar of incense, that was before the veil.

"And Aaron shall lay both his hands upon the head of the live goat, and confess over him all the iniquities of the children of Israel, and all their transgressions in all their sins, putting them upon the head of the goat, and shall send him away by the hand of a fit man into the wilderness; and the goat shall bear upon him all their iniquities unto a land not inhabitated." (*Lev.* 16:21, 22) The scape-goat came no more into the camp of Israel, and the man who led him away was required to wash himself and his clothing with water before returning to the camp.

The whole ceremony was designed to impress the Israelites with the holiness of God and His abhorrence of sin, and, further, to show them that they could not come in contact with sin without becoming polluted. Every man was required to afflict his soul while this work of atonement was going forward. All business was to be laid aside, and the whole congregation of Israel were to spend the day in solemn humiliation before God, with prayer, fasting, and deep searching of heart.

Important truths concerning the atonement are taught by the typical service. A substitute was accepted in the sinner's stead; but the sin was not canceled by the blood of the victim. A means was thus provided by which it was transferred to the sanctuary. By the offering of blood, the sinner acknowledged the authority of the law, confessed his guilt in transgression, and expressed his desire for pardon through faith in a Redeemer to come; but he was not yet entirely released from the condemnation of the law. On the day of atonement the high priest, having taken an offering from the congregation, went into the most holy place with the blood of this offering, and sprinkled it upon the mercy-seat, directly over the law, to make satisfaction for its claims. Then, in his character of mediator, he took the sins upon himself, and bore them from the sanctuary. Placing his hands upon the head of the scape-goat, he confessed over him all these sins, thus in figure transferring them from himself to the goat. The goat then bore them away, and they were regarded as forever separated from the people.

Such was the service performed "unto the example and shadow of heavenly things." And what was done in type in the ministration of the earthly sanctuary, is done in reality in the ministration of the heavenly sanctuary. After his ascension, our Saviour began His work as our high priest. Says Paul, "Christ is not entered into the holy places made with hands, which are the figures of the true; but into Heaven itself, now to appear in the presence of God for us." (*Heb.* 9:24)

The ministration of the priest throughout the year in the first apartment of the sanctuary, "within the veil" which formed the door and separated the holy place from the outer court, represents the work of ministration upon

which Christ entered at His ascension. It was the work of
the priest in the daily ministration to present before God
the blood of the sin-offering, also the incense which ascended with the prayers of Israel. So did Christ plead His
blood before the Father in behalf of sinners, and present
before Him also, with the precious fragrance of His own
righteousness, the prayers of penitent believers. Such was
the work of ministration in the first apartment of the
sanctuary in Heaven.

Thither the faith of Christ's disciples followed Him as
he ascended from their sight. Here their hopes centered,
"which hope we have," said Paul, "as an anchor of the
soul, both sure and steadfast, and which entereth into that
within the veil; whither the forerunner is for us entered,
even Jesus, made an high priest forever." "Neither by the
blood of goats and calves, but by His own blood He entered in once into the holy place, having obtained eternal
redemption for us." (*Heb.* 6:19, 20; 9:12)

For eighteen centuries this work of ministration continued in the first apartment of the sanctuary. The blood of
Christ, pleaded in behalf of penitent believers, secured
their pardon and acceptance with the Father, yet their
sins still remained upon the books of record. As in the
typical service there was a work of atonement at the close
of the year, so before Christ's work for the redemption of
men is completed, there is a work of atonement for the
removal of sin from the sanctuary. This is the service
which began when the 2300 days ended. At that time, as
foretold by Daniel the prophet, our High Priest entered
the most holy, to perform the last division of His solemn
work,—to cleanse the sanctuary.

As anciently the sins of the people were by faith placed
upon the sin-offering, and through its blood transferred in
figure, to the earthly sanctuary, so in the new covenant
the sins of the repentant are by faith placed upon Christ,
and transferred, in fact, to the heavenly sanctuary. And as
the typical cleansing of the earthly was accomplished by
the removal of the sins by which it had been polluted, so

the actual cleansing of the heavenly is to be accomplished by the removal, or blotting out, of the sins which are there recorded. But, before this can be accomplished, there must be an examination of the books of record to determine who, through repentance of sin and faith in Christ, are entitled to the benefits of His atonement. The cleansing of the sanctuary therefore involves a work of investigation,—a work of judgment. This work must be performed prior to the coming of Christ to redeem His people; for when He comes, His reward is with Him to give to every man according to his works. (Rev. 22:12)

Thus those who followed in the light of the prophetic word was, that, instead of coming to the earth at the termination of the 2300 days in 1844, Christ then entered the most holy place of the heavenly sanctuary, to perform the closing work of atonement, preparatory to His coming.

It was seen, also, that while the sin-offering pointed to Christ as a sacrifice, and the high priest represented Christ as a mediator, the scape-goat typified Satan, the author of sin, upon whom the sins of the truly penitent will finally be placed. When the high priest, by virtue of the blood of the sin-offering, removed the sins from the sanctuary, he placed them upon the scape-goat. When Christ, by virtue of His own blood removes the sins of His people from the heavenly sanctuary at the close of His ministration, He will place them upon Satan, who, in the execution of the judgment, must bear the final penalty. The scape-goat was sent away into a land not inhabited, never to come again into the congregation of Israel. So will Satan be forever banished from the presence of God and His people, and he will be blotted from existence in the final destruction of sin and sinners.

Chapter 8

SPIRITUALISM

THE MINISTRATION OF HOLY ANGELS, as presented in the Scriptures, is a truth most comforting and precious to every follower of Christ. But the Bible teaching upon this point has been obscured and perverted by the errors of popular theology. The doctrine of natural immortality, first borrowed from the pagan philosophy, and in the darkness of the great apostasy incorporated into the Christian faith, has supplanted the truth, so plainly taught in Scripture, that "the dead know not anything." Multitudes have come to believe that it is the spirits of the dead who are the "ministering spirits sent forth to minister for them who shall be heirs of salvation." And this notwithstanding the testimony of Scripture to the existence of heavenly angels, and their connection with the history of man, before the death of a human being.

The doctrine of man's consciousness in death, especially the belief that the spirits of the dead return to minister to the living, has prepared the way for modern Spiritualism. If the dead are admitted to the presence of God and holy angels, and privileged with knowledge far exceeding what they before possessed, why should they not return to the earth to enlighten and instruct the living? If, as taught by popular theologians, the spirits of the dead are hovering about their friends on earth, why should they not be permitted to communicate with them, to warn them against evil, or to comfort them in sorrow? How can those who believe in man's consciousness in death reject what comes to them as divine light communicated by glorified spirits? Here is a channel regarded as sacred, through which Satan works for the accomplishment of his purposes. The fallen angels who do his bidding appear as messengers from the spirit world. While professing to bring the living into communication with the dead, the prince of evil exercises his bewitching influence upon their minds.

He has power to bring before men the appearance of their departed friends. The counterfeit is perfect; the familiar look, the words, the tone, are reproduced with marvelous distinctness. Many are comforted with the assurance that their loved ones are enjoying the bliss of Heaven; and without suspicion of danger, they give ear to "seducing spirits, and doctrines of devils."

When they have been led to believe that the dead actually return to communicate with them, Satan causes those to appear who went into the grave unprepared. They claim to be happy in Heaven, and even to occupy exalted positions there; and thus the error is widely taught, that no difference is made between the righteous and the wicked. The pretended visitants from the world of spirits sometimes utter cautions and warnings which prove to be correct. Then, as confidence is gained, they present doctrines that directly undermine faith in the Scriptures. With an appearance of deep interest in the well-being of their friends on earth, they insinuate the most dangerous errors. The fact that they state some truths, and are able at times to foretell future events, gives to their statements an appearance of reliability; and their false teachings are accepted by the multitudes as readily, and believed as implicitly, as if they were the most sacred truths of the Bible. The law of God is set aside, the Spirit of grace despised, the blood of the covenant counted an unholy thing. The spirits deny the divinity of Christ, and place even the Creator on a level with themselves. Thus under a new disguise the great rebel still carries forward his warfare against God, begun in Heaven, and for nearly six thousand years continued upon the earth.

Many endeavor to account for spiritual manifestations by attributing them wholly to fraud and sleight of hand on the part of the medium. But while it is true that the results of trickery have often been palmed off as genuine manifestations, there have been, also, marked exhibitions of supernatural power. The mysterious rapping with which modern Spiritualism began was not the result of human trickery or cunning, but was the direct work of evil angels, who thus introduced one of the most successful of soul-destroying delusions. Many will be ensnared through the belief that Spiritualism is a merely human imposture; when brought face to face with manifestations which they cannot but regard as supernatural, they will be deceived, and will be led to accept them as the great power of God.

These persons overlook the testimony of the Scriptures concerning the wonders wrought by Satan and his agents. It was by Satanic aid that Pharaoh's magicians were enabled to counterfeit the work of God. Paul testifies that before the second advent of Christ there will be similar manifestations of Satanic power. The coming of the Lord is to be preceded by "the working of Satan with all power and signs and lying wonders, and with all deceivableness of unrighteousness." (2 *Thess.* 2:9,10) And the apostle John, describing the miracle-working power that will be manifested in the last days, declares: "He doeth great wonders, so that he maketh fire come down from heaven on the earth in the sight of men, and deceiveth them that dwell on the earth by the means of those miracles which he had power to do." (*Rev.* 13:13, 14) No mere impostures are held foretold. Men are deceived by the miracles which Satan's agents have power to do, not which they pretend to do.

The prince of darkness, who has so long bent the powers of his master-mind to the work of deception, skillfully adapts his temptations to men of all classes and conditions. To persons of culture and refinement he presents Spiritualism in its more refined and intellectual aspects, and thus succeeds in drawing many into his snare. The wisdom which Spiritualism imparts is that described by the apostle James, which "descendeth not from above, but is earthly, sensual, devilish." (*Jas.* 3:15) This, however, the great deceiver conceals, when concealment will best suit his purpose. He who could appear clothed with the brightness of the heavenly seraphs before Christ in the wilderness of temptation, comes to men in the most attractive manner, as an angel of light. He appeals to the reason by the presentation of elevating themes, he delights the fancy with enrapturing scenes, and he enlists the affections by his eloquent portrayals of love and charity. He excites the imagination to lofty flights, leading men to take so great pride in their own wisdom that in their hearts they despise the Eternal One. That mighty being who could take the world's Redeemer to an exceedingly high mountain, and bring before Him all the kingdoms of the earth and the glory of them, will present his temptations to men in a manner to pervert the senses of all who are not shielded by divine power.

Satan beguiles men now as he beguiled Eve in Eden, by flattery, by kindling a desire to obtain forbidden knowledge, by exciting ambition for self-exaltation. It was cherishing these evils that caused his fall, and through them he aims to compass the ruin of men. "Ye shall be as gods," he declares, "knowing good and evil." (*Gen.* 3:5) Spiritualism teaches "that man is the creature of progression; that it is his destiny from his birth to progress, even to eternity, toward the Godhead." And again: "Each mind will judge itself and not another. The judgment will be right, because it is the judgment of self. . . . The throne is within you." Said a Spiritualistic teacher, as the "spiritual consciousness" awoke within him, "My fellowmen, all were unfallen demigods." And another declares, "Any just and perfect being is Christ."

Thus, in place of the righteousness and perfection of the infinite God, the true object of adoration; in place of the perfect righteousness of His law, the true standard of human attainment, Satan has substituted the sinful, erring nature of man himself, as the only object of adoration, the only rule of judgment, or standard of character. This is progress, not upward, but downward.

It is a law both of the intellectual and the spiritual nature, that by beholding, we become changed. The mind gradually adapts itself to the subjects upon which it is allowed to dwell. It becomes assimilated to that which it is accustomed to love and reverence. Man will never rise higher than his standard of purity or goodness or truth. If self is his loftiest ideal, he will never attain to anything more exalted. Rather, he will constantly sink lower and lower. The grace of God alone has power to exalt man. Left to himself, his course must inevitably be downward.

To the self-indulgent, the pleasure-loving, the sensual, Spiritualism presents itself under a less subtle disguise than to the more refined and intellectual; in its grosser forms they find that which is in harmony with their inclinations. Satan studies every indication of the frailty of human nature, he marks the sins which each individual is inclined to commit, and then he takes care that opportunities shall not be wanting to gratify the tendency to evil. He tempts men to excess in that which is in itself lawful, causing them, through intemperance, to weaken physical, mental, and moral power. He has destroyed and is destroying thousands through the indulgence of the passions, thus brutalizing the entire nature of man. And to complete his work, he declares, through the spirits, that "true knowledge places man above all law;" that "whatsoever is, is right;" that "God doth not condemn;" and that "all sins which are committed are innocent." When the people are thus led to believe that desire is the highest law, that liberty is license, and that man is accountable only to himself, who can wonder that corruption and depravity teem on every hand? Multitudes eagerly accept teachings that leave them at liberty to obey the promptings of the carnal heart. The reins of self-control are laid upon the neck of lust, the powers of mind and soul are made subject to the animal propensities, and Satan exultingly sweeps into his net thousands who profess to be followers of Christ.

But none need be deceived by the lying claims of Spiritualism. God has given the world sufficient light to enable them to discover the snare. As already shown, the theory which forms the very foundation of Spiritualism is at war with the plainest statements of Scripture. The Bible declares that the dead know not anything, that their thoughts have perished; they have no part in anything that is done under the sun; they know nothing of the joys or sorrows of those who were dearest to them on earth.

Furthermore, God has expressly forbidden all pretended communication with departed spirits. In the days of the Hebrews there was a class of people who claimed, as do the Spiritualists of to-day, to hold communication with the dead. But the "familiar spirits," as these visitants from other worlds were called, are declared by the Bible to be the "spirits of devils." (Compare *Num.* 25:1-3; *Ps.* 106:28; *1 Cor.* 10:20; *Rev.* 16:14) The work of dealing with familiar spirits was pronounced an abomination to the Lord, and was solemnly forbidden under penalty of death. (*Lev.* 19:31; 20:27) The very name of witchcraft is now held in contempt. The claim that men can hold intercourse with evil spirits is regarded as a fable of the Dark Ages. But Spiritualism, which numbers its converts by hundreds of thousands, yea, by millions, which has made its way into scientific circles, which has invaded churches, and has found favor in legislative bodies, and even in the courts of kings—this mammoth deception is but a revival, in a new disguise, of the witchcraft condemned and prohibited of old.

If there were no other evidence of the real character of Spiritualism, it should be enough for the Christian that the spirits make no difference between righteousness and sin, between the noblest and purest of the apostles of Christ and the most corrupt of the servants of Satan. By representing the basest of men as in Heaven, and highly exalted there, Satan says to the world: "No matter how wicked you are; no matter whether you believe or disbelieve God and the Bible, live as you please; Heaven is your home." The Spiritualist teachers virtually declare, "Every one that doeth evil is good in the sight of the Lord, and He delighteth in them; or, Where is the God of judgment?" (*Mal.* 2:17) Saith the Word of God, "Woe unto them that call evil good, and good evil; that put darkness for light, and light for darkness." (*Isa.* 5:20)

The apostles, as personated by these lying spirits, are made to contradict what they wrote at the dictation of the Holy Spirit when on earth. They deny the divine origin of the Bible, and thus tear away the foundation of the Christian's hope, and put out the light that reveals the way to Heaven. Satan is making the world believe that the Bible is a mere fiction, or at least a book suited to the infancy of the race, but now to be lightly regarded, or cast aside as obsolete. And to take the place of the Word of God he holds out spiritual manifestations. Here is a channel wholly under his control; by this means he can make the world believe what he will. The Book that is to judge him and his followers he puts in the shade, just where he wants it; the Saviour of the world he makes to be no more than a common man. And as the Roman guard that watched the tomb of Jesus spread the lying report which the priests and elders put into their mouths to disprove His resurrection, so do the believers in spiritual manifestations try to make it appear that there is nothing miraculous in the circumstances of our Saviour's life. After thus seeking to put Jesus in the background, they call attention to their own miracles, declaring that these far exceed the works of Christ.

It is true that Spiritualism is now changing its form, and, veiling some of its more objectionable features, is assuming a Christian guise. But its utterances from the platform and the press have been before the public for nearly forty years, and in these its real character stands revealed. These teachings cannot be denied or hidden.

Even in its present form, so far from being more worthy of toleration than formerly, it is really a more dangerous, because a more subtle deception. While it formerly denounced Christ and the Bible, it now *professes* to accept both. But the Bible is interpreted in a manner that is pleasing to the unrenewed heart, while its solemn and vital truths are made of no effect. Love is dwelt upon as the chief attribute of God, but it is degraded to a weak sentimentalism making little distinction between good and evil. God's justice, His denunciations of sin, the requirements of His holy law, are all kept out of sight. The people are taught to regard the decalogue as a dead letter. Pleasing, bewitching fables captivate the senses, and lead men to reject the Bible as the foundation of their faith. Christ is as verily denied as before; but Satan has so blinded the eyes of the people that the deception is not discerned.

There are few who have any just conception of the deceptive power of Spiritualism and the danger of coming under its influence. Many tamper with it, merely to gratify their curiosity. They have no real faith in it, and would be filled with horror at the thought of yielding themselves to the spirits' control. But they venture upon the forbidden ground, and the mighty destroyer exercises his power upon them against their will. Let them once be induced to submit their minds to his direction, and he holds them captive. It is impossible, in their own strength, to break away from the bewitching, alluring spell. Nothing but the power of God, granted in answer to the earnest prayer of faith, can deliver these ensnared souls.

All who indulge sinful traits of character, or willfully cherish a known sin, are inviting the temptations of Satan. They separate themselves from God and from the watch-care of His angels; as the evil one presents his deceptions, they are without defense, and fall an easy prey. Those who thus place themselves in his power, little realize where their course will end. Having achieved their overthrow, the tempter will employ them as his agents to lure others to ruin.

Says the prophet Isaiah: "When they shall say unto you, Seek unto them that have familiar spirits, and unto wizards that peep, and that mutter: should not a people seek unto their God? for the living to the dead? To the law and to the testimony: if they speak not according to this word, it is because there is no light in them." (*Isa.* 8:19, 20) If men had been willing to receive the truth so plainly stated in the Scriptures concerning the nature of man and the state of the dead, they would see in the claims and manifestations of Spiritualism the working of Satan with power and signs and lying wonders. But rather than yield the liberty so agreeable to the carnal heart and renounce the sins which they love, multitudes close their eyes to the light, and walk straight on, regardless of warnings, while Satan weaves his snares about them, and they become his prey. "Because they received not the love of the truth, that they might be saved," therefore "God shall send them strong delusion, that they should believe a lie." (*2 Thess.* 2:10, 11)

Those who oppose the teachings of Spiritualism are assailing, not men alone, but Satan and his angels. They have entered upon a contest against principalities and powers and wicked spirits in high places. Satan will not yield one inch of ground except as he is driven back by the power of heavenly messengers. The people of God should be able to meet him, as did our Saviour, with the words, "It is written." Satan can quote Scripture now as in the days of Christ, and he will pervert its teachings to sustain his delusions. Those who would stand in this time of peril must understand for themselves the testimony of the Scriptures.

Many will be confronted by the spirits of devils personating beloved relatives or friends and declaring the most dangerous heresies. These visitants will appeal to our tenderest sympathies and will work miracles to sustain their pretensions. We must be prepared to withstand them with the Bible truth that the dead know not anything, and that they who thus appear are the spirits of devils.

Just before us is the "hour of temptation, which shall come upon all the world, to try them that dwell upon the earth." (*Rev.* 3:10) All whose faith is not firmly established upon the Word of God will be deceived and overcome. Satan "works with all deceivableness of unrighteousness" to gain control of the children of men; and his deceptions will continually increase. But he can gain his object only as men voluntarily yield to his temptations.

Those who are earnestly seeking a knowledge of truth, and are striving to purify their souls through obedience, thus doing what they can to prepare for the conflict, will find, in the God of truth, a sure defense. "Because thou hast kept the word of My patience, I also will keep thee," (*Rev.* 3:10) is the Saviour's promise. He would sooner send every angel out of Heaven to protect His people, than leave one soul that trusts in Him to be overcome by Satan.

The prophet Isaiah brings to view the fearful deception which will come upon the wicked, causing them to count themselves secure from the judgments of God: "We have made a covenant with death, and with hell are we at agreement; when the overflowing scourge shall pass through, it shall not come unto us; for we have made lies our refuge, and under falsehood have we hid ourselves." (*Isa.* 28:15) In the class here described are included those who in their stubborn impenitence comfort themselves with the assurance that there is to be no punishment for the sinner; that all mankind, it matters not how corrupt, are to be exalted to Heaven, to become as the angels of God. But still more emphatically are those making a covenant with death and an agreement with hell who renounce the truths which Heaven has provided as a defense for the righteous in the day of trouble and accept the refuge of lies offered by Satan in its stead, the delusive pretensions of Spiritualism.

Marvelous beyond expression is the blindness of the people of this generation. Thousands reject the Word of God as unworthy of belief and with eager confidence receive the deceptions of Satan. Skeptics and scoffers denounce the bigotry of those who contend for the faith of prophets and apostles, and they divert themselves by holding up to ridicule the solemn declarations of the Scriptures concerning Christ and the plan of salvation, and the retribution to be visited upon the rejecters of the truth. They affect great pity for minds so narrow, weak, and superstitious as to acknowledge the claims of God, and obey the requirements of His law. They manifest as much assurance as if, indeed, they had made a covenant with death and an agreement with hell—as if they had erected an impassable, impenetrable barrier between themselves and the vengeance of God. Nothing can arouse their fears. So fully have they yielded to the tempter, so closely are they united with him, and so thoroughly imbued with his spirit, that they have no power and no inclination to break away from his snare.

Satan has long been preparing for his final effort to deceive the world. The foundation of his work was laid by the assurance given to Eve in Eden, "Ye shall not surely die." In the day ye eat thereof, then your eyes shall be opened, and ye shall be as gods, knowing good and evil." (*Gen.* 3:4, 5) Little by little he has prepared the way for his master-piece of deception in the development of Spiritualism. He has not yet reached the full accomplishment of his designs; but it will be reached in the last remnant of time. Says the prophet: "I saw three unclean spirits like frogs; . . . they are the spirits of devils, working miracles, which go forth unto the kings of the earth and of the whole world, to gather them to the battle of that great day of God Almighty." (*Rev.* 16:13, 14) Except those who are kept by the power of God through faith in His Word the whole world will be swept into the ranks of this delusion. The people are fast being lulled to a fatal security, to be awakened only by the outpouring of the wrath of God.

Saith the Lord God: "Judgment also will I lay to the line, and righteousness to the plummet; and the hail shall sweep away the refuge of lies, and the waters shall overflow the hiding-place. And your covenant with death shall be disannulled, and your agreement with hell shall not stand; when the overflowing scourge shall pass through, then ye shall be trodden down by it." (*Isa.* 28:17, 18)

Chapter 9

LIBERTY THREATENED

ROMANISM IS NOW REGARDED by Protestants with far greater favor than in former years. In those countries where Catholicism is not in the ascendency, and the papists are taking a conciliatory course in order to gain influence, there is an increasing indifference concerning the doctrines that separate the reformed churches from the papal hierarchy; the opinion is gaining ground, that, after all, we do not differ so widely upon vital points as has been supposed, and that a little concession on our part will bring us into a better understanding with Rome. The time was when Protestants placed a high value upon the liberty of conscience which has been so dearly purchased. They taught their children to abhor popery and held that to seek harmony with Rome would be disloyalty to God. But how widely different are the sentiments now expressed.

The defenders of popery declare that the church has been maligned; and the Protestant world are inclined to accept the statement. Many urge that it is unjust to judge the church of to-day by the abominations and absurdities that marked her reign during the centuries of ignorance and darkness. They excuse her horrible cruelty as the result of the barbarism of the times and plead that the influence of modern civilization has changed her sentiments.

Have these persons forgotten the claim of infallibility put forth for eight hundred years by this haughty power? So far from being relinquished, this claim has been affirmed in the nineteenth century with greater positiveness than ever before. As Rome asserts that she *"never erred, and never can err,"* how can she renounce the principles which governed her course in past ages?

The papal church will never relinquish her claim to infallibility. All that she has done in her persecution of those who reject her dogmas, she holds to be right; and would she not repeat the same acts, should the opportunity be presented? Let the restraints now imposed by secular governments be removed, and Rome be re-instated in her former power, and there would speedily be a revival of her tyranny and persecution.

A well-known writer (Josiah Strong, D.D., in "Our Country," pp. 46-48.) speaks thus of the attitude of the papal hierarchy as regards freedom of conscience, and of the perils which especially threaten the United States from the success of her policy:—

"There are many who are disposed to attribute any fear of Roman Catholicism in the United States to bigotry or childishness. Such see nothing in the character and attitude of Romanism that is hostile to our free institutions, or find nothing portentous in its growth. Let us, then, first compare some of the fundamental principles of our government with those of the Catholic Church.

"The Constitution of the United States guarantees *liberty of conscience.* Nothing is dearer or more fundamental. Pope Pius IX., in his Encyclical Letter of August 15, 1854, said: 'The absurd and erroneous doctrines or ravings in defense of liberty of conscience, are a most pestilential error—a pest, of all others, most to be dreaded in a State.' The same pope, in his Encyclical Letter of December 8, 1864, anathematized 'those who assert the liberty of conscience and of religious worship,' also 'all such as maintain that the church may not employ force.'

"The pacific tone of Rome in the United States does not imply a change of heart. She is tolerant where she is helpless. Says Bishop O'Connor: 'Religious liberty is merely endured until the opposite can be carried into effect without peril to the Catholic world.' The archbishop of St. Louis once said: 'Heresy and unbelief are crimes; and in Christian countries, as in Italy and Spain, for instance, where all the people are Catholics, and where the Catholic religion is an essential part of the law of the land, they are punished as other crimes.'

"Every cardinal, archbishop, and bishop in the Catholic Church takes an oath of allegiance to the pope, in which occur the following words: 'Heretics, schismatics, and rebels to our said lord the pope, or his aforesaid successors, I will to my utmost persecute and oppose.' "

It is true that there are real Christians in the Roman Catholic communion. Thousands in that church are serving God according to the best light they have. They are not allowed access to His Word, and therefore they do not discern the truth. They have never seen the contrast between a living heart-service and a round of mere forms and ceremonies. God looks with pitying tenderness upon these souls, educated as they are in a faith that is delusive and unsatisfying. He will cause rays of light to penetrate the dense darkness that surrounds them. He will reveal to them the truth, as it is in Jesus, and many will yet take their position with His people.

But Romanism as a system is no more in harmony with the gospel of Christ now than at any former period in her history. The Protestant churches are in great darkness, or they would discern the signs of the times. The Roman Church is far-reaching in her plans and modes of operation. She is employing every device to extend her influence and increase her power in preparation for a fierce and determined conflict to regain control of the world, to re-establish persecution, and to undo all that Protestantism has done. Catholicism is gaining ground upon every side. See the increasing number of her churches and chapels in Protestant countries. Look at the popularity of her colleges and seminaries in America, so widely patronized by Protestants. Look at the growth of ritualism in England, and the frequent defections to the ranks of the Catholics. These things should awaken the anxiety of all who prize the pure principles of the gospel.

Protestants have tampered with and patronized popery; they have made compromises and concessions which papists themselves are surprised to see, and fail to understand. Men are closing their eyes to the real character of Romanism and the dangers to be apprehended from her supremacy. The people need to be aroused to resist the advances of this most dangerous foe to civil and religious liberty.

Many Protestants suppose that the Catholic religion is unattractive, and that its worship is a dull, meaningless round of ceremony. Here they mistake. While Romanism is based upon deception, it is not a coarse and clumsy imposture. The religious service of the Roman Church is a most impressive ceremonial. Its gorgeous display and solemn rites fascinate the senses of the people, and silence the voice of reason and of conscience. The eye is charmed. Magnificent churches, imposing processions, golden altars, jeweled shrines, choice paintings, and exquisite sculpture appeal to the love of beauty. The ear also is captivated. The music is unsurpassed. The rich notes of the deep-toned organ, blending with the melody of many voices as it swells through the lofty domes and pillared aisles of her grand cathedrals, cannot fail to impress the mind with awe and reverence.

This outward splendor, pomp, and ceremony, that only mocks the longings of the sin-sick soul, is an evidence of inward corruption. The religion of Christ needs not such attractions to recommend it. In the light shining from the cross, true Christianity appears so pure and lovely that no external decorations can enhance its true worth. It is the beauty of holiness, a meek and quiet spirit, which is of value with God.

Brilliancy of style is not necessarily an index of pure, elevated thought. High conceptions of art, delicate refinement of taste, often exist in minds that are earthly and sensual. They are often employed by Satan to lead men to forget the necessities of the soul, to lose sight of the future, immortal life, to turn away from their infinite Helper, and to live for this world alone.

A religion of externals is attractive to the unrenewed heart. The pomp and ceremony of the Catholic worship have a seductive, bewitching power, by which many are deceived; and they come to look upon the Roman Church as the very gate of Heaven. None but those who have planted their feet firmly upon the foundation of truth, and whose hearts are renewed by the Spirit of God, are proof against her influence. Thousands who have not an experimental knowledge of Christ will be led to accept the forms of godliness without the power. Such a religion is just what the multitudes desire.

The church's claim to the right to pardon causes the Romanist to feel at liberty to sin; and the ordinance of confession, without which her pardon is not granted, tends also to give license to evil. He who kneels before fallen man and opens in confession the secret thoughts and imaginations of his heart is debasing his manhood, and degrading every noble instinct of his soul. In unfolding the sins of his life to a priest—an erring sinful mortal, and too often corrupted with wine and licentiousness—his standard of character is lowered, and he is defiled in consequence. His thought of God is degraded to the likeness of fallen humanity; for the priest stands as a representative of God. This degrading confession of man to man is the secret spring from which has flowed much of the evil that is defiling the world and fitting it for the final destruction. Yet. to him who loves self-indulgence, it is more pleasing to confess to a fellow-mortal than to open the soul to God. It is more palatable to human nature to do penance than to renounce sin; it is easier to mortify the flesh by sackcloth and nettles and galling chains than to crucify fleshly lusts. Heavy is the yoke which the carnal heart is willing to bear rather than bow to the yoke of Christ.

There is a striking similarity between the Church of Rome and the Jewish Church at the time of Christ's first advent. While the Jews secretly trampled upon every principle of the law of God, they were outwardly rigorous in the observance of its precepts, loading it down with exactions and tranditions that made obedience painful and burdensome. As the Jews professed to revere the law, so do Romanists claim to reverence the cross. They exalt the symbol of Christ's sufferings, while in their lives they deny Him whom it represents.

Papists place crosses upon their churches, upon their altars, and upon their garments. Everywhere is seen the insignia of the cross. Everywhere it is outwardly honored and exalted. But the teachings of Christ are buried beneath a mass of senseless traditions, false interpretations, and rigorous exactions. The Saviour's words concerning the bigoted Jews, apply with still greater force to the Roman leaders: "They bind heavy burdens and grievous to be borne, and lay them on men's shoulders; but they themselves will not move them with one of their fingers." (*Matt.* 23:4) Conscientious souls are kept in constant terror, fearing the wrath of an offended God, while the dignitaries of the church are living in luxury and sensual pleasure.

The worship of images and relics, the invocation of saints, and the exaltation of the pope, are devices of Satan to attract the minds of the people from God and from His Son. To accomplish their ruin, he endeavors to turn their attention from Him through whom alone they can find salvation. He will direct them to any object that can be substituted for the One who has said. "Come unto Me all ye that labor and are heavy-laden, and I will give you rest." (*Matt.* 11:28)

It is Satan's constant effort to misrepresent the character of God, the nature of sin, and the real issues at stake in the great controversy. His sophistry lessens the obligation of the divine law, and gives men license to sin. At the same time he causes them to cherish false conceptions of God, so that they regard Him with fear and hate, rather than with love. The cruelty inherent in his own character is attributed to the Creator; it is embodied in systems of religion and expressed in modes of worship. Thus the minds of men are blinded, and Satan secures them as his agents to war against God. By perverted conceptions of the divine attributes heathen nations were led to believe human sacrifices necessary to secure the favor of Deity;

and horrible cruelties have been perpetrated under the various forms of idolatry. The Roman Church, uniting the form of paganism and Christianity, and, unlike paganism, misrepresenting the character of God, has resorted to practices no less cruel and revolting. In the days of Rome's supremacy, there were instruments of torture to compel assent to her doctrines. There was the stake for those who would not concede to her claims. There were massacres on a scale that will never be known until revealed in the Judgment. Dignitaries of the church studied, under Satan their master, to invent means to cause the greatest possible torture, and not end the life of their victim. The infernal process was repeated to the utmost limit of human endurance, until nature gave up the struggle, and the sufferer hailed death as a sweet release.

Such was the fate of Rome's opponents. For her adherents she had the discipline of the scourge, of famishing hunger, of bodily austerities in every conceivable, heartsickening form. To secure the favor of Heaven, penitents violated the laws of God by violating the laws of nature. They were taught to sunder every tie which He has formed to bless and gladden man's earthly sojourn. The churchyard contains millions of victims, who spent their lives in vain endeavors to subdue their natural affections, to repress, as offensive to God, every thought and feeling of sympathy with their fellow-creatures.

If we desire to understand the determined cruelty of Satan, manifested for hundreds of years, not among those who never heard of God, but in the very heart and throughout the extent of Christendom, we have only to look at the history of Romanism. Through this mammoth system of deception the prince of evil achieves his purpose of bringing dishonor to God and wretchedness to man. And as we see how he succeeds in disguising himself, and accomplishing his work through the leaders of the church, we may better understand why he has so great antipathy to the Bible. If that book is read, the mercy and love of God will be revealed; it will be seen that He lays upon men none of these heavy burdens. All that He asks is a broken and contrite heart, a humble, obedient spirit.

Christ gives no example in His life for men and women to shut themselves in monasteries in order to become fitted for Heaven. He has never taught that love and sympathy must be repressed. The Saviour's heart overflowed with love. The nearer man approaches to moral perfection, the keener are his sensibilities, the more acute is his perception of sin, and the deeper his sympathy for the afflicted. The pope claims to be the vicar of Christ; but how does his character bear comparison with that of our Saviour? Was Christ ever known to consign men to the prison or the rack because they did not pay Him homage as the King of Heaven? Was His voice heard condemning to death those who did not accept Him? When He was slighted by the people of a Samaritan village, the apostle John was filled with indignation, and inquired, "Lord, wilt Thou that we command fire to come down from heaven, and consume them, even as Elias did?" Jesus looked with pity upon His disciple, and rebuked his harsh spirit, saying, "The Son of man is not come to destroy men's lives, but to save them." (*Luke* 9:54, 56) How different from the spirit manifested by Christ is that of His professed vicar.

The Roman Church now presents a fair front to the world, covering with apologies her record of horrible cruelties. She has clothed herself in Christ-like garments; but she is unchanged. Every principle of popery that existed in past ages exists to-day. The doctrines devised in the darkest ages are still held. Let none deceive themselves. The popery that Protestants are now so ready to honor is the same that ruled the world in the days of the Reformation, when men of God stood up at the peril of their lives to expose her iniquity. She possesses the same pride and arrogant assumption that lorded it over kings and princes and claimed the prerogatives of God. Her spirit is no less cruel and despotic now than when she crushed out human liberty and slew the saints of the Most High.

Popery is just what prophecy declared that she would

be, the apostasy of the latter times. (*2 Thess.* 2:3, 4) It is a part of her policy to assume the character which will best accomplish her purpose; but beneath the variable appearance of the chameleon, she conceals the invariable venom of the serpent. "We are not bound to keep faith and promises to heretics," she declares. Shall this power, whose record for a thousand years is written in the blood of the saints, be now acknowledged as a part of the church of Christ?

It is not without reason that the claim has been put forth in Protestant countries, that Catholicism differs less widely from Protestantism than in former times. There has been a change; but the change is not in the papacy. Catholicism indeed resembles much of the Protestantism that now exists, because Protestantism has so greatly degenerated since the days of the reformers.

As the Protestant churches have been seeking the favor of the world, false charity has blinded their eyes. They do not see but that it is right to believe good of all evil; and as the inevitable result, they will finally believe evil of all good. Instead of standing in defense of the faith once delivered to the saints, they are now, as it were, apologizing to Rome for their uncharitable opinion of her, begging pardon for their bigotry.

A large class, even of those who look upon Romanism with no favor, apprehend little danger from her power and influence. Many urge that the intellectual and moral darkness prevailing during the Middle Ages favored the spread of her dogmas, superstitions, and oppression, and that the greater intelligence of modern times, the general diffusion of knowledge, and the increasing liberality in matters of religion, forbid a revival of intolerance and tyranny. The very thought that such a state of things will exist in this enlightened age is ridiculed. It is true that great light, intellectual, moral, and religious, is shining upon this generation. In the open pages of God's holy Word light from Heaven has been shed upon the world. But it should be remembered that the greater the light bestowed, the greater the darkness of those who pervert or reject it.

A prayerful study of the Bible would show Protestants the real character of the papacy, and would cause them to abhor and to shun it; but many are so wise in their own conceit that they feel no need of humbly seeking God that they may be led into the truth. Although priding themselves on their enlightenment, they are ignorant both of the Scriptures and of the power of God. They must have some means of quieting their consciences; and they seek that which is least spiritual and humiliating. What they desire is a method of forgetting God which shall pass as a method of remembering Him. The papacy is well adapted to meet the wants of all these. It is prepared for two classes of mankind, embracing nearly the whole world—those who would be saved by their merits, and those who would be saved in their sins. Here is the secret of its power.

A day of great intellectual darkness has been shown to be favorable to the success of popery. It will yet be demonstrated that a day of great intellectual light is equally favorable for its success. In past ages, when men were without God's Word, and without the knowledge of the truth, their eyes were blindfolded, and thousands were ensnared, not seeing the net spread for their feet. In this generation there are many whose eyes become dazzled by the glare of human speculations, "science falsely so-called;" they discern not the net and walk into it as readily as if blindfolded. God designed that man's intellectual powers should be held as a gift from his Maker and should be employed in the service of truth and righteousness; but when pride and ambition are cherished, and men exalt their own theories above the Word of God, then intelligence can accomplish greater harm than ignorance. Thus the false science of the nineteenth century, which undermines faith in the Bible, will prove as successful in preparing the way for the acceptance of the papacy, with its pleasing forms, as did the withholding of knowledge in opening the way for its aggrandizement in the Dark Ages.

In the movements now in progress in the United States to secure for the institutions and usages of the church the support of the State, Protestants are following in the steps of papists. Nay, more, they are opening the door for popery to regain in Protestant America the supremacy which she has lost in the Old World. And that which gives greater significance to his movement is the fact that the principal object contemplated is the enforcement of Sunday observance—a custom which originated with Rome, and which she claims as the sign of her authority. It is the spirit of the papacy—the spirit of conformity to worldly customs, the veneration for human traditions above the commandments of God—that is permeating the Protestant churches and leading them on to do the same work of Sunday exaltation which the papacy has done before them.

If the reader would understand the agencies to be employed in the soon-coming contest, he has but to trace the record of the means which Rome employed for the same object in ages past. If he would know how papists and Protestants united will deal with those who reject their dogmas, let him see the spirit which Rome manifested toward the Sabbath and its defenders.

Royal edicts, general councils, and church ordinances sustained by secular power, were the steps by which the pagan festival attained its position of honor in the Christian world. The first public measure enforcing Sunday observance was the law enacted by Constantine. (A.D. 321) This edict required townspeople to rest on "the venerable day of the sun," but permitted countrymen to continue their agricultural pursuits. Though virtually a heathen statute, it was enforced by the emperor after his nominal acceptance of Christianity.

The royal mandate not proving a sufficient substitute for divine authority, Eusebius, a bishop who sought the favor of princes, and who was the special friend and flatterer of Constantine, advanced the claim that Christ had transferred the Sabbath to Sunday. Not a single testimony of the Scriptures was produced in proof of the new doctrine. Eusebius himself unwittingly acknowledges its falsity and points to the real authors of the change. "All things," he says, "whatsoever that it was duty to do on the Sabbath, these *we* have transferred to the Lord's day." But the Sunday argument, groundless as it was, served to embolden men in trampling upon the Sabbath of the Lord. All who desired to be honored by the world accepted the popular festival.

As the papacy became firmly established, the work of Sunday exaltation was continued. For a time the people engaged in agricultural labor when not attending church, and the seventh day was still regarded as the Sabbath. But steadily a change was effected. Those in holy office were forbidden to pass judgment in any civil controversy on the Sunday. Soon after, all persons, of whatever rank, were commanded to refrain from common labor, on pain of a fine for freemen, and stripes in the case of servants. Later it was decreed, that rich men should be punished with the loss of half of their estates; and finally, that if still obstinate they should be made slaves. The lower classes were to suffer perpetual banishment.

Miracles also were called into requisition. Among other wonders it was reported that as a husbandman who was about to plow his field on Sunday, cleaned his plow with an iron, the iron stuck fast in his hand, and for two years he carried it about with him, "to his exceeding great pain and shame."

Later, the pope gave directions that the parish priest should admonish the violators of Sunday, and wish them to go to church and say their prayers, lest they bring some great calamity on themselves and neighbors. An ecclesiastical council brought forward the argument, since so widely employed, even by Protestants, that because persons had been struck by lightning while laboring on Sunday, it must be the Sabbath. "It is apparent," said the prelates, "how high the displeasure of God was upon their neglect of this day." An appeal was then made that priests and ministers, kings and princes, and all faithful people, "use their utmost endeavors and care that the day be restored to its honor, and, for the credit of Christianity, more devoutly observed for time to come."

The decrees of councils proving insufficient, the secular authorities were besought to issue an edict that would strike terror to the hearts of the people, and force them to refrain from labor on the Sunday. At a synod held in Rome, all previous decisions were reaffirmed with greater force and solemnity. They were also incorporated into the ecclesiastical law, and enforced by the civil authorities throughout nearly all Christendom.

Still the absence of scriptural authority for Sunday-keeping occasioned no little embarrassment. The people questioned the right of their teachers to set aside the positive declaration of Jehovah, "The seventh day is the Sabbath of the Lord thy God," in order to honor the day of the sun. To supply the lack of Bible testimony, other expedients were necessary. A zealous advocate of Sunday, who about the close of the twelfth century visited the churches of England, was resisted by faithful witnesses for the truth; and so fruitless were his efforts that he departed from the country for a season and cast about him for some means to enforce his teachings. When he returned, the lack was supplied, and in his after-labors he met with greater success. He brought with him a roll purporting to be from God Himself, which contained the needed command for Sunday observance, with awful threats to terrify the disobedient. This precious document—as base a counterfeit as the institution it supported—was said to have fallen from Heaven, and to have been found in Jerusalem, upon the altar of St. Simeon in Golgotha. But in fact, the pontifical palace at Rome was the source whence it proceeded. Frauds and forgeries to advance the power and prosperity of the church have in all ages been esteemed lawful by the papal hierarchy.

The roll forbade labor from the ninth hour, three o'clock, on Saturday afternoon, till sunrise on Monday; and its authority was declared to be confirmed by many miracles. It was reported that persons laboring beyond the appointed hour were stricken with paralysis. A miller who attempted to grind his corn, saw instead of flour, a torrent of blood come forth, and the mill wheel stood still, notwithstanding the strong rush of the water. A woman who placed dough in the oven, found it raw when taken out, though the oven was very hot. Another who had dough prepared for baking at the ninth hour, but determined to set it aside till Monday, found, the next day, that it had been made into loaves and baked by divine power. A man who baked bread after the ninth hour on Saturday, found, when he broke it the next morning, that blood started therefrom. By such absurd and superstitious fabrications did the advocates of Sunday endeavor to establish its sacredness.

In Scotland, as in England, a greater regard for Sunday was secured by uniting with it a portion of the ancient Sabbath. But the time required to be kept holy varied. An edict from the king of Scotland declared that Saturday from twelve at noon ought to be accounted holy, and that no man, from that time till Monday morning, should engage in worldly business.

But notwithstanding all the efforts to establish Sunday sacredness, papists themselves publicly confessed the divine authority of the Sabbath, and the human origin of the institution by which it had been supplanted. In the sixteenth century a papal council plainly declared: "Let all Christians remember that the seventh day was consecrated by God, and hath been received and observed, not only by the Jews, but by all others who pretend to worship God; though we Christians have changed their Sabbath into the Lord's day." Those who were tampering with the divine law were not ignorant of the character of their work. They were deliberately setting themselves above God.

A striking illustration of Rome's policy toward those who disagree with her was given in the long and bloody persecution of the Waldenses, some of whom were observers of the Sabbath. Others suffered in a similar manner for their fidelity to the fourth commandment. The history of the churches of Ethiopia and Abyssinia is especially significant. Amid the gloom of the Dark Ages, the Christians of Central Africa were lost sight of and forgotten by the world, and for many centuries they enjoyed freedom in the exercise of their faith. But at last Rome learned of their existence, and the emperor of Abyssinia was soon beguiled into an acknowledgment of the pope as the vicar of Christ. Other concessions followed. An edict was issued forbidding the observance of the Sabbath under the severest penalties. But papal tyranny soon became a yoke so galling that the Abyssinians determined to break it from their necks. After a terrible struggle, the Romanists were banished from their dominions, and the ancient faith was restored. The churches rejoiced in their freedom, and they never forgot the lesson they had learned concerning the deception, the fanaticism, and the despotic power of Rome. Within their solitary realm they were content to remain, unknown to the rest of Christendom.

The churches of Africa held the Sabbath as it was held by the papal church before her complete apostasy. While they kept the seventh day in obedience to the commandment of God, they abstained from labor on the Sunday in conformity to the custom of the church. Upon obtaining supreme power, Rome had trampled upon the Sabbath of God to exalt her own; but the churches of Africa, hidden for nearly a thousand years, did not share in this apostasy. When brought under the sway of Rome, they were forced to set aside the true and exalt the false Sabbath; but no sooner had they regained their independence than they returned to obedience to the fourth commandment.

These records of the past clearly reveal the enmity of Rome toward the true Sabbath and its defenders and the means which she employs to honor the institution of her creating. The Word of God teaches that these scenes are to be repeated as Catholics and Protestants shall unite for the exaltation of the Sunday.

The prophecy of Revelation 13 declares that the power represented by the beast with lamb-like horns shall cause "the earth and them which dwell therein" to worship the papacy—there symbolized by the beast "like unto a leopard." The beast with two horns is also to say "to them that dwell on the earth, that they should make an image to the beast;" and, furthermore, it is to command all, "both small and great, rich and poor, free and bond," to receive "the mark of the beast." (*Rev.* 13:11-16) It has been shown that the United States is the power represented by the beast with lamb-like horns, and that this prophecy will be fulfilled when the United States shall enforce Sunday observance, which Rome claims as the special acknowledgment of her supremacy. But in this homage to the papacy the United States will not be alone. The influence of Rome in the countries that once acknowledged her dominion is still far from being destroyed. And prophecy foretells a restoration of her power. "I saw one of his heads as it were wounded to death; and his deadly wound was healed; and all the world wondered after the beast." (*Rev.* 13:3) The infliction of the deadly wound points to the abolition of the papacy in 1798. After this, says the prophet, "His deadly wound was healed; and all the world wondered after the beast." Paul states plainly that the man of sin will continue until the second advent. (2 *Thess.* 2:8) To the very close of time he will carry forward his work of deception. And the Revelator declares, also referring to the papacy, "All that dwell upon the earth shall worship him, whose names are not written in the book of life." (*Rev.* 13:8) In both the Old and the New World, the papacy will receive homage in the honor paid to the Sunday institution that rests solely upon the authority of the Roman Church.

Since the middle of the nineteenth century students of prophecy in the United States have presented this testimony to the world. In the events now taking place is seen a rapid advance toward the fulfillment of the prediction. With Protestant teachers there is the same claim of divine authority for Sunday-keeping, and the same lack of scriptural evidence, as with the papal leaders who fabricated miracles to supply the place of a command from God. The assertion that God's judgments are visited upon men for ther violation of the Sunday-sabbath, will be repeated; already it is beginning to be urged. And a movement to enforce Sunday observance is fast gaining ground.

Marvelous in her shrewdness and cunning is the Roman Church. She can read what is to be. She bides her time, seeing that the Protestant churches are paying her homage in their acceptance of the false Sabbath, and that they are preparing to enforce it by the very means which she herself employed in by-gone days. Those who reject the light of truth will yet seek the aid of this self-styled infallible power to exalt an institution that originated with her. How readily she will come to the help of Protestants in this work, it is not difficult to conjecture. Who understands better than the papal leaders how to deal with those who are disobedient to the church?

The Roman Church, with all its ramifications throughout the world, forms one vast organization, under the control, and designed to serve the interests, of the papal see. Its millions of communicants, in every country on the globe, are instructed to hold themselves as bound in allegiance to the pope. Whatever their nationality or their government, they are to regard the authority of the church as above all other. Though they may take the oath pledging their loyalty to the State, yet back of this lies the vow of obedience to Rome, absolving them from every pledge inimical to her interests.

Protestants little know what they are doing when they propose to accept the aid of Rome in the work of Sunday exaltation. While they are bent upon the accomplishment of their purpose, Rome is aiming to re-establish her power, to recover her lost supremacy. Let history testify of her artful and persistent efforts to insinuate herself into the affairs of nations; and having gained a foothold, to further her own aims, even at the ruin of princes and people. Romanism openly puts forth the claim that the pope "can pronounce sentences and judgments in contradiction to the *right of nations, to the law of God and man.*" (The "Decretalia")

And let it be remembered, it is the boast of Rome that she never changes. The principles of Gregory VII and Innocent III are still the principles of the Roman Church. And had she but the power, she would put them in practice with as much vigor now as in past centuries. Let the principle once be established in the United States, that the church may employ or control the power of the State; that religious observances may be enforced by secular laws; in short, that the authority of the church and State is to dominate the conscience, and the triumph of Rome in this country is assured.

God's Word has given warning of the impending danger; let this be unheeded, and the Protestant world will learn what the purposes of Rome really are, only when it is too late to escape the snare. She is silently growing into power. Her doctrines are exerting their influence in legislative halls, in the churches, and in the hearts of men. She is piling up her lofty and massive structures in the secret recesses of which her former persecutions will be repeated. Stealthily and unsuspectedly she is strengthening her forces to further her own ends when the time shall come for her to strike. All that she desires is vantage-ground, and this is already being given her. We shall soon see and shall feel what the purpose of the Roman element is. Whoever shall believe and obey the Word of God will thereby incur reproach and persecution.

Chapter 10

THE IMPENDING CONFLICT

FROM THE VERY BEGINNING of the great controversy in Heaven, it has been Satan's purpose to overthrow the law of God. It was to accomplish this that he entered upon his rebellion against the Creator; and though he was cast out of Heaven, he has continued the same warfare upon the earth. To deceive men, and thus lead them to transgress God's law, is the object which he has steadfastly pursued. Whether this be accomplished by casting aside the law altogether, or by rejecting one of its precepts, the result will be ultimately the same. He that offends "in one point," manifests contempt for the whole law; his influence and example are on the side of transgression; he becomes "guilty of all." (*James* 2:10).

In seeking to cast contempt upon the divine statues, Satan has perverted the doctrines of the Bible, and errors have thus become incorporated into the faith of thousands who profess to believe the Scriptures. The last great conflict between truth and error is but the final struggle of the long-standing controversy concerning the law of God. Upon this battle we are now entering—a battle between the laws of men and the precepts of Jehovah, between the religion of the Bible and the religion of fable and tradition.

The agencies which will unite against truth and righteousness in this contest are now actively at work. God's holy Word, which has been handed down to us at such a cost of suffering and blood, is but little valued. The Bible is within the reach of all, but there are few who really accept it as the guide of life. Infidelity prevails to an alarming extent, not in the world merely, but in the church. Many have come to deny doctrines which are the very pillars of the Christian faith. The great facts of creation as presented by the inspired writers, the fall of man, the atonement, and the perpetuity of the law of God, are practically rejected, either wholly or in part, by a large share of the professedly Christian world. Thousands who pride themselves upon their widsom and independence regard it an evidence of weakness to place implicit confidence in the Bible; they think it a proof of superior talent and learning to cavil at the Scriptures, and to spiritualize and explain away their most important truths. Many ministers are teaching their people, and many professors and teachers are instructing their students, that the law of God has been changed or abrogated; and those who regard its requirements as still valid, to be literally obeyed, are thought to be deserving only of ridicule or contempt.

In rejecting the truth, men reject its Author. In trampling upon the law of God, they deny the authority of the Lawgiver. It is as easy to make an idol of false doctrines and theories as to fashion an idol of wood or stone. By misrepresenting the attributes of God, Satan leads men to conceive of Him in a false character. With many, a philosophical idol is enthroned in the place of Jehovah; while the living God, as He is revealed in His Word, in Christ, and in the works of creation, is worshiped by but few. Thousands deify nature, while they deny the God of nature. Though in a different form, idolatry exists in the Christian world to-day as verily as it existed among ancient Israel in the days of Elijah. The god of many professedly wise men, of philosophers, poets, politicians, journalists—the god of polished fashionable circles, of many colleges and universities, even of some theological institutions—is little better than Baal, the sun-god of Phenicia.

No error accepted by the Christian world strikes more boldly against the authority of Heaven, none is more directly opposed to the dictates of reason, none is more pernicious in its results, than the modern doctrine, so rapidly gaining ground, that God's law is no longer binding upon men. Every nation has its laws, which command respect and obedience; no government could exist without them; and can it be conceived that the Creator of the heavens and the earth has no law to govern the beings He has made? Suppose that prominent ministers were publicly to teach that the statutes which govern their land and protect the rights of its citizens were not obligatory—that they restricted the liberties of the people, and therefore ought not to be obeyed; how long would such men be tolerated in the pulpit? But is it a graver offense to disregard the laws of States and nations than to trample upon those divine precepts which are the foundation of all government?

It would be far more consistent for nations to abolish their statutes, and permit the people to do as they please, than for the Ruler of the universe to annul His law and leave the world without a standard to condemn the guilty or justify the obedient. Would we know the result of making void the law of God? The experiment has been tried. Terrible were the scenes enacted in France when atheism became the controlling power. It was then demonstrated to the world that to throw off the restraints which God has imposed is to accept the rule of the cruelest of tyrants. When the standard of righteousness is set aside, the way is open for the prince of evil to establish his power in the earth.

Wherever the divine precepts are rejected, sin ceases to appear sinful, or righteousness desirable Those who refuse to submit to the government of God are wholly unfitted to govern themselves. Through their pernicious teachings, the spirit of insubordination is implanted in the hearts of children and youth, who are naturally impatient of control; and a lawless, licentious state of society results. While scoffing at the credulity of those who obey the requirements of God, the multitudes eagerly accept the delusions of Satan. They give the rein to lust, and practice the sins which have called down judgments upon the heathen.

Those who teach the people to lightly regard the commandments of God, sow disobedience, to reap disobedience. Let the restraint imposed by the divine law be wholly cast aside, and human laws would soon be disregarded. Because God forbids dishonest practices, coveting, lying, and defrauding, men are ready to trample upon His statutes as a hindrance to their worldly prosperity; but the results of banishing these precepts would be such as they do not anticipate. If the law were not binding, why should any fear to transgress? Property would no longer be safe. Men would obtain their neighbor's possessions by violence; and the strongest would become richest. Life itself would not be respected. The marriage vow would no longer stand as a sacred bulwark to protect the family. He who had the power, would, if he desired, take his neighbor's wife by violence. The fifth commandment would be set aside with the fourth. Children would not shrink from taking the life of their parents, if by so doing they could obtain the desire of their corrupt hearts. The civilized world would become a horde of robbers and assassins; and peace, rest, and happiness would be banished from the earth.

Already the doctrine that men are released from obedience to God's requirements has weakened the force of moral obligation and opened the flood-gates of iniquity upon the world. Lawlessness, dissipation, and corruption are sweeping in upon us like an overwhelming tide. In the family Satan is at work. His banner waves, even in professedly Christian households. There is envy, evil surmising, hypocrisy, estrangement, emulation, strife, betrayal of sacred trusts, indulgence of lust. The whole system of religious principles and doctrines, which should form the foundation and frame-work of social life, seems to be a tottering mass, ready to fall to ruin. The vilest of criminals, when thrown into prison for their offenses, are often made the recipients of gifts and attentions, as if they had attained an enviable distinction. Great publicity is given to their character and crimes. The press publishes the revolting details of vice, thus initiating others into the practice of fraud, robbery, and murder; and Satan exults in the success of his hellish schemes. The infatuation of vice, the wanton taking of life, the terrible increase of intemperance and iniquity of every order and degree, should arouse all who fear God, to inquire what can be done to stay the tide of evil.

Courts of justice are corrupt. Rulers are actuated by desire for gain and love of sensual pleasure. Intemperance has beclouded the faculties of many, so that Satan has almost complete control of them. Jurists are perverted, bribed, deluded. Drunkenness and revelry, passion, envy, dishonesty of every sort, are represented among those who administer the laws. "Justice standeth afar off; for truth is fallen in the street, and equity cannot enter." (*Isa.* 59:14)

The iniquity and spiritual darkness that prevailed under the supremacy of Rome were the inevitable result of her suppression of the Scriptures; but where is to be found the cause of the widespread infidelity, the rejection of the law of God, and the consequent corruption, under the full blaze of gospel light in an age of religious freedom? Now that Satan can no longer keep the world under his control by withholding the Scriptures, he resorts to other means to accomplish the same object. To destroy faith in the Bible serves his purpose as well as to destroy the Bible itself. By introducing the belief that God's law is not binding, he as effectually leads men to transgress as if they were wholly ignorant of its precepts. And now, as in former ages, he has worked through the church to further his designs. The religious organizations of the day have refused to listen to unpopular truths plainly brought to view in the Scriptures, and in combating them they have adopted interpretations and taken positions which have sown broadcast the seeds of skepticism. Clinging to the papal error of natural immortality and man's consciousness in death, they have rejected the only defense against the delusions of Spiritualism. The doctrine of eternal torment has led many to disbelieve the Bible. And as the claims of the fourth commandment are urged upon the people, it is found that the observance of the seventh-day Sabbath is enjoined; and as the only way to free themselves from a duty which they are unwilling to perform, popular teachers declare that the law of God is no longer binding. Thus they cast away the law and the Sabbath together. As the work of Sabbath reform extends, this rejection of the divine law to avoid the claims of the fourth commandment will become well-nigh universal. The teachings of religious leaders have opened the door to infidelity, to Spiritualism, and to contempt for God's holy law, and upon these leaders rests a fearful responsibility for the iniquity that exists in the Christian world.

Yet this very class put forth the claim that the fast-spreading corruption is largely attributable to the desecration of the so-called "Christian Sabbath," and that the enforcement of Sunday observance would greatly improve the morals of society. This claim is especially urged in America, where the doctrine of the true Sabbath has been most widely preached. Here the temperance work, one of the most prominent and important of moral reforms, is often combined with the Sunday movement, and the advocates of the latter represent themselves as laboring to promote the highest interest of society; and those who refuse to unite with them are denounced as the enemies of temperance and reform. But the fact that a movement to establish error is connected with a work which is in itself good, is not an argument in favor of the error. We may disguise poison by mingling it with wholesome food, but we do not change its nature. On the contrary, it is rendered more dangerous, as it is more likely to be taken unawares. It is one of Satan's devices to combine with falsehood just enough truth to give it plausibility. The leaders of the Sunday movement may advocate reforms which the people need, principles which are in harmony with the Bible, yet while there is with these a requirement which is contrary to God's law, his servants cannot unite with them. Nothing can justify them in setting aside the commandments of God for the precepts of men.

Through the two great errors, the immortality of the

soul and Sunday sacredness, Satan will bring the people under his deceptions. While the former lays the foundation of Spiritualism, the latter creates a bond of sympathy with Rome. The Protestants of the United States will be foremost in stretching their hands across the gulf to grasp the hand of Spiritualism; they will reach over the abyss to clasp hands with the Roman power; and under the influence of this threefold union this country will follow in the steps of Rome in trampling on the rights of conscience.

As Spiritualism more closely imitates the nominal Christianity of the day, it has greater power to deceive and ensnare. Satan himself is converted, after the modern order of things. He will appear in the character of an angel of light. Through the agency of Spiritualism, miracles will be wrought, the sick will be healed, and many undeniable wonders will be performed. And as the spirits will profess faith in the Bible, and manifest respect for the institutions of the church, their work will be accepted as a manifestation of divine power.

The line of distinction between professed Christians and the ungodly is now hardly distinguishable. Church-members love what the world loves, and are ready to join with them; and Satan determines to unite them in one body, and thus strengthen his cause by sweeping all into the ranks of Spiritualism. Papists, who boast of miracles as a certain sign of the true church, will be readily deceived by this wonder-working power; and Protestants, having cast away the shield of truth, will also be deluded. Papists, Protestants, and worldlings will alike accept the form of godliness without the power, and they will see in this union a grand movement for the conversion of the world, and the ushering in of the long-expected millennium.

Through Spiritualism, Satan appears as a benefactor of the race, healing the diseases of the people, and professing to present a new and more exalted system of religious faith; but at the same time he works as a destroyer. His temptations are leading multitudes to ruin. Intemperance dethrones reason; sensual indulgence, strife, and bloodshed follow. Satan delights in war, for it excites the worst passions of the soul, and then sweeps into eternity its victims steeped in vice and blood. It is his object to incite the nations to war against one another; for he can thus divert the minds of the people from the work of preparation to stand in the day of God.

Satan works through the elements also to garner his harvest of unprepared souls. He has studied the secrets of the laboratories of nature, and he uses all his power to control the elements as far as God allows. When he was suffered to afflict Job, how quickly flocks and herds, servants, houses, children, were swept away, one trouble succeeding another as in a moment. It is God that shields His creatures, and hedges them in from the power of the destroyer. But the Christian world have shown contempt for the law of Jehovah; and the Lord will do just what He has declared that He would, He will withdraw His blessings from the earth, and remove His protecting care from those who are rebelling against His law, and teaching and forcing others to do the same. Satan has control of all whom God does not especially guard. He will favor and prosper some, in order to further his own designs, and he will bring trouble upon others and lead men to believe that it is God who is afflicting them.

While appearing to the children of men as a great physician who can heal all their maladies, he will bring disease and disaster, until populous cities are reduced to ruin and desolation. Even now he is at work. In accidents and calamities by sea and by land, in great conflagrations, in fierce tornadoes and terrific hail-storms, in tempests, floods, cyclones, tidal waves, and earthquakes, in every place and in a thousand forms, Satan is exercising his power. He sweeps away the ripening harvest, and famine and distress follow. He imparts to the air a deadly taint, and thousands perish by the pestilence. These visitations are to become more and more frequent and disastrous. Destruction will be upon both man and beast. "The earth mourneth and fadeth away, the haughty people . . . do languish. The earth also is defiled under the inhabitants thereof; because they have transgressed the laws, changed the ordinance, broken the everlasting covenant." (*Isa.* 24:4, 5)

And then the great deceiver will persuade men that those who serve God are causing these evils. The class that have provoked the displeasure of Heaven will charge all their troubles upon those whose obedience of God's commandments is a perpetual reproof to transgressors. It will be declared that men are offending God by the violation of the Sunday-sabbath, that this sin has brought calamities which will not cease until Sunday observance shall be strictly enforced, and that those who present the claims of the fourth commandment, thus destroying reverence for Sunday, are troublers of the people, preventing their restoration to divine favor and temporal prosperity. Thus the accusation urged of old against the servant of God will be repeated, and upon grounds equally well established. "And it came to pass, when Ahab saw Elijah, that Ahab said unto him, Art thou he that troubleth Israel? And he answered, I have not troubled Israel; but thou, and thy father's house, in that ye have forsaken the commandments of the Lord, and thou hast followed Baalim." (1 *Kings* 18:17, 18) As the wrath of the people shall be excited by false charges, they will pursue a course toward God's ambassadors very similar to that which apostate Israel pursued toward Elijah.

The miracle-working power manifested through Spiritualism will exert its influence against those who choose to obey God rather than men. Communications from the spirits will declare that God has sent them to convince the rejecters of Sunday of their error, affirming that the laws of the land should be obeyed as the law of God. They will lament the great wickedness in the world, and second the testimony of religious teachers, that the degraded state of morals is caused by the desecration of Sunday. Great will be the indignation excited against all who refuse to accept their testimony.

Satan's policy in this final conflict with God's people is the same that he employed in the opening of the great controversy in Heaven. He professed to be seeking to promote the stability of the divine government, while secretly bending every effort to secure its overthrow. And the very work which he was thus endeavoring to accomplish, he charged upon the loyal angels. The same policy of deception has marked the history of the Roman Church. It has professed to act as the vicegerent of Heaven, while seeking to exalt itself above God and to change His law. Under the rule of Rome, those who suffered death for their fidelity to the gospel were denounced as evil-doers; they were declared to be in league with Satan; and every possible means was employed to cover them with reproach, to cause them to appear, in the eyes of the people, and even to themselves, as the vilest of criminals. So it will be now. While Satan seeks to destroy those who honor God's law, he will cause them to be accused as law-breakers, as men who are dishonoring God and bringing judgments upon the world.

God never forces the will or the conscience; but Satan's constant resort—to gain control of those whom he cannot otherwise seduce—is compulsion by cruelty. Through fear or force he endeavors to rule the conscience and to secure homage to himself. To accomplish this he works through both religious and secular authorities, moving them to the enforcement of human laws in defiance of the law of God.

Those who honor the Bible Sabbath will be denounced as enemies of law and order, as breaking down the moral restraints of society, causing anarchy and corruption and calling down the judgments of God upon the earth. Their conscientious scruples will be pronounced obstinacy, stubbornness, and contempt of authority. They will be accused of disaffection toward the government. Ministers who deny the obligation of the divine law will present from the pulpit the duty of yielding obedience to the civil authorities as ordained of God. In legislative halls and courts of justice, commandment-keepers will be misrepresented and condemned. A false coloring will be given to their words; the worst construction will be put upon their motives.

As the Protestant churches reject the clear, scriptural arguments in defense of God's law, they will long to silence those whose faith they cannot overthrow by the Bible. Though they blind their own eyes to the fact, they are now adopting a course which will lead to the persecution of those who conscientiously refuse to do what the rest of the Christian world are doing and acknowledge the claims of the papal Sabbath.

The dignitaries of church and state will unite to bribe, persuade, or compel all classes to honor the Sunday. The lack of divine authority will be supplied by oppressive enactments. Political corruption is destroying love of justice and regard for truth; and even in free America, rulers and legislators, in order to secure public favor, will yield to the popular demand for a law enforcing Sunday observance. Liberty of conscience, which has cost so great a sacrifice, will no longer be respected. In the soon-coming conflict we shall see exemplified the prophet's words: "The dragon was wroth with the woman, and went to make war with the remnant of her seed, which keep the commandments of God, and have the testimony of Jesus Christ." (*Rev.* 12:17)

Chapter 11

THE SCRIPTURES A SAFEGUARD

"To the law and to the testimony. If they speak not according to this word, it is because there is no light in them." (*Isa.* 8:20) The people of God are directed to the Scriptures as their safeguard against the influence of false teachers and the delusive power of spirits of darkness. Satan employs every possible device to prevent men from obtaining a knowledge of the Bible; for its plain utterances reveal his deceptions. At every revival of God's work the prince of evil is aroused to more intense activity; he is now putting forth his utmost efforts for a final struggle against Christ and His followers. The last great delusion is soon to open before us. Antichrist is to perform his marvelous works in our sight. So closely will the counterfeit resemble the true, that it will be impossible to distinguish between them except by the Holy Scriptures. By their testimony every statement and every miracle must be tested.

Those who endeavor to obey all the commandments of God will be opposed and derided. They can stand only in God. In order to endure the trial before them, they must understand the will of God as revealed in His Word; they can honor Him only as they have a right conception of His character, government, and purposes, and act in accordance with them. None but those who have fortified the mind with the truths of the Bible will stand through the last great conflict. To every soul will come the searching test, Shall I obey God rather than men? The decisive hour is even now at hand. Are our feet planted on the rock of God's immutable Word? Are we prepared to

135

stand firm in defense of the commandments of God and the faith of Jesus?

Before His crucifixion, the Saviour explained to His disciples that He was to be put to death, and to rise again from the tomb; and angels were present to impress His words on minds and hearts. But the disciples were looking for temporal deliverance from the Roman yoke, and they could not tolerate the thought that He in whom all their hopes centered should suffer an ignominious death. The words which they needed to remember were banished from their minds; and when the time of trial came, it found them unprepared. The death of Jesus as fully destroyed their hopes as if He had not forewarned them. So in the prophecies the future is opened before us as plainly as it was opened to the disciples by the words of Christ. The events connected with the close of probation and the work of preparation for the time of trouble are clearly presented. But multitudes have no more understanding of these important truths than if they had never been revealed. Satan watches to catch away every impression that would make them wise unto salvation, and the time of trouble will find them unready.

When God sends to men warnings so important that they are represented as proclaimed by holy angels flying in the midst of heaven, He requires every person endowed with reasoning powers to heed the message. The fearful judgments denounced against the worship of the beast and his image, (*Rev.* 14:9-11) should lead all to a diligent study of the prophecies to learn what the mark of the beast is, and how they are to avoid receiving it. But the masses of the people turn away their ears from hearing the truth and are turned unto fables. The apostle Paul declared, looking down to the last days, "The time will come when they will not endure sound doctrine." (2 *Tim.* 4:3) That time has fully come The multitudes do not want Bible truth because it interferes with the desires of the sinful, world-loving heart; and Satan supplies the deceptions which they love.

But God will have a people upon the earth to maintain

the Bible, and the Bible only, as the standard of all doctrines, and the basis of all reforms. The opinions of learned men, the deductions of science, the creeds or decisions of ecclesiastical councils, as numerous and discordant as are the churches which they represent, the voice of the majority—not one or all of these should be regarded as evidence for or against any point of religious faith. Before accepting any doctrine or precept, we should demand a plain "Thus saith the Lord" in its support.

Satan is constantly endeavoring to attract attention to man in the place of God. He leads the people to look to bishops, to pastors, to professors of theology, as their guides instead of searching the Scriptures to learn their duty for themselves. Then, by controlling the minds of these leaders, he can influence the multitudes according to his will.

When Christ came to speak the words of life, the common people heard Him gladly; and many, even of the priests and rulers, believed in Him. But the chief of the priesthood and the leading men of the nation were determined to condemn and repudiate His teachings. Though they were baffled in all their efforts to find accusations against Him, though they could not but feel the influence of the divine power and wisdom attending His words, yet they encased themselves in prejudice; they rejected the clearest evidence of His Messiahship, lest they should be forced to become His disciples. These opponents of Jesus were men whom the people had been taught from infancy to reverence, to whose authority they had been accustomed implicitly to bow. "How is it," they asked, "that our rulers and learned scribes do not believe on Jesus? Would not these pious men receive Him if He were the Christ?" It was the influence of such teachers that led the Jewish nation to reject their Redeemer.

The spirit which actuated those priests and rulers is still manifested by many who make a high profession of piety. They refuse to examine the testimony of the Scriptures concerning the special truths for this time. They point to their own numbers, wealth, and popularity, and look with contempt upon the advocates of truth as few, poor, and unpopular, having a faith that separates them from the world.

Christ foresaw that the undue assumption of authority indulged by the scribes and Pharisees would not cease with the dispersion of the Jews. He had a prophetic view of the work of exalting human authority to rule the conscience, which has been so terrible a curse to the church in all ages And His fearful denunciations of the scribes and Pharisees, and His warnings to the people not to follow these blind leaders, were placed on record as an admonition to future generations.

The Roman Church reserves to the clergy the right to interpret the Scriptures. On the ground that ecclesiastics alone are competent to explain God's Word, it is withheld from the common people. Though the Reformation gave the Scriptures to all, yet the self-same principle which was maintained by Rome prevents multitudes in Protestant churches from searching the Bible for themselves. They are taught to accept its teachings *as interpreted by the church;* and there are thousands who dare receive nothing, however plainly revealed in Scripture, that is contrary to their creed, or the established teaching of their church.

Notwithstanding the Bible is full of warnings against false teachers, many are ready thus to commit the keeping of their souls to the clergy. There are to-day thousands of professors of religion who can give no other reason for points of faith which they hold than that they were so instructed by their religious leaders. They pass by the Saviour's teachings almost unnoticed and place implicit confidence in the words of the ministers. But are ministers infallible? How can we trust our souls to their guidance unless we know from God's Word that they are light-bearers? A lack of moral courage to step aside from the beaten track of the world, leads many to follow in the steps of learned men; and by their reluctance to investigate for themselves, they are becoming hopelessly fastened in the chains of error. They see that the truth for this time is plainly brought to view in the Bible, and they feel the power of the Holy Spirit attending its proclamation; yet they allow the opposition of the clergy to turn them from the light. Though reason and conscience are convinced, these deluded souls dare not think differently from the minister; and their individual judgment, their eternal interests, are sacrificed to the unbelief, the pride and prejudice, of another.

Many are the ways by which Satan works through human influence to bind his captives. He secures multitudes to himself by attaching them by the silken cords of affection to those who are enemies of the cross of Christ. Whatever this attachment may be, parental, filial, conjugal, or social, the effect is the same; the opposers of truth exert their power to control the conscience, and the souls held under their sway have not sufficient courage or independence to obey their own convictions of duty.

The truth and the glory of God are inseparable; it is impossible for us with the Bible within our reach to honor God by erroneous opinions. Many claim that it matters not what one believes, if his life is only right. But the life is moulded by the faith If light and truth are within our reach, and we neglect to improve the privilege of hearing and seeing it, we virtually reject it; we are choosing darkness rather than light.

"There is a way that seemeth right unto a man, but the end thereof are the ways of death." (*Prov.* 16:25) Ignorance is no excuse for error or sin, when there is every opportunity to know the will of God. A man is traveling and comes to a place where there are several roads, and a guide-board indicating where each one leads. If he disregards the guideboard and takes whichever road seems to him to be right, he may be ever so sincere but will in all probability find himself on the wrong road.

God has given us His Word that we may become acquainted with its teachings and know for ourselves what He requires of us. When the lawyer came to Jesus with the inquiry, "What shall I do to inherit eternal life?" the Saviour referred him to the Scriptures, saying, "What is written in the law? how readest thou?" Ignorance will not excuse young or old or release them from the punishment due for the transgression of God's law, because there is in their hands a faithful presentation of that law and of its principles and its claims. It is not enough to have good intentions; it is not enough to do what a man thinks is right or what the minister tells him is right. His soul's salvation is at stake, and he should search the Scriptures for himself. However strong may be his conviction, however confident he may be that the minister knows what is truth, this is not his foundation. He has a chart pointing out every waymark on the heavenward journey, and he ought not to guess at anything.

It is the first and highest duty of every rational being to learn from the Scriptures what is truth, and then to walk in the light and encourage others to follow his example. We should day by day study the Bible diligently, weighing every thought and comparing scripture with scripture. With divine help we are to form our opinions for ourselves, as we are to answer for ourselves before God.

The truths most plainly revealed in the Bible have been involved in doubt and darkness by learned men, who, with a pretense of great wisdom, teach that the Scriptures have a mystical, a secret, spiritual meaning not apparent in the language employed. These men are false teachers It was to such a class that Jesus declared, "Ye know not the Scriptures, neither the power of God." (*Mark* 12:24) The language of the Bible should be explained according to its obvious meaning, unless a symbol or figure is employed. Christ has given the promise, "If any man will do His will, he shall know of the doctrine." (*John* 7:17) If men would but take the Bible as it reads, if there were no false teachers to mislead and confuse their minds, a work would be accomplished that would make angels glad, and that would bring into the fold of Christ thousands upon thousands who are now wandering in error.

We should exert all the powers of the mind in the study of the Scriptures and should task the understanding to comprehend, as far as mortals can, the deep things of God; yet we must not forget that the docility and submission of a child is the true spirit of the learner. Scriptural difficulties can never be mastered by the same methods that are employed in grappling with philosophical problems. We should not engage in the study of the Bible with that self-reliance with which so many enter the domains of science, but with a prayerful dependence upon God and a sincere desire to learn His will. We must come with a humble and teachable spirit to obtain knowledge from the great I AM. Otherwise, evil angels will so blind our minds and harden our hearts that we shall not be impressed by the truth.

Many a portion of Scripture which learned men pronounce a mystery, or pass over as unimportant, is full of comfort and instruction to him who has been taught in the school of Christ. One reason why many theologians have no clearer understanding of God's Word is, they close their eyes to truths which they do not wish to practice. An understanding of Bible truth depends not so much on the power of intellect brought to the search as on the singleness of purpose, the earnest longing after righteousness.

The Bible should never be studied without prayer. The Holy Spirit alone can cause us to feel the importance of those things easy to be understood, or prevent us from wresting truths difficult of comprehension. It is the office of heavenly angels to prepare the heart to so comprehend God's Word that we shall be charmed with its beauty, admonished by its warnings, or animated and strengthened by its promises. We should make the psalmist's petition our own: "Open Thou mine eyes, that I may behold wondrous things out of Thy law." (*Ps* 119:18) Temptations often appear irresistible because, through neglect of prayer and the study of the Bible, the tempted one cannot readily remember God's promises and meet Satan with the Scripture weapons. But angels are round about those who are willing to be taught in divine things; and in the time of great necessity they will bring to their remembrance the very truths which are needed. Thus "when the enemy shall come in like a flood, the Spirit of the Lord shall lift up a standard against him." (*Isa.* 59:19)

Jesus promised His disciples, "The Comforter, the Holy Ghost, whom the Father will send in My name, He shall teach you all things, and bring all things to your remembrance, whatsoever I have said unto you." (*John* 14:26) But the teachings of Christ must previously have been stored in the mind in order for the Spirit of God to bring them to our remembrance in the time of peril. "Thy Word have I hid in mine heart," said David, "that I might not sin against Thee." (*Ps.* 119:11)

All who value their eternal interests should be on their guard against the inroads of skepticism. The very pillars of truth will be assailed. It is impossible to keep beyond the reach of the sarcasms and sophisms, the insidious and pestilent teachings of modern infidelity. Satan adapts his temptations to all classes. He assails the illiterate with a jest or sneer, while he meets the educated with scientific objections and philosophical reasoning, alike calculated to excite distrust or contempt of the Scriptures. Even youth of little experience presume to insinuate doubts concerning the fundamental principles of Christianity. And this youthful infidelity, shallow as it is, has its influence. Many are thus led to jest at the faith of their fathers and to do despite to the Spirit of grace (*Heb.* 10:29) Many a life that promised to be an honor to God and a blessing to the world has been blighted by the foul breath of infidelity. All who trust to the boastful decisions of human reason and imagine that they can explain divine mysteries and arrive at truth unaided by the wisdom of God, are entangled in the snare of Satan.

We are living in the most solemn period of this world's history. The destiny of earth's teeming multitudes is about to be decided. Our own future well-being, and also the salvation of other souls, depends upon the course which we now pursue. We need to be guided by the Spirit of truth. Every follower of Christ should earnestly inquire, "Lord, what wilt Thou have me to do?" We need to humble ourselves before the Lord with fasting and prayer and to meditate much upon His Word, especially upon the scenes of the Judgment. We should now seek a deep and living experience in the things of God. We have not a moment to lose. Events of vital importance are taking place around us; we are on Satan's enchanted ground. Sleep not, sentinels of God; the foe is lurking near, ready at any moment, should you become lax and drowsy, to spring upon you and make you his prey.

Many are deceived as to their true condition before God. They congratulate themselves upon the wrong acts which they do not commit and forget to enumerate the good and noble deeds which God requires of them, but which they have neglected to perform. It is not enough that they are trees in the garden of God. They are to answer His expectation by bearing fruit. He holds them accountable for their failure to accomplish all the good which they could have done through His grace strengthening them. In the books of Heaven they are registered as cumberers of the ground. Yet the case of even this class is not utterly hopeless. With those who have slighted God's mercy and abused His grace, the heart of long-suffering love yet pleads. "Wherefore He saith, Awake, thou that sleepest, and arise from the dead, and Christ shall give thee light. See then that ye walk circumspectly, . . . redeeming the time, because the days are evil." (*Eph.* 5:14-16)

When the testing time shall come, those who have made God's Word their rule of life will be revealed. In summer there is no noticeable difference between evergreens and other trees; but when the blasts of winter come, the evergreens remain unchanged, while other trees are stripped of their foliage. So the false-hearted professor may not now be distinguished from the real Christian, but the time is just upon us when the difference will be apparent. Let opposition arise, let bigotry and intolerance again bear sway, let persecution be kindled, and the half-hearted and hypocritical will waver and yield the faith; but the true Christian will stand firm as a rock, his faith stronger, his hope brighter, than in days of prosperity.

Says the psalmist: "Thy testimonies are my meditation. Through Thy percepts I get understanding, therefore I hate every false way." (*Ps.* 119:99, 104)

"Happy is the man that findeth wisdom." "He shall be as a tree planted by the waters, and that spreadeth out her roots by the river, and shall not see when heat cometh, but her leaf shall be green; and shall not be careful in the year of drought, neither shall cease from yielding fruit" (*Prov.* 3:13; *Jer.* 17:8)

The Final War

Says the psalmist: "Thy testimonies are my meditation. Through Thy precepts I get understanding; therefore I hate every false way." (*Ps.* 119:99, 104)
"He that is the man that findeth wisdom." "He shall be

Chapter 12

THE FINAL WARNING

"I SAW ANOTHER ANGEL come down from Heaven, having
great power; and the earth was lightened with his glory.
And he cried mightily with a strong voice, saying, Babylon the great is fallen, is fallen, and is become the habitation of devils, and the hold of every foul spirit, and a cage
of every unclean and hateful bird. And I heard another
voice from Heaven, saying, Come out of her, My people,
that ye be not partakers of her sins, and that ye receive
not of her plagues." (*Rev.* 18:1, 2, 4)

This scripture points forward to a time when the announcement of the fall of Babylon, as made by the second
angel (*Rev.* 14:8) of Revelation 14, is to be repeated,
with the additional mention of the corruptions which have
been entering the various organizations that constitute
Babylon, since that message was first given in the summer of 1844. A terrible condition of the religious world is
here described. With every rejection of truth the minds of
the people will become darker, their hearts more stubborn,
until they are entrenched in an infidel hardihood. In defiance of the warnings which God has given they will continue to trample upon one of the precepts of the
decalogue, until they are led to persecute those who hold
it sacred. Christ is set at naught in the contempt placed
upon His Word and His people. As the teachings of Spiritualism are accepted by the churches, the restraint imposed upon the carnal heart is removed, and the
profession of religion will become a cloak to conceal the
basest iniquity. A belief in spiritual manifestations opens
the door to seducing spirits and doctrines of devils, and

thus the influence of evil angels will be felt in the churches.

Of Babylon, at the time brought to view in this prophecy, it is declared, "Her sins have reached unto heaven, and God hath remembered her iniquities." (*Rev.* 18:5) She has filled up the measure of her guilt, and destruction is about to fall upon her. But God still has a people in Babylon; and before the visitation of His judgments these faithful ones must be called out, that they "partake not of her sins, and receive not of her plagues." Hence the movement symbolized by the angel coming down from Heaven, lightening the earth with his glory, and crying mightily with a strong voice, announcing the sins of Babylon In connection with his message the call is heard, "Come out of her, My people." These announcements, uniting with the third angel's message, constitute the final warning to be given to the inhabitants of the earth.

Fearful is the issue to which the world is to be brought. The powers of earth, uniting to war against the commandments of God, will decree that all, "both small and great, rich and poor, free and bond," (*Rev.* 13:16) shall conform to the customs of the church by the observance of the false sabbath. All who refuse compliance will be visited with civil penalties, and it will finally be declared that they are deserving of death. On the other hand, the law of God enjoining the Creator's rest-day demands obedience and threatens wrath against all who transgress its precepts.

With the issue thus clearly brought before him, whoever shall trample upon God's law to obey a human enactment, receives the mark of the beast; he accepts the sign of allegiance to the power which he chooses to obey instead of God. The warning from Heaven is, "If any man worship the beast and his image, and receive his mark in his forehead, or in his hand, the same shall drink of the wine of the wrath of God, which is poured out without mixture into the cup of His indignation." (*Rev.* 14:9, 10)

But not one is made to suffer the wrath of God until

the truth has been brought home to his mind and conscience and has been rejected. There are many who have never had an opportunity to hear the special truths for this time. The obligation of the fourth commandment has never been set before them in its true light. He who reads every heart and tries every motive will leave none who desire a knowledge of the truth to be deceived as to the issues of the controversy. The decree is not to be urged upon the people blindly. Every one is to have sufficient light to make his decision intelligently.

The Sabbath will be the great test of loyalty; for it is the point of truth especially controverted. When the final test shall be brought to bear upon men, then the line of distinction will be drawn between those who serve God and those who serve Him not. While the observance of the false sabbath in compliance with the law of the State, contrary to the fourth commandment, will be an avowal of allegiance to a power that is in opposition to God, the keeping of the true Sabbath, in obedience to God's law, is an evidence of loyalty to the Creator. While one class, by accepting the sign of submission to earthly powers, receive the mark of the beast, the other, choosing the token of allegiance to divine authority, receive the seal of God.

Heretofore those who presented the truths of the third angel's message have often been regarded as mere alarmists. Their predictions that religious intolerance would gain control in the United States, that church and State would unite to persecute those who keep the commandments of God, have been pronounced groundless and absurd. It has been confidently declared that this land could never become other than what it has been, the defender of religious freedom. But as the question of enforcing Sunday observance is widely agitated, the event so long doubted and disbelieved is seen to be approaching, and the third message will produce an effect which it could not have had before.

In every generation God has sent His servants to rebuke sin, both in the world and in the church. But the people desire smooth things spoken to them, and the pure, unvarnished truth is not acceptable. Many reformers, in entering upon their work, determined to exercise great prudence in attacking the sins of the church and the nation. They hoped, by the example of a pure Christian life, to lead the people back to the doctrines of the Bible. But the Spirit of God came upon them as it came upon Elijah, moving him to rebuke the sins of a wicked king and an apostate people; they could not refrain from preaching the plain utterances of the Bible—doctrines which they had been reluctant to present. They were impelled to zealously declare the truth and the danger which threatened souls. The words which the Lord gave them they uttered, fearless of consequences, and the people were compelled to hear the warning.

Thus the message of the third angel will be proclaimed. As the time comes for it to be given with greatest power, the Lord will work through humble instruments, leading the minds of those who consecrate themselves to His service. The laborers will be qualified rather by the unction of His Spirit than by the training of literary institutions. Men of faith and prayer will be constrained to go forth with holy zeal, declaring the words which God gives them. The sins of Babylon will be laid open. The fearful results of enforcing the observances of the church by civil authority, the inroads of Spiritualism, the stealthy but rapid progress of the papal power—all will be unmasked. By these solemn warnings the people will be stirred. Thousands upon thousands will listen who have never heard words like these. In amazement they hear the testimony that Babylon is the church, fallen because of her errors and sins, because of her rejection of the truth sent to her from Heaven. As the people go to their former teachers with the eager inquiry, Are these things so? the ministers present fables, prophesy smooth things, to soothe their fears and quiet the awakened conscience. But since many refuse to be satisfied with the mere authority of men and demand a plain "Thus saith the Lord," the popular ministry, like the Pharisees of old, filled with anger as their authority is questioned, will denounce the message as of

Satan and stir up the sin-loving multitudes to revile and persecute those who proclaim it.

As the controversy extends into new fields and the minds of the people are called to God's down-trodden law, Satan is astir. The power attending the message will only madden those who oppose it. The clergy will put forth almost superhuman efforts to shut away the light lest it should shine upon their flocks. By every means at their command they will endeavor to suppress the discussion of these vital questions. The church appeals to the strong arm of civil power, and in this work papists and Protestants unite. As the movement for Sunday enforcement becomes more bold and decided, the law will be invoked against commandment-keepers. They will be threatened with fines and imprisonment, and some will be offered positions of influence and other rewards and advantages as inducements to renounce their faith. But their steadfast answer is, "Show us from the Word of God our error"—the same plea that was made by Luther under similar circumstances. Those who are arraigned before the courts make a strong vindication of the truth, and some who hear them are led to take their stand to keep all the commandments of God Thus light will be brought before thousands who otherwise would know nothing of these truths.

Conscientious obedience to the Word of God will be treated as rebellion. Blinded by Satan, the parent will exercise harshness and severity toward the believing child; the master or mistress will oppress the commandment-keeping servant. Affection will be alienated; children will be disinherited and driven from home. The words of Paul will be literally fulfilled, "All that will live godly in Christ Jesus shall suffer persecution." (2 *Tim.* 3:12) As the defenders of truth refuse to honor the Sunday-sabbath, some of them will be thrust into prison, some will be exiled, some will be treated as slaves. To human wisdom all this now seems impossible; but as the restraining Spirit of God shall be withdrawn from men, and they shall be under the control of Satan, who hates the divine precepts, there will be strange developments. The heart can be very cruel when God's fear and love are removed.

As the storm approaches, a large class who have professed faith in the third angel's message, but have not been sanctified through obedience to the truth, abandon their position, and join the ranks of the opposition. By uniting with the world and partaking of its spirit, they have come to view matters in nearly the same light; and when the test is brought, they are prepared to choose the easy, popular side. Men of talent and pleasing address, who once rejoiced in the truth, employ their powers to deceive and mislead souls. They become the most bitter enemies of their former brethren. When Sabbath-keepers are brought before the courts to answer for their faith, these apostates are the most efficient agents of Satan to misrepresent and accuse them, and by false reports and insinuations to stir up the rulers against them.

In this time of persecution the faith of the Lord's servants will be tried. They have faithfully given the warning, looking to God and to His Word alone. God's Spirit, moving upon their hearts, has constrained them to speak. Stimulated with holy zeal, and with the divine impulse strong upon them, they entered upon the performance of their duties without coldly calculating the consequences of speaking to the people the word which the Lord had given them. They have not consulted their temporal interests, or sought to preserve their reputation or their lives. Yet when the storm of opposition and reproach bursts upon them, some, overwhelmed with consternation, will be ready to exclaim, "Had we foreseen the consequences of our words, we would have held our peace." They are hedged in with difficulties. Satan assails them with fierce temptations. The work which they have undertaken seems far beyond their ability to accomplish. They are threatened with destruction. The enthusiasm which animated them is gone; yet they cannot turn back. Then, feeling their utter helplessness, they flee to the Mighty One for strength. They remember that the words which they have spoken were not theirs, but His who bade them give the warning. God put the truth into their hearts, and they could not forbear to proclaim it.

The same trials have been experienced by men of God in ages past. Wycliffe, Huss, Luther, Tyndale, Baxter, Wesley, urged that all doctrines be brought to the test of the Bible and declared that they would renounce everything which it condemned. Against these men persecution raged with relentless fury; yet they ceased not to declare the truth. Different periods in the history of the church have each been marked by the development of some special truth, adapted to the necessities of God's people at that time. Every new truth has made its way against hatred and opposition; those who were blessed with its light were tempted and tried. The Lord gives a special truth for the people in an emergency. Who dare refuse to publish it? He commands His servants to present the last invitation of mercy to the world. They cannot remain silent, except at the peril of their souls. Christ's ambassadors have nothing to do with consequences. They must perform their duty and leave results with God.

As the opposition rises to a fiercer height, the servants of God are again perplexed; for it seems to them that they have brought the crisis. But conscience and the Word of God assure them that their course is right; and although the trials continue, they are strengthened to bear them. The contest grows closer and sharper, but their faith and courage rise with the emergency. Their testimonies, "We dare not tamper with God's Word, dividing His holy law, calling one portion essential and another non-essential, to gain the favor of the world. The Lord whom we serve is able to deliver us. Christ has conquered the powers of earth; and shall we be afraid of a world already conquered?"

Persecution in its varied forms is the development of a principle which will exist as long as Satan exists and Christianity has vital power. No man can serve God without enlisting against himself the opposition of the hosts of darkness. Evil angels will assail him, alarmed that his influence is taking the prey from their hands. Evil men, rebuked by his example, will unite with them in seeking to separate him from God by alluring temptations. When these do not succeed, then a compelling power is employed to force the conscience.

But so long as Jesus remains man's intercessor in the sanctuary above, the restraining influence of the Holy Spirit is felt by rulers and people. It still controls, to some extent, the laws of the land. Were it not for these laws, the condition of the world would be much worse than it now is. While many of our rulers are active agents of Satan, God also has His agents among the leading men of the nation. The enemy moves upon his servants to propose measures that would greatly impede the work of God; but statesmen who fear the Lord are influenced by holy angels to oppose such propositions with unanswerable arguments. Thus a few men will hold in check a powerful current of evil. The opposition of the enemies of truth will be restrained that the third angel's message may do its work. When the final warning shall be given, it will arrest the attention of these leading men through whom the Lord is now working, and some of them will accept it and will stand with the people of God through the time of trouble.

The angel who unites in the proclamation of the third angel's message is to lighten the whole earth with his glory. A work of world-wide extent and unwonted power is here foretold. The Advent movement of 1840-44 was a glorious manifestation of the power of God; the first angel's message was carried to every missionary station in the world, and in some countries there was the greatest religious interest which has been witnessed in any land since the Reformation of the sixteenth century; but these are to be far exceeded by the mighty movement under the last warning of the third angel.

The work will be similar to that of the day of Pentecost. As the "former rain" was given, in the outpouring of the Holy Spirit at the opening of the gospel, to cause the upspringing of the precious seed, so the "latter rain" will be given at its close, for the ripening of the harvest.

"Then shall we know, if we follow on to know the Lord; His going forth is prepared as the morning; and He shall come unto us as the rain, as the latter and former rain unto the earth." (*Hosea* 6:3) "Be glad then, ye children of Zion, and rejoice in the Lord your God; for He hath given you the former rain moderately, and He will cause to come down for you the rain, the former rain, and the latter rain." (*Joel* 2:23) "In the last days, saith God, I will pour out of My Spirit upon all flesh. And it shall come to pass, that whosoever shall call on the name of the Lord shall be saved." (*Acts* 2:17, 21) The great work of the gospel is not to close with less manifestation of the power of God than marked its opening. The prophecies which were fulfilled in the outpouring of the former rain at the opening of the gospel are again to be fulfilled in the latter rain at its close. Here are "the times of refreshing" to which the apostle Peter looked forward when he said, "Repent ye therefore, and be converted, that your sins may be blotted out [in the investigative Judgment], when the times of refreshing shall come from the presence of the Lord; and He shall send Jesus." (*Acts* 3:19, 20)

Servants of God, with their faces lighted up and shining with holy consecration, will hasten from place to place to proclaim the message from Heaven. By thousands of voices, all over the earth, the warning will be given. Miracles will be wrought, the sick will be healed, and signs and wonders will follow the believers. Satan also works with lying wonders, even bringing down fire from heaven in the sight of men. (*Rev.* 13:13) Thus the inhabitants of the earth will be brought to take their stand.

The message will be carried not so much by argument as by the deep conviction of the Spirit of God, The arguments have been presented. The seed has been sown, and now it will spring up and bear fruit. The publications distributed by missionary workers have exerted their influence, yet many whose minds were impressed have been prevented from fully comprehending the truth or from yielding obedience. Now the rays of light penetrate everywhere, the truth is seen in its clearness, and the honest children of God sever the bands which have held them. Family connections, church relations, are powerless to stay them now. Truth is more precious than all besides. Notwithstanding the agencies combined against the truth, a large number take their stand upon the Lord's side.

Chapter 13

"THE TIME OF TROUBLE"

"AT THAT TIME SHALL Michael stand up, the great prince which standeth for the children of thy people; and there shall be a time of trouble, such as never was since there was a nation even to that same time; and at that time thy people shall be delivered, every one that shall be found written in the book." (*Dan.* 12:1)

When the third angel's message closes, mercy no longer pleads for the guilty inhabitants of the earth. The people of God have accomplished their work. They have received "the latter rain," "the refreshing from the presence of the Lord," and they are prepared for the trying hour before them. Angels are hastening to and fro in Heaven. An angel returning from the earth announces that his work is done; the final test has been brought upon the world, and all who have proved themselves loyal to the divine precepts have received "the seal of the living God." Then Jesus ceases His intercession in the sanctuary above. He lifts His hands and with a loud voice says, "It is done;" and all the angelic host lay off their crowns as He makes the solemn announcement: "He that is unjust, let him be unjust still; and he which is filthy, let him be filthy still; and he that is righteous, let him be righteous still; and he that is holy, let him be holy still." (*Rev.* 22:11) Every case has been decided for life or death. Christ has made the atonement for His people and blotted out their sins. The number of His subjects is made up; "the kingdom and dominion, and the greatness of the kingdom under the whole heaven," is about to be given to the heirs of salvation, and Jesus is to reign as King of kings and Lord of lords.

When He leaves the sanctuary, darkness covers the inhabitants of the earth. In that fearful time the righteous must live in the sight of a holy God without an intercessor. The restraint which has been upon the wicked is removed, and Satan has entire control of the finally impenitent. God's long-suffering has ended. The world has rejected His mercy, despised His love, and trampled upon His law. The wicked have passed the boundary of their probation; the Spirit of God, persistently resisted, has been at last withdrawn. Unsheltered by divine grace, they have no protection from the wicked one. Satan will then plunge the inhabitants of the earth into one great, final trouble. As the angels of God cease to hold in check the fierce winds of human passion, all the elements of strife will be let loose. The whole world will be involved in ruin more terrible than that which came upon Jerusalem of old.

A single angel destroyed all the first-born of the Egyptians and filled the land with mourning. When David offended against God by numbering the people, one angel caused that terrible destruction by which his sin was punished. The same destructive power exercised by holy angels when God commands, will be exercised by evil angels when He permits. There are forces now ready, and only waiting the divine permission, to spread desolation everywhere.

Those who honor the law of God have been accused of bringing judgments upon the world, and they will be regarded as the cause of the fearful convulsions of nature and the strife and bloodshed among men that are filling the earth with woe. The power attending the last warning has enraged the wicked; their anger is kindled against all who have received the message, and Satan will excite to still greater intensity the spirit of hatred and persecution.

When God's presence was finally withdrawn from the Jewish nation, priests and people knew it not. Though under the control of Satan, and swayed by the most horrible and malignant passions, they still regarded themselves as the chosen of God. The ministration in the temple continued; sacrifices were offered upon its polluted altars, and daily the divine blessing was invoked upon a people guilty of the blood of God's dear Son and seeking to slay His ministers and apostles. So when the irrevocable decision of the sanctuary has been pronounced, and the destiny of the world has been forever fixed, the inhabitants of the earth will know it not. The forms of religion will be continued by a people from whom the Spirit of God has been finally withdrawn; and the Satanic zeal with which the prince of evil will inspire them for the accomplishment of his malignant designs will bear the semblance of zeal for God.

As the Sabbath has become the special point of controversy throughout Christendom, and religious and secular authorities have combined to enforce the observance of the Sunday, the persistent refusal of a small minority to yield to the popular demand will make them objects of universal execration. It will be urged that the few who stand in opposition to an institution of the church and a law of the State ought not to be tolerated; that it is better for them to suffer than for whole nations to be thrown into confusion and lawlessness. The same argument eighteen hundred years ago was brought against Christ by the "rulers of the people." "It is expedient for us," said the wily Caiaphas, "that one man should die for the people, and that the whole nation perish not " (*John* 11:50) This argument will appear conclusive; and a decree will finally be issued against those who hallow the Sabbath of the fourth commandment, denouncing them as deserving of the severest punishment and giving the people liberty, after a certain time, to put them to death. Romanism in the Old World and apostate Protestantism in the New will pursue a similar course toward those who honor all the divine percepts.

The people of God will then be plunged into those scenes of affliction and distress described by the prophet as the time of Jacob's trouble. "Thus saith the Lord: We have heard a voice of trembling, of fear, and not of peace. All faces are turned into paleness. Alas! for that day is great, so that none is like it; it is even the time of Jacob's trouble; but he shall be saved out of it." (*Jer.* 30:5-7)

Jacob's night of anguish, when he wrestled in prayer for deliverance from the hand of Esau, (*Gen.* 32:24-30) represents the experience of God's people in the time of trouble. Because of the deception practiced to secure his father's blessing, intended for Esau, Jacob had fled for his life, alarmed by his brother's deadly threats. After remaining for many years in exile, he had set out, at God's command, to return with his wives and children, his flocks and herds, to his native country. On reaching the borders of the land, he was filled with terror by the tidings of Esau's approach at the head of a band of warriors, doubtless bent upon revenge. Jacob's company, unarmed and defenseless, seemed about to fall helpless victims of violence and slaughter. And to the burden of anxiety and fear was added the crushing weight of self-reproach; for it was his own sin that had brought his danger. His only hope was in the mercy of God; his only defense must be prayer. Yet he leaves nothing undone on his own part to atone for the wrong to his brother and to avert the threatened danger. So should the followers of Christ, as they approach the time of trouble, make every exertion to place themselves in a proper light before the people, to disarm prejudice, and to avert the danger which threatens liberty of conscience

Having sent his family away, that they may not witness his distress, Jacob remains alone to intercede with God. He confesses his sin and gratefully acknowledges the mercy of God toward him, while with deep humiliation he pleads the covenant made with his fathers, and the promises to himself in the night vision at Bethel and in the land of his exile. The crisis in his life has come; everything is at stake. In the darkness and solitude he continues praying and humbling himself before God. Suddenly a hand is laid upon his shoulder. He thinks that an enemy is seeking his life, and with all the energy of despair he wrestles with his assailant. As the day begins to break, the stranger puts forth his superhuman power; at his touch the strong man seems paralyzed, and he falls, a helpless, weeping suppliant, upon the neck of his mysterious antagonist. Jacob knows now that it is the Angel of the covenant with whom he has been in conflict. Though disabled and suffering the keenest pain, he does not relinquish his purpose. Long has he endured perplexity, remorse, and trouble for his sin; now he must have the assurance that it is pardoned. The divine visitant seems about to depart; but Jacob clings to Him pleading for a blessing. The Angel urges, "Let Me go; for the day breaketh;" but the patriarch exclaims, "I will not let Thee go, except Thou bless me." What confidence, what firmness and perserverance, are here displayed! Had this been a boastful, presumptuous claim, Jacob would have been instantly destroyed; but his was the assurance of one who confesses his weakness and unworthiness, yet trusts the mercy of a covenant-keeping God.

"He had power over the Angel, and prevailed." (*Hos.* 12:4) Through humiliation, repentance, and self-surrender, this sinful, erring mortal prevailed with the Majesty of Heaven. He had fastened his trembling grasp upon the promises of God, and the heart of Infinite Love could not turn away the sinner's plea. As an evidence of his triumph, and an encouragement to others to imitate his example, his name was changed from one which was a reminder of his sin, to one that commemorated his victory. And the fact that Jacob had prevailed with God was an assurance that he would prevail with men. He no longer feared to encounter his brother's anger; for the Lord was his defense.

Satan had accused Jacob before the angels of God, claiming the right to destroy him because of his sin; he had moved upon Esau to march against him; and during the patriarch's long night of wrestling, Satan endeavored to force upon him a sense of his guilt in order to discourage him and break his hold upon God. Jacob was driven almost to despair; but he knew that without help from Heaven he must perish. He had sincerely repented of his great sin, and he appealed to the mercy of God. He would not be turned from his purpose, but held fast the Angel and urged his petition with earnest, agonizing cries, until he prevailed.

As Satan influenced Esau to march against Jacob, so he will stir up the wicked to destroy God's people in the time of trouble. And as he accused Jacob, he will urge his accusations against the people of God. He numbers the world as his subjects; but the little company who keep the commandments of God are resisting his supremacy. If he could blot them from the earth, his triumph would be complete. He sees that holy angels are guarding them, and he infers that their sins have been pardoned; but he does not know that their cases have been decided in the sanctuary above. He has an accurate knowledge of the sins which he had tempted them to commit, and he presents these before God in the most exaggerated light, representing this people to be just as deserving as himself of exclusion from the favor of God. He declares that the Lord cannot in justice forgive their sins and yet destroy him and his angels. He claims them as his prey and demands that they be given into his hands to destroy.

As Satan accuses the people of God on account of their sins, the Lord permits him to try them to the uttermost. Their confidence in God, their faith and firmness, will be severely tested. As they review the past, their hopes sink; for in their whole lives they can see little good. They are fully conscious of their weakness and unworthiness. Satan endeavors to terrify them with the thought that their cases are hopeless, that the stain of their defilement will never be washed away. He hopes to so destroy their faith that they will yield to his temptations and turn from their allegiance to God.

Though God's people will be surrounded by enemies who are bent upon their destruction, yet the anguish which they suffer is not a dread of persecution for the truth's sake; they fear that every sin has not been repented of and that through some fault in themselves they shall fail to realize the fulfillment of the Saviour's promise, "I will keep thee from the hour of temptation which shall come upon all the world." (*Rev.* 3:10) If they could have the assurance of pardon, they would not shrink from torture or death; but should they prove unworthy and lose their lives because of their own defects of character, then God's holy name would be reproached.

On every hand they hear the plottings of treason and see the active working of rebellion; and there is aroused within them an intense desire, an earnest yearning of soul, that this great apostasy may be terminated and the wickedness of the wicked may come to an end. But while they plead with God to stay the work of rebellion, it is with a keen sense of self-reproach that they themselves have no more power to resist and urge back the mighty tide of evil. They feel that had they always employed all their ability in the service of Christ, going forward from strength to strength, Satan's forces would have less power to prevail against them.

They afflict their souls before God, pointing to their past repentance of their many sins and pleading the Saviour's promise, "Let him take hold of My strength, that he may make peace with Me and he shall make peace with Me." (*Isa.* 27:5) Their faith does not fail because their prayers are not immediately answered. Though suffering the keenest anxiety, terror, and distress, they do not cease their intercessions. They lay hold of the strength of God as Jacob laid hold of the Angel; and the language of their souls is, "I will not let Thee go, except Thou bless me."

Had not Jacob previously repented of his sin in obtaining the birthright by fraud, God would not have heard his prayer and mercifully preserved his life. So, in the time of trouble, if the people of God had unconfessed sins to appear before them while tortured with fear and anguish, they would be overwhelmed; despair would cut off their faith and they could not have confidence to plead with God for deliverance. But while they have a deep sense of their unworthiness, they have no concealed wrongs to reveal. Their sins have gone beforehand to Judgment and have been blotted out; and they cannot bring them to remembrance.

Satan leads many to believe that God will overlook their unfaithfulness in the minor affairs of life; but the Lord shows in His dealings with Jacob that He will in nowise sanction or tolerate evil. All who endeavor to excuse or conceal their sins and permit them to remain upon the books of Heaven, unconfessed and unforgiven, will be overcome by Satan. The more exalted their profession and the more honorable the position which they hold, the more grievous is their course in the sight of God, and the more sure the triumph of their great adversary. Those who delay a preparation for the day of God cannot obtain it in the time of trouble or at any subsequent time. The case of all such is hopeless.

Those professed Christians who come up to that last fearful conflict unprepared, will, in their despair, confess their sins in words of burning anguish, while the wicked exult over their distress. These confessions are of the same character as was that of Esau or of Judas. Those who make them lament the *result* of transgression, but not its guilt. They feel no true contrition, no abhorrence of evil. They acknowledge their sin through fear of punishment; but like Pharaoh of old they would return to their defiance of Heaven, should the judgments be removed.

Jacob's history is also an assurance that God will not cast off those who have been deceived and tempted and betrayed into sin, but who have returned unto Him with true repentance. While Satan seeks to destroy this class, God will send His angels to comfort and protect them in the time of peril. The assaults of Satan are fierce and determined, his delusions are terrible; but the Lord's eye is upon His people, and His ear listens to their cries. Their affliction is great, the flames of the furnace seem about to consume them; but the Refiner will bring them forth as gold tried in the fire. God's love for His children during the period of their severest trial is as strong and tender as in the days of their sunniest prosperity; but it is needful for them to be placed in the furnace fire; their earthliness must be consumed that the image of Christ may be perfectly reflected.

The season of distress and anguish before us will require a faith that can endure weariness, delay, and hunger—a faith that will not faint, though severely tried. The period of probation is granted to all to prepare for that time. Jacob prevailed because he was persevering and determined. His victory is an evidence of the power of importunate prayer. All who will lay hold of God's promises as he did, and be as earnest and persevering as he was, will succeed as he succeeded. Those who are unwilling to deny self, to agonize before God, to pray long and earnestly for His blessing, will not obtain it. Wrestling with God—how few know what it is! How few have ever had their souls drawn out after God with intensity of desire until every power is on the stretch. When waves of despair which no language can express sweep over the suppliant, how few cling with unyielding faith to the promises of God.

Those who exercise but little faith now are in the greatest danger of falling under the power of Satanic delusions and the decree to compel the conscience. And even if they endure the test, they will be plunged into deeper distress and anguish in the time of trouble because they have never made it a habit to trust in God. The lessons of faith which they have neglected, they will be forced to learn under a terrible pressure of discouragement.

We should now acquaint ourselves with God by proving His promises. Angels record every prayer that is earnest and sincere. We should rather dispense with selfish gratifications than neglect communion with God. The deepest poverty, the greatest self-denial, with His approval, is better than riches, honors, ease, and friendship without it. We must take time to pray. If we allow our minds to be absorbed by worldly interest, the Lord may give us time by removing from us our idols of gold, of houses, or of fertile lands.

The young would not be seduced into sin if they would

refuse to enter any path save that upon which they could ask God's blessing. If the messengers who bear the last solemn warning to the world would pray for the blessing of God, not in a cold, listless, lazy manner, but fervently and in faith, as did Jacob, they would find many places where they could say, "I have seen God face to face, and my life is preserved." (*Gen.* 32:30) They would be accounted of Heaven as princes, having power to prevail with God and with men.

The "time of trouble such as never was" is soon to open upon us; and we shall need an experience which we do not now possess, and which many are too indolent to obtain. It is often the case that trouble is greater in anticipation than in reality; but this is not true of the crisis before us. The most vivid presentation cannot reach the magnitude of the ordeal. In that time of trial every soul must stand for himself before God. Though Noah, Daniel, and Job were in the land, "as I live, saith the Lord God, they shall deliver neither son nor daughter; they shall but deliver their own souls by their righteousness." (*Eze.* 14:20)

Now, while our great High Priest is making the atonement for us, we should seek to become perfect in Christ. Not even by a thought could our Saviour be brought to yield to the power of temptation. Satan finds in human hearts some point where he can gain a foot-hold; some sinful desire is cherished by means of which his temptations assert their power. But Christ declared of Himself, "The prince of this world cometh, and hath nothing in Me." (*John* 14:30) Satan could find nothing in the Son of God that would enable him to gain the victory. He had kept His Father's commandments, and there was no sin in Him that Satan could use to his advantage. This is the condition in which those must be found who shall stand in the time of trouble.

It is in this life that we are to separate sin from us through faith in the atoning blood of Christ. Our precious Saviour invites us to join ourselves to Him, to unite our weakness to His strength, our ignorance to His wisdom, our unworthiness to His merits. God's providence is the school in which we are to learn the meekness and lowliness of Jesus. The Lord is ever setting before us, not the way we would choose, which seems easier and pleasanter to us, but the true aims of life. It rests with us to co-operate with the agencies which Heaven employs in the work of conforming our characters to the divine model. None can neglect or defer this work but at the most fearful peril to their souls.

The apostle John in vision heard a loud voice in Heaven exclaiming, "Woe to the inhabiters of the earth and of the sea! for the devil is come down unto you, having great wrath, because he knoweth that he hath but a short time." (*Rev.* 12:12) Fearful are the scenes which call forth this exclamation from the heavenly voice. The wrath of Satan increases as his time grows short, and his work of deceit and destruction will reach its culmination in the time of trouble.

Fearful sights of a supernatural character will soon be revealed in the heavens, in token of the power of miracle-working demons. The spirits of devils will go forth to the kings of the earth and to the whole world to fasten them in deception and urge them on to unite with Satan in his last struggle against the government of Heaven. By these agencies rulers and subjects will be alike deceived. Persons will arise pretending to be Christ Himself and claiming the title and worship which belong to the world's Redeemer. They will perform wonderful miracles of healing and will profess to have revelations from Heaven contradicting the testimony of the Scriptures.

As the crowning act in the great drama of deception Satan himself will personate Christ. The church has long professed to look to the Saviour's advent as the consummation of her hopes. Now the great deceiver will make it appear that Christ has come. In different parts of the earth Satan will manifest himself among men as a majestic being of dazzling brightness, resembling the description of the Son of God given by John in the Revelation. (*Rev.* 1:13-15) The glory that surrounds him is unsurpassed by anything that mortal eyes have yet beheld. The shout of triumph rings out upon the air, "Christ has come! Christ has come!" The people prostrate themselves in adoration before him, while he lifts up his hands and pronounces a blessing upon them, as Christ blessed His disciples when He was upon the earth. His voice is soft and subdued, yet full of melody. In gentle, compassionate tones he presents some of the same gracious, heavenly truths which the Saviour uttered; he heals the diseases of the people, and then in his assumed character of Christ he claims to have changed the Sabbath to Sunday and commands all to hallow the day which he has blessed. He declares that those who persist in keeping holy the seventh day are blaspheming his name by refusing to listen to his angels sent to them with light and truth. This is the strong, almost overmastering delusion. Like the Samaritans who were deceived by Simon Magus, the multitudes from the least to the greatest give heed to these sorceries, saying, This is "the great power of God." (*Acts* 8:10)

But the people of God will not be misled. The teachings of this false christ are not in accordance with the Scriptures. His blessing is pronounced upon the worshipers of the beast and his image—the very class upon whom the Bible declares that God's unmingled wrath shall be poured out.

And, furthermore, Satan is not permitted to counterfeit the manner of Christ's advent. The Saviour has warned His people against deception upon this point and has clearly foretold the manner of His second coming. "There shall arise false christs, and false prophets, and shall show great signs and wonders; insomuch that, if it were possible, they shall deceive the very elect. . . . Wherefore if they shall say unto you, Behold, He is in the desert; go not forth: behold, He is in the secret chambers; believe it not. For as the lightning cometh out of the east, and shineth even unto the west; so shall also the coming of the Son of man be." (*Matt.* 24:24-27, 31; 25:31; *Rev.* 1:7; 1 *Thess.* 4:16, 17) This coming there is no possibility of counterfeiting. It will be universally known—witnessed by the whole world.

Only those who have been diligent students of the Scriptures and who have received the love of the truth will be shielded from the powerful delusion that takes the world captive. By the Bible testimony these will detect the deceiver in his disguise. To all, the testing time will come. By the sifting of temptation the genuine Christian will be revealed. Are the people of God now so firmly established upon His Word that they would not yield to the evidence of their senses? Would they in such a crisis cling to the Bible and the Bible only? Satan will, if possible, prevent them from obtaining a preparation to stand in that day. He will so arrange affairs as to hedge up their way, entangle them with earthly treasures, cause them to carry a heavy, wearisome burden, that their hearts may be overcharged with the cares of this life, and the day of trial may come upon them as a thief.

As the decree issued by the various rulers of Christendom against commandment-keepers shall withdraw the protection of government and abandon them to those who desire their destruction, the people of God will flee from the cities and villages and associate together in companies, dwelling in the most desolate and solitary places. Many will find refuge in the strongholds of the mountains. Like the Christians of the Piedmont valleys they will make the high places of the earth their sanctuaries and will thank God for the "munitions of rocks." (*Isa.* 33:16) But many of all nations and all classes, high and low, rich and poor, black and white, will be cast into the most unjust and cruel bondage. The beloved of God pass weary days, bound in chains, shut in by prison bars, sentenced to be slain, some apparently left to die of starvation in dark and loathsome dungeons. No human ear is open to hear their moans; no human hand is ready to lend them help.

Will the Lord forget His people in this trying hour? Did He forget faithful Noah when judgments were visited upon the antediluvian world? Did He forget Lot when the fire came down from Heaven to consume the cities of the plain? Did He forget Joseph surrounded by idolaters in Egypt? Did He forget Elijah when the oath of Jezebel threatened him with the fate of the prophets of Baal? Did He forget Jeremiah in the dark and dismal pit of his prison-house? Did He forget the three worthies in the fiery furnace? or Daniel in the den of lions?

"But Zion said, The Lord hath foresaken me, and my Lord hath forgotten me. Can a woman forget her sucking child, that she should not have compassion on the son of her womb? yea, they may forget, yet will I not forget thee. Behold, I have graven thee upon the palms of My hands." (*Isa*. 49:14-16) The Lord of hosts has said, "He that toucheth you toucheth the apple of His eye." (*Zech*. 2:8)

Though enemies may thrust them into prison, yet dungeon walls cannot cut off the communication between their souls and Christ. One who sees their every weakness, who is acquainted with every trial, is above all earthly powers; and angels will come to them in lonely cells, bringing light and peace from Heaven. The prison will be as a palace; for the rich in faith dwell there, and the gloomy walls will be lighted up with heavenly light, as when Paul and Silas prayed and sang praises at midnight in the Philippian dungeon.

God's judgments will be visited upon those who are seeking to oppress and destroy His people. His long forbearance with the wicked emboldens men in transgression, but their punishment is none the less certain and terrible because it is long delayed. "The Lord shall rise up as in Mount Perazim, He shall be wroth as in the valley of Gibeon, that He may do His work, His strange work; and bring to pass His act, His strange act." (*Isa*. 28:21) To our merciful God the act of punishment is a strange act. "As I live, saith the Lord God, I have no pleasure in the death of the wicked." (*Eze*. 33:11) The Lord is "merciful and gracious, long-suffering, and abundant in goodness and truth, forgiving iniquity and transgression and sin." Yet He will "by no means clear the guilty."

"The Lord is slow to anger, and great in power, and will not at all acquit the wicked." (*Ex.* 34:6, 7; *Nah.* 1:3) By terrible things in righteousness He will vindicate the authority of His downtrodden law. The severity of the retribution awaiting the transgressor may be judged by the Lord's reluctance to execute justice. The nation with which He bears long and which He will not smite until it has filled up the measure of its iniquity in God's account will finally drink the cup of wrath unmixed with mercy.

When Christ ceases His intercession in the sanctuary, the unmingled wrath threatened against those who worship the beast and his image and receive his mark (*Rev.* 14:9, 10) will be poured out. The plagues upon Egypt when God was about to deliver Israel were similar in character to those more terrible and extensive judgments which are to fall upon the world just before the final deliverance of God's people. Says the Revelator in describing these terrific scourges, "There fell a noisome and grievous sore upon the men which had the mark of the beast, and upon them which worshiped his image." The sea "became as the blood of a dead man, and every living soul died in the sea." And "the rivers and fountains of waters became blood." (*Rev.* 16:2-6, 8, 9) Terrible as these inflictions are, God's justice stands fully vindicated. The angel of God declares, "Thou art righteous, O Lord . . . because Thou has judged thus. For they have shed the blood of saints and prophets, and Thou hast given them blood to drink; for they are worthy." (*Rev.* 16:2-6, 8, 9) By condemning the people of God to death they have as truly incurred the guilt of their blood as if it had been shed by their hands. In like manner Christ declared the Jews of His time guilty of all the blood of holy men which had been shed since the days of Abel; for they possessed the same spirit and were seeking to do the same work with these murderers of the prophets.

In the plague that follow power is given to the sun "to scorch men with fire. And men were scorched with great heat." (*Rev.* 16:2-6, 8, 9) The prophets thus describe the condition of the earth at this fearful time:

"The land mourneth; . . . because the harvest of the field is perished. All the trees of the field are withered; because joy is withered away from the sons of men. The seed is rotten under their clods, the garners are laid desolate. How do the beasts groan! the herds of cattle are perplexed, because they have no pasture. . . . The rivers of waters are dried up, and the fire hath devoured the pastures of the wilderness." "The songs of the temple shall be howlings in that day, saith the Lord God; there shall be many dead bodies in every place; they shall cast them forth with silence." (*Joel* 1:10-12, 17-20; *Amos* 8:3)

These plagues are not universal, or the inhabitants of the earth would be wholly cut off. Yet they will be the most awful scourges that have ever been known to mortals. All the judgments upon men prior to the close of probation have been mingled with mercy. The pleading blood of Christ has shielded the sinner from receiving the full measure of his guilt; but in the final Judgment wrath is poured out unmixed with mercy.

In that day multitudes will desire the shelter of God's mercy which they have so long despised. "Behold, the days come, saith the Lord God, that I will send a famine in the land, not a famine of bread, nor a thirst for water, but of hearing the words of the Lord. And they shall wander from sea to sea, and from the north even to the east, they shall run to and fro to seek the word of the Lord, and shall not find it." (*Amos* 8:11, 12)

The people of God will not be free from suffering; but while persecuted and distressed, while they endure privation and suffer for want of food, they will not be left to perish. That God who cared for Elijah will not pass by one of His self-sacrificing children. He who numbers the hairs of their head will care for them, and in time of famine they shall be satisfied. While the wicked are dying from hunger and pestilence, angels will shield the righteous and supply their wants. To him that "walketh righteously" is the promise, "Bread shall be given him; his waters shall be sure. When the poor and needy seek water, and there is none, and their tongue faileth for thirst, I the Lord will hear them, I the God of Israel will not forsake them." (*Isa.* 33:16; 41:17)

"Although the fig-tree shall not blossom, neither shall fruit be in the vines; the labor of the olive shall fail, and the fields shall yield no meat; the flock shall be cut off from the fold, and there shall be no herd in the stalls;" yet shall they that fear Him "rejoice in the Lord," and joy in the God of their salvation. (*Hab.* 3:17, 18)

"The Lord is thy keeper; the Lord is thy shade upon thy right hand. The sun shall not smite thee by day, nor the moon by night. The Lord shall preserve thee from all evil; He shall preserve thy soul. He shall deliver thee from the snare of the fowler, and from the noisome pestilence. He shall cover thee with His feathers, and under His wings shalt thou trust; His truth shall be thy shield and buckler. Thou shalt not be afraid for the terror by night; nor for the arrow that flieth by day; nor for the pestilence that walketh in darkness; nor for the destruction that wasteth at noonday. A thousand shall fall at thy side, and ten thousand at thy right hand; but it shall not come nigh thee. Only with thine eyes shalt thou behold and see the reward of the wicked. Because thou hast made the Lord, which is my refuge, even the Most High, thy habitation; there shall no evil befall thee, neither shall any plague come nigh thy dwelling." (*Ps.* 121:5-7; 91:3-10)

Yet to human sight it will appear that the people of God must soon seal their testimony with their blood, as did the martyrs before them. They themselves begin to fear that the Lord has left them to fall by the hand of their enemies. It is a time of fearful agony. Day and night they cry unto God for deliverance. The wicked exult, and the jeering cry is heard, "Where now is your faith? Why does not God deliver you out of our hands if you are indeed His people?" But the waiting ones remember Jesus dying upon Calvary's cross and the chief priests and rulers shouting in mockery, "He saved others; Himself He cannot save. If He be the King of Israel, let Him now

come down from the cross, and we will believe Him."
(*Matt.* 27:42) Like Jacob, all are wrestling with God.
Their countenances express their internal struggle.
Paleness sits upon every face. Yet they cease not their
earnest intercession.

Could men see with heavenly vision, they would behold
companies of angels that excel in strength stationed about
those who have kept the word of Christ's patience. With
sympathizing tenderness angels have witnessed their distress and have heard their prayers. They are waiting
the word of their Commander to snatch them from their
peril. But they must wait yet a little longer. The people of
God must drink of the cup and be baptized with the baptism. The very delay, so painful to them, is the best answer to their petitions. As they endeavor to wait trustingly
for the Lord to work, they are led to exercise faith, hope,
and patience, which have been too little exercised during
their religious experience. Yet for the elect's sake the
time of trouble will be shortened. "Shall not God avenge
His own elect, which cry day and night unto Him? . . . I
tell you that He will avenge them speedily." (*Luke* 18:7,
8) The end will come more quickly than men expect. The
wheat will be gathered and bound in sheaves for the garner of God; the tares will be bound as fagots for the fires
of destruction.

The heavenly sentinels, faithful to their trust, continue
their watch. Though a general decree has fixed the time
when commandment-keepers may be put to death, their
enemies will in some cases anticipate the decree, and, before the time specified, will endeavor to take their lives.
But none can pass the mighty guardians stationed about
every faithful soul. Some are assailed in their flight from
the cities and villages; but the swords raised against them
break and fall as powerless as a straw. Others are defended by angels in the form of men of war.

In all ages God has wrought through holy angels for
the succor and deliverance of His people. Celestial beings
have taken an active part in the affairs of men. They have
appeared clothed in garments that shone as the lightning;

they have come as men in the garb of wayfarers. Angels have appeared in human form to men of God. They have rested, as if weary, under the oaks at noon. They have accepted the hospitalities of human homes. They have acted as guides to benighted travelers. They have with their own hands kindled the fires of the altar. They have opened prison doors and set free the servants of the Lord. Clothed with the panoply of Heaven, they came to roll away the stone from the Saviour's tomb.

In the form of men angels are often in the assemblies of the righteous, and they visit the assemblies of the wicked, as they went to Sodom, to make a record of their deeds to determine whether they have passed the boundary of God's forbearance. The Lord delights in mercy; and for the sake of a few who really serve Him He restrains calamities and prolongs the tranquillity of multitudes. Little do sinners against God realize that they are indebted for their own lives to the faithful few whom they delight to ridicule and oppress.

Though the rulers of this world know it not, yet often in their councils angels have been spokesmen. Human eyes have looked upon them; human ears have listened to their appeals; human lips have opposed their suggestions and ridiculed their counsels; human hands have met them with insult and abuse. In the council hall and the court of justice these heavenly messengers have shown an intimate acquaintance with human history; they have proved themselves better able to plead the cause of the oppressed than were their ablest and most eloquent defenders. They have defeated purposes and arrested evils that would have greatly retarded the work of God and would have caused great suffering to His people. In the hour of peril and distress "the angel of the Lord encampeth round about them that fear Him, and delivereth them." (*Ps.* 34:7)

With earnest longing God's people await the tokens of their coming King. As the watchmen are accosted, "What of the night?" the answer is given unfalteringly, "The morning cometh, and also the night." (*Isa.* 21:11, 12) Light is gleaming upon the clouds above the mountain tops. Soon there will be a revealing of His glory. The Sun of Righteousness is about to shine forth. The morning and the night are both at hand—the opening of endless day to the righteous, the settling down of eternal night to the wicked.

As the wrestling ones urge their petitions before God, the veil separating them from the unseen seems almost withdrawn. The heavens glow with the dawning of eternal day, and, like the melody of angel songs the words fall upon the ear, "Stand fast to your allegiance. Help is coming." Christ, the almighty victor, holds out to His weary soldiers a crown of immortal glory; and His voice comes from the gates ajar: "Lo, I am with you. Be not afraid. I am acquainted with all your sorrows; I have borne your griefs. You are not warring against untried enemies. I have fought the battle in your behalf, and in My name you are more than conquerors."

The precious Saviour will send help just when we need it. The way to Heaven is consecrated by His foot-prints. Every thorn that wounds our feet has wounded His. Every cross that we are called to bear, He has borne before us. The Lord permits conflicts, to prepare the soul for peace. The time of trouble is a fearful ordeal for God's people; but it is the time for every true believer to look up and by faith he may see the bow of promise encircling him.

"The redeemed of the Lord shall return, and come with singing unto Zion; and everlasting joy shall be upon their head; they shall obtain gladness and joy, and sorrow and mourning shall flee away. I, even I, am He that comforteth you; who art thou, that thou shouldst be afraid of a man that shall die, and of the son of man which shall be made as grass; and forgettest the Lord thy Maker; . . . and hast feared continually every day because of the fury of the oppressor, as if he were ready to destroy? and where is the fury of the oppressor? The captive exile hasteneth that he may be loosed, and that he should not die in the pit, nor that his bread should fail. But I am the Lord thy God, that divided the sea, whose waves roared. The Lord of hosts is His name. And I have put My words in thy mouth, and I have covered thee in the shadow of Mine hand."

"Therefore hear now this, thou afflicted, and drunken, but not with wine: Thus saith thy Lord Jehovah, and thy God that pleadeth the cause of His people, Behold, I have taken out of thine hand the cup of trembling, even the dregs of the cup of My fury; thou shalt no more drink it again. But I will put it into the hand of them that afflict thee; which have said to thy soul, Bow down, that we may go over; and thou hast laid thy body as the ground, and as the street, to them that went over." (*Isa.* 51:11-16, 21-23)

The eye of God looking down the ages was fixed upon the crisis which His people are to meet when earthly powers shall be arrayed against them. Like the captive exile they will be in fear of death by starvation or by violence. But the Holy One who divided the Red Sea before Israel will manifest His mighty power and turn their captivity. "They shall be Mine, saith the Lord of hosts, in that day when I make up My jewels; and I will spare them, as a man spareth his own son that serveth him." (*Mal.* 3:17) If the blood of Christ's faithful witnesses were shed at this time, it would not, like the blood of the martyrs, be as seed sown to yield a harvest for God. Their fidelity would not be a testimony to convince others of the truth; for the obdurate heart has beaten back the waves of mercy until they return no more. If the righteous were now left to fall a prey to their enemies, it would be a triumph for the prince of darkness. Says the psalmist, "In the time of trouble He shall hide me in His pavilion; in the secret of His tabernacle shall He hide me." (*Ps.* 27:5) Christ has spoken: "Come, My people, enter thou into thy chambers, and shut thy doors about thee; hide thyself as it were for a little moment, until the indignation be overpast. For, behold, the Lord cometh out of His place to punish the inhabitants of the earth for their iniquity." (*Isa.* 26:20, 21) Glorious will be the deliverance of those who have patiently waited for His coming and whose names are written in the book of life.

Chapter 14

GOD'S PEOPLE DELIVERED

WHEN THE PROTECTION OF human laws shall be withdrawn from those who honor the law of God, there will be in different lands a simultaneous movement for their destruction. As the time appointed in the decree draws near the people will conspire to root out the hated sect. It will be determined to strike in one night a decisive blow which shall utterly silence the voice of dissent and reproof.

The people of God—some in prison cells, some hidden in solitary retreats in the forests and the mountains—still plead for divine protection while in every quarter companies of armed men, urged on by hosts of evil angels, are preparing for the work of death. It is now in the hour of utmost extremity that the God of Israel will interpose for the deliverance of His chosen. Saith the Lord: "Ye shall have a song, as in the night when a holy solemnity is kept; and gladness of heart, as when one goeth . . . to come into the mountain of Jehovah, to the Mighty One of Israel. And the Lord shall cause His glorious voice to be heard, and shall show the lighting down of His arm, with the indignation of His anger, and with the flame of a devouring fire, with scattering, and tempest, and hailstones." (*Isa.* 30:29, 30)

With shouts of triumph, jeering, and imprecation, throngs of evil men are about to rush upon their prey, when lo, a dense blackness, deeper than the darkness of the night, falls upon the earth. Then a rainbow, shining with the glory from the throne of God, spans the heavens and seems to encircle each praying company. The angry

176

multitudes are suddenly arrested. Their mocking cries die away. The objects of their murderous rage are forgotten. With fearful forebodings they gaze upon the symbol of God's covenant and long to be shielded from its over-powering brightness.

By the people of God a voice, clear and melodious, is heard saying, "Look up," and lifting their eyes to the heavens, they behold the bow of promise. The black, angry clouds that covered the firmament are parted, and like Stephen they look up steadfastly into Heaven and see the glory of God and the Son of man seated upon His throne. In His divine form they discern the marks of His humiliation; and from His lips they hear the request, presented before His Father and the holy angels, "I will that they also, whom Thou hast given Me, be with Me where I am." (*John* 17:24) Again a voice, musical and triumphant, is heard saying, "They come! they come! holy, harmless, and undefiled. They have kept the word of My patience, they shall walk among the angels;" and the pale, quivering lips of those who have held fast their faith, utter a shout of victory.

It is at midnight that God manifests His power for the deliverance of His people. The sun appears, shining in its strength. Signs and wonders follow in quick succession. The wicked look with terror and amazement upon the scene, while the righteous behold with solemn joy the to-kens of their deliverance. Everything in nature seems turned out of its course. The streams cease to flow. Dark, heavy clouds come up and clash against each other. In the midst of the angry heavens is one clear space of in-describable glory, whence comes the voice of God like the sound of many waters, saying, "It is done." (*Rev.* 16:17, 18)

That voice shakes the heavens and the earth. There is a mighty earthquake, "such as was not since men were upon the earth, so mighty an earthquake and so great." (*Rev.* 16:17, 18) The firmament appears to open and shut. The glory from the throne of God seems flashing through. The mountains shake like a reed in the wind, and ragged rocks are scattered on every side. There is a roar as of a coming tempest. The sea is lashed into fury. There is heard the shriek of the hurricane like the voice of demons upon a mission of destruction. The whole earth heaves and swells like the waves of the sea. Its surface is breaking up. Its very foundations seem to be giving way. Mountain chains are sinking. Inhabited islands disappear. The seaports that have become like Sodom for wickedness are swallowed up by the angry waters. Babylon the Great has come in remembrance before God, "to give unto her the cup of the wine of the fierceness of His wrath." (*Rev.* 16:19, 21) Great hailstones, every one "about the weight of a talent," are doing their work of destruction. The proudest cities of the earth are laid low. The lordly palaces upon which the world's great men have lavished their wealth in order to glorify themselves are crumbling to ruin before their eyes. Prison walls are rent asunder, and God's people, who have been held in bondage for their faith, are set free.

Graves are opened and "many of them that sleep in the dust of the earth awake, some to everlasting life, and some to shame and everlasting contempt." (*Dan.* 12:2) All who have died in the faith of the third angel's message come forth from the tomb glorified to hear God's covenant of peace with those who have kept His law. "They also which pierced Him," (*Rev.* 1:7) those that mocked and derided Christ's dying agonies, and the most violent opposers of His truth and His people, are raised to behold Him in His glory and to see the honor placed upon the loyal and obedient.

Thick clouds still cover the sky; yet the sun now and then breaks through, appearing like the avenging eye of Jehovah. Fierce lightnings leap from the heavens, enveloping the earth in a sheet of flame. Above the terrific roar of thunder voices, mysterious and awful, declare the doom of the wicked. The words spoken are not comprehended by all: but they are distinctly understood by the false teachers. Those who a little before were so reckless, so boastful and defiant, so exultant in their cruelty to God's commandment-keeping people, are now overwhelmed with consternation and shuddering in fear. Their wails are heard above the sound of the elements. Demons acknowledge the divinity of Christ and tremble before His power, while men are supplicating for mercy and groveling in abject terror.

Said the prophets of old as they beheld in holy vision the day of God: "Howl ye; for the day of the Lord is at hand; it shall come as a destruction from the Almighty." (*Isa.* 13:6) "Enter into the rock, and hide thee in the dust, for fear of the Lord, and for the glory of His majesty. The lofty looks of man shall be humbled, and the haughtiness of men shall be bowed down; and the Lord alone shall be exalted in that day. For the day of the Lord of hosts shall be upon every one that is proud and lofty, and upon every one that is lifted up; and he shall be brought low. In that day a man shall cast the idols of his silver, and the idols of his gold, which they made each one for himself to worship, to the moles and to the bats; to go into the clefts of the rocks; and into the tops of the ragged rocks, for fear of the Lord, and for the glory of His majesty, when He ariseth to shake terribly the earth." (*Isa.* 2:10-12, 20, 21 (margin).

Through a rift in the clouds, there beams a star whose brilliancy is increased fourfold in contrast with the darkness. It speaks hope and joy to the faithful, but severity and wrath to the transgressors of God's law. Those who have sacrificed all for Christ are now secure, hidden as in the secret of the Lord's pavilion. They have been tested and before the world and the despisers of truth they have evinced their fidelity to Him who died for them. A marvelous change has come over those who have held fast their integrity in the very face of death. They have been suddenly delivered from the dark and terrible tyranny of men transformed to demons. Their faces, so lately pale, anxious, and haggard, are now aglow with wonder, faith, and love. Their voices rise in triumphant song: "God is our refuge and strength, a very present help in trouble. Therefore will not we fear, though the earth be removed, and though the mountains be carried into the midst of the sea; though the waters thereof roar and be troubled, though the mountains shake with the swelling thereof." (*Ps.* 46:1-3)

While these words of holy trust ascend to God, the clouds sweep back, and the starry heavens are seen, unspeakably glorious in contrast with the black and angry firmament on either side. The glory of the celestial city streams from the gates ajar. Then there appears against the sky a hand holding two tables of stone folded together. Says the prophet, "The heavens shall declare His righteousness; for God is judge Himself." (*Ps.* 50:6) That holy law, God's righteousness, that amid thunder and flame was proclaimed from Sinai as the guide of life, is now revealed to men as the rule of judgment. The hand opens the tables, and there are seen the precepts of the decalogue, traced as with a pen of fire. The words are so plain that all can read them. Memory is aroused, the darkness of superstition and heresy is swept from every mind, and God's ten words, brief, comprehensive, and authoritative, are presented to the view of all the inhabitants of the earth.

It is impossible to describe the horror and despair of those who have trampled upon God's holy requirements. The Lord gave them His law; they might have compared their characters with it and learned their defects while there was yet opportunity for repentance and reform; but in order to secure the favor of the world, they set aside its precepts and taught others to transgress. They have endeavored to compel God's people to profane His Sabbath. Now they are condemned by that law which they have despised. With awful distinctness they see that they are without excuse. They chose whom they would serve and worship. "Then shall ye return, and discern between the righteous and the wicked, between him that serveth God and him that serveth Him not." (*Mal.* 3:18)

The enemies of God's law, from the ministers down to the least among them, have a new conception of truth and duty. Too late they see that the Sabbath of the fourth commandment is the seal of the living God. Too late they see the true nature of their spurious sabbath and the sandy foundation upon which they have been building. They find that they have been fighting against God. Religious teachers have led souls to perdition while professing to guide them to the gates of Paradise. Not until the day of final accounts will it be known how great is the responsibility of men in holy office and how terrible are the results of their unfaithfulness. Only in eternity can we rightly estimate the loss of a single soul. Fearful will be the doom of him to whom God shall say, Depart, thou wicked servant.

The voice of God is heard from Heaven, declaring the day and hour of Jesus' coming and delivering the everlasting covenant to His people. Like peals of loudest thunder His words roll through the earth. The Israel of God stand listening with their eyes fixed upward. Their countenances are lighted up with His glory and shine as did the face of Moses when he came down from Sinai. The wicked cannot look upon them. And when the blessing is pronounced on those who have honored God by keeping His Sabbath holy, there is a mighty shout of victory.

Soon there appears in the east a small black cloud, about half the size of a man's hand. It is the cloud which surrounds the Saviour and which seems in the distance to be shrouded in darkness. The people of God know this to be the sign of the Son of man. In solemn silence they gaze upon it as it draws nearer the earth, becoming lighter and more glorious, until it is a great white cloud, its base a glory like consuming fire, and above it the rainbow of the covenant. Jesus rides forth as a mighty conqueror. Not now a "man of sorrows," to drink the bitter cup of shame and woe, He comes, victor in Heaven and earth, to judge the living and the dead. "Faithful and True, in righteousness He doth judge and make war." And "the armies in Heaven follow Him." (*Rev.* 19:11, 14) With anthems of celestial melody the holy angels, a vast, unnumbered throng, attend Him on His way. The firmament seems filled with radiant forms—"ten thousand times ten thousand, and thousands of thousands." No human pen can portray the scene; no mortal mind is adequate to conceive its splendor. "His glory covered the heavens, and the earth was full of His praise. And His brightness was as the light." (*Heb.* 3:3, 4) As the living cloud comes still nearer every eye beholds the Prince of life. No crown of thorns now mars that sacred head, but a diadem of glory rests on His holy brow. His countenance outshines the dazzling brightness of the noonday sun. "And He hath on His vesture and on His thigh a name written, King of kings, and Lord of lords." (*Rev.* 19:16)

Before His presence "all faces are turned into paleness;" upon the rejecters of God's mercy falls the terror of eternal despair. "The heart melteth, and the knees smite together," "and the faces of them all gather blackness." (*Jer.* 30:6; *Nah.* 2:10) The righteous cry with trembling, "Who shall be able to stand?" The angels' song is hushed and there is a period of awful silence. Then the voice of Jesus is heard saying, "My grace is sufficient for you." The faces of the righteous are lighted up and joy fills every heart. And the angels strike a note higher and sing again, as they draw still nearer to earth.

The King of kings descends upon the cloud, wrapped in flaming fire. The heavens are rolled together as a scroll, the earth trembles before Him, and every mountain and island is moved out of its place. "Our God shall come, and shall not keep silence; a fire shall devour before Him, and it shall be very tempestous round about Him. He shall call to the heavens from above, and to the earth, that He may judge His people." (*Ps.* 50:3, 4)

"And the kings of the earth, and the great men, and the rich men, and the chief captains, and the mighty men, and every bondman, and every freeman, hid themselves in the dens and in the rocks of the mountains; and said to the mountains and rocks, Fall on us, and hide us from the face of Him that sitteth on the throne, and from the wrath of the Lamb; for the great day of His wrath is come; and who shall be able to stand?" (*Rev.* 6:15-17)

The derisive jests have ceased. Lying lips are hushed into silence. The clash of arms, the tumult of battle, "with confused noise, and garments rolled in blood," (*Isa.* 9:5) is stilled. Naught now is heard but the voice of prayer and the sound of weeping and lamentation. The cry bursts forth from lips so lately scoffing, "The great day of His wrath is come; and who shall be able to stand?" The wicked pray to be buried beneath the rocks of the mountains rather than meet the face of Him whom they have despised and rejected.

That voice which penetrates the ear of the dead, they know. How often have its plaintive, tender tones called them to repentance. How often has it been heard in the touching entreaties of a friend, a brother, a Redeemer. To the rejecters of His grace no other could be so full of condemnation, so burdened with denunciation, as that voice which has so long pleaded, "Turn ye, turn ye from your evil ways; for why will ye die?" (*Eze.* 33:11) Oh that it were to them the voice of a stranger! Says Jesus: "I have called, and ye refused; I have stretched out My hand, and no man regarded. But ye have set at naught all My counsel, and would none of My reproof." (*Prov.* 1:24, 25) That voice awakens memories which they would fain blot out—warnings despised, invitations refused, privileges slighted.

There are those who mocked Christ in His humiliation. With thrilling power come to their minds the Sufferer's words, when, adjured by the high priest, He solemnly declared, "Hereafter shall ye see the Son of man sitting on the right hand of power, and coming in the clouds of heaven." (*Matt.* 26:64) Now they behold Him in His glory, and they are yet to see Him sitting on the right hand of power.

Those who derided His claim to be the Son of God are speechless now. There is the haughty Herod who jeered at His royal title and bade the mocking soldiers crown Him king. There are the very men who with impious hands placed upon His form the purple robe, upon His sacred brow the thorny crown, and in His unresisting hand the mimic scepter, and bowed before Him in blasphemous mockery. The men who smote and spit upon the Prince of life now turn from His piercing gaze and seek to flee from the overpowering glory of His presence. Those who drove the nails through His hands and feet, the soldier who pierced His side, behold these marks with terror and remorse.

With awful distinctness do priests and rulers recall the events of Calvary. With shuddering horror they remember how, wagging their heads in Satanic exultation, they exclaimed, "He saved others; Himself He cannot save. If He be the King of Israel, let Him now come down from the cross, and we will believe Him. He trusted in God; let Him deliver Him now, if He will have Him." (*Matt.* 27:42, 43)

Vividly they recall the Saviour's parable of the husbandmen who refused to render to their lord the fruit of the vineyard, who abused his servants and slew his son. They remember, too, the sentence which they themselves pronounced: The lord of the vineyard will miserably destroy those wicked men. In the sin and punishment of those unfaithful men the priests and elders see their own course and their own just doom. And now there rises a cry of mortal agony. Louder than the shout, "Crucify Him! crucify Him!" which rang through the streets of Jerusalem, swells the awful, despairing wail, "He is the Son of God! He is the true Messiah!" They seek to flee from the presence of the King of kings. In the deep caverns of the earth, rent asunder by the warring of the elements, they vainly attempt to hide.

In the lives of all who reject truth, there are moments when conscience awakens, when memory represents the torturing recollection of a life of hypocrisy, and the soul is harassed with vain regrets. But what are these compared with the remorse of that day when "fear cometh as desolaton," when "destruction cometh as a whirlwind!" (*Prov.* 1:27) Those who would have destroyed Christ and His faithful people now witness the glory which rests upon them. In the midst of their terror they hear the voices of the saints in joyful strains exclaiming, "Lo, this is our God; we have waited for Him, and He will save us." (*Isa.* 25:9)

Amid the reeling of the earth, the flash of lightning, and the roar of thunder, the voice of the Son of God calls forth the sleeping saints. He looks upon the graves of the righteous, then raising His hands to heaven He cries, "Awake, awake, awake, ye that sleep in the dust, and arise!" Throughout the length and breadth of the earth, the dead shall hear that voice; and they that hear shall live. And the whole earth shall ring with the tread of the exceeding great army of every nation, kindred, tongue, and people. From the prison-house of death they come, clothed with immortal glory, crying, "O death, where is thy sting? O grave, where is thy victory?" (1 *Cor.* 15:55) And the living righteous and the risen saints unite their voices in a long, glad shout of victory.

All come forth from their graves the same in stature as when they entered the tomb. Adam, who stands among the risen throng, is of lofty height and majestic form, in stature but little below the Son of God. He presents a marked contrast to the people of later generations; in this one respect is shown the great degeneracy of the race. But all arise with the freshness and vigor of eternal youth. In the beginning man was created in the likeness of God, not only in character, but in form and feature. Sin defaced and almost obliterated the divine image; but Christ came to restore that which had been lost. He will change our vile bodies and fashion them like unto His glorious body. The mortal, corruptible form, devoid of comeliness, once polluted with sin, becomes perfect, beautiful, and immortal. All blemishes and deformities are left in the grave. Restored to the tree of life in the long-lost Eden, the redeemed will "grow up" (*Mal.* 4:2) to the full stature of the race in its primeval glory. The last lingering traces of the curse of sin will be removed and Christ's faithful ones will appear "in the beauty of the Lord our God;" in mind and soul and body reflecting the perfect image of their

Lord. Oh, wonderful redemption! long talked of, long hoped for, contemplated with eager anticipation, but never fully understood.

The living righteous are changed "in a moment, in the twinkling of an eye." At the voice of God they were glorified; now they are made immortal, and with the risen saints are caught up to meet their Lord in the air. Angels "gather together the elect from the four winds, from one end of heaven to the other." Little children are borne by holy angels to their mothers' arms. Friends long separated by death are united, nevermore to part; and with songs of gladness ascend together to the city of God.

On each side of the cloudy chariot are wings, and beneath it are living wheels; and as the chariot rolls upward, the wheels cry, "Holy," and the wings, as they move, cry, "Holy," and the retinue of angels cry, "Holy, holy, holy, Lord God Almighty." And the redeemed shout "Alleluia!" as the chariot moves onward toward the New Jerusalem.

Before entering the city of God the Saviour bestows upon His followers the emblems of victory and invests them with the insignia of their royal state. The glittering ranks are drawn up in the form of a hollow square about their King, whose form rises in majesty high above saint and angel, whose countenance beams upon them full of benignant love. Throughout the unnumbered host of the redeemed every glance is fixed upon Him, every eye beholds His glory whose "visage was so marred more than any man, and His form more than the sons of men." Upon the heads of the overcomers Jesus with His own right hand places the crown of glory. For each there is a crown bearing his own "new name" (*Rev.* 2:17) and the inscription, "Holiness to the Lord." In every hand are placed the victor's palm and the shining harp. Then, as the commanding angels strike the note, every hand sweeps the harp strings with skillful touch, awaking sweet music in rich, melodious strains. Rapture unutterable thrills every heart and each voice is raised in grateful praise: "Unto Him that loved us, and washed us from our sins in

His own blood, and hath made us kings and priests unto God and His Father; to Him be glory and dominion forever and ever." (*Rev.* 1:5, 6)

Before the ransomed throng is the holy city. Jesus opens wide the pearly gates, and the nations that have kept the truth enter in. There they behold the Paradise of God, the home of Adam in his innocency. Then that voice, richer than any music that ever fell on mortal ear, is heard, saying, "Your conflict is ended. Come, ye blessed of My Father, inherit the kingdom prepared for you from the foundation of the world."

Now is fulfilled the Saviour's prayer for His disciples, "I will that they also whom Thou hast given Me be with Me where I am." "Faultless before the presence of His glory with exceeding joy," (*Jude* 24) Christ presents to the Father the purchase of His blood, declaring, "Here am I, and the children whom Thou hast given Me. Those that Thou gavest Me I have kept." Oh, the wonders of redeeming love! the rapture of that hour when the infinite Father, looking upon the ransomed, shall behold His image, sin's discord banished, its blight removed, and the human once more in harmony with the divine!

With unutterable love Jesus welcomes His faithful ones to the "joy of their Lord." The Saviour's joy is in seeing in the kingdom of glory the souls that have been saved by His agony and humiliation. And the redeemed will be sharers in His joy as they behold among the blessed, those who have been won to Christ through their prayers, their labors, and loving sacrifice. As they gather about the great white throne, gladness unspeakable will fill their hearts when they behold those whom they have won for Christ and see that one has gained others, and these still others, all brought into the haven of rest, there to lay their crowns at Jesus' feet and praise Him through the endless cycles of eternity.

As the ransomed ones are welcomed to the city of God, there rings out upon the air an exultant cry of adoration. The two Adams are about to meet. The Son of God is standing with outstretched arms to receive the father of our race—the being whom He created, who sinned against his Maker, and for whose sin the marks of the crucifixion are borne upon the Saviour's form. As Adam discerns the prints of the cruel nails, he does not fall upon the bosom of his Lord, but in humiliation casts himself at His feet, crying, "Worthy, worthy is the Lamb that was slain!" Tenderly the Saviour lifts him up and bids him look once more upon the Eden home from which he has so long been exiled.

After his expulsion from Eden Adam's life on earth was filled with sorrow. Every dying leaf, every victim of sacrifice, every blight upon the fair face of nature, every stain upon man's purity, was a fresh reminder of his sin. Terrible was the agony of remorse as he beheld iniquity abounding and in answer to his warnings, met the reproaches cast upon himself as the cause of sin. With patient humility he bore for nearly a thousand years the penalty of transgression. Faithfully did he repent of his sin and trust in the merits of the promised Saviour, and he died in the hope of a resurrection. The Son of God redeemed man's failure and fall, and now through the work of the atonement Adam is re-instated in his first dominion.

Transported with joy he beholds the trees that were once his delight—the very trees whose fruit he himself had gathered in the days of his innocence and joy. He sees the vines that his own hands trained, the very flowers that he once loved to care for. His mind grasps the reality of the scene; he comprehends that this is indeed Eden restored, more lovely now than when he was banished from it. The Saviour leads him to the tree of life and plucks the glorious fruit and bids him eat. He looks about him and beholds a multitude of his family redeemed, standing in the Paradise of God. Then he casts his glittering crown at the feet of Jesus, and falling upon His breast embraces the Redeemer. He touches the golden harp and the vaults of Heaven echo the triumphant song, "Worthy, worthy, worthy is the Lamb that was slain, and lives again!" The family of Adam take up the strain and cast their crowns at the Saviour's feet as they bow before Him in adoration.

This reunion is witnessed by the angels who wept at the fall of Adam and rejoiced when Jesus after His resurrection ascended to Heaven, having opened the grave for all who should believe on His name. Now they behold the work of redemption accomplished and they unite their voices in the song of praise.

Upon the crystal sea before the throne, that sea of glass as it were mingled with fire—so resplendent is it with the glory of God—are gathered the company that have "gotten the victory over the beast, and over his image, and over his mark, and over the number of his name." (*Rev.* 15:2) With the Lamb upon Mount Zion, "having the harps of God," they stand, the hundred and forty and four thousand that were redeemed from among men; and there is heard, as the sound of many waters and as the sound of a great thunder, "the voice of harpers harping with their harps." (*Rev.* 14:1-5; 15:3; 7:14-17) And they sing "a new song" before the throne, a song which no man can learn save the hundred and forty and four thousand. It is the song of Moses and the Lamb—a song of deliverance. None but the hundred and forty-four thousand can learn that song; for it is the song of their experience—an experience such as no other company have ever had. "These are they which follow the Lamb whithersoever He goeth." These, having been translated from the earth, from among the living, are counted as "the first-fruits unto God and to the Lamb. These are they which came out of great tribulation;" (*Rev.* 14:1-5; 15:3; 7:14-17) they have passed through the time of trouble such as never was since there was a nation; they have endured the anguish of the time of Jacob's trouble; they have stood without an intercessor through the final outpouring of God's judgments. But they have been delivered, for they have "washed their robes, and made them white in the blood of the Lamb. In their mouth was found no guile; for they are without fault" before God. "Therefore are they before the throne of God, and

serve Him day and night in His temple; and He that sitteth on the throne shall dwell among them." (*Rev.* 14:1-
5; 15:3; 7:14-17) They have seen the earth wasted with
famine and pestilence, the sun having power to scorch
men with great heat, and they themselves have endured
suffering, hunger, and thirst. But "they shall hunger no
more; neither thirst any more; neither shall the sun light
on them, nor any heat; for the Lamb which is in the midst
of the throne shall feed them, and shall lead them unto
living fountains of waters; and God shall wipe away all
tears from their eyes." (*Rev.* 14:1-5; 15:3; 7:14-17)

In all ages the Saviour's chosen have been educated
and disciplined in the school of trial. They walked in narrow paths on earth; they were purified in the furnace of
affliction. For Jesus' sake they endured opposition, hatred,
calumny. They followed Him through conflicts sore; they
endured self-denial and experienced bitter disappointments. By their own painful experience they learned the
evil of sin, its power, its guilt, its woe; and they look upon
it with abhorrence. A sense of the infinite sacrifice made
for its cure humbles them in their own sight and fills
their hearts with gratitude and praise which those who
have never fallen cannot appreciate. They love much because they have been forgiven much. Having been partakers of Christ's sufferings, they are fitted to be partakers
with Him of His glory.

The heirs of God have come from garrets, from hovels,
from dungeons, from scaffolds, from mountains, from
deserts, from the caves of the earth, from the caverns of
the sea. On earth they were "destitute, afflicted, tormented." Millions went down to the grave loaded with infamy because they steadfastly refused to yield to the
deceptive claims of Satan. By human tribunals they were
adjudged the vilest of criminals. But now "God is judge
Himself." (*Ps.* 50:6) Now the decisions of earth are reversed. "The rebuke of His people shall He take away."
(*Isa.* 25:8) "They shall call them, The holy people, The
redeemed of the Lord." He hath appointed "to give unto
them beauty for ashes, the oil of joy for mourning, the

garment of praise for the spirit of heaviness." (*Isa.* 62:12; 61:3) They are no longer feeble, afflicted, scattered, and oppressed. Henceforth they are to be ever with the Lord. They stand before the throne clad in richer robes than the most honored of the earth have ever worn. They are crowned with diadems more glorious than were ever placed upon the brow of earthly monarchs. The days of pain and weeping are forever ended. The King of glory has wiped the tears from all faces; every cause of grief has been removed. Amid the waving of palm-branches they pour forth a song of praise, clear, sweet, and harmonious; every voice takes up the strain until the anthem swells through the vaults of Heaven, "Salvation to our God which sitteth upon the throne, and unto the Lamb." And all the inhabitants of Heaven respond in the ascription, "Amen: Blessing and glory, and wisdom, and thanksgiving, and honor, and power, and might, be unto our God forever and ever." (*Rev.* 7:10, 12)

In this life we can only begin to understand the wonderful theme of redemption. With our finite comprehension we may consider most earnestly the shame and the glory, the life and the death, the justice and the mercy, that meet in the cross; yet with the utmost stretch of our mental powers we fail to grasp its full significance. The length and the breadth, the depth and the height of redeeming love are but dimly comprehended. The plan of redemption will not be fully understood, even when the ransomed see as they are seen and know as they are known; but through the eternal ages, new truth will continually unfold to the wondering and delighted mind. Though the griefs and pains and temptations of earth are ended and the cause removed, the people of God will ever have a distinct, intelligent knowledge of what their salvation has cost.

The cross of Christ will be the science and the song of the redeemed through all eternity. In Christ glorified they will behold Christ crucified. Never will it be forgotten that He whose power created and upheld the unnumbered worlds through the vast realms of space, the Beloved of

God, the Majesty of Heaven, He whom cherub and shining seraph delighted to adore—humbled Himself to uplift fallen man; that He bore the guilt and shame of sin and the hiding of His Father's face till the woes of a lost world broke His heart and crushed out His life on Calvary's cross. That the Maker of all worlds, the Arbiter of all destinies, should lay aside His glory and humiliate Himself from love to man, will ever excite the wonder and adoration of the universe. As the nations of the saved look upon their Redeemer and behold the eternal glory of the Father shining in His countenance; as they behold His throne, which is from everlasting to everlasting, and know that His kingdom is to have no end, they break forth in rapturous song, "Worthy, worthy is the Lamb that was slain, and hath redeemed us to God by His own most precious blood!"

The mystery of the cross explains all other mysteries. In the light that streams from Calvary the attributes of God which had filled us with fear and awe appear beautiful and attractive. Mercy, tenderness, and parental love are seen to blend with holiness, justice, and power. While we behold the majesty of His throne, high and lifted up, we see His character in its gracious manifestations and comprehend as never before the significance of that endearing title, our Father.

It will be seen that He who is infinite in wisdom could devise no plan for our salvation except the sacrifice of His Son. The compensation for this sacrifice is the joy of peopling the earth with ransomed beings, holy, happy, and immortal. The result of the Saviour's conflict with the powers of darkness is joy to the redeemed, redounding to the glory of God throughout eternity. And such is the value of the soul that the Father is satisfied with the price paid; and Christ Himself, beholding the fruits of His great sacrifice, is satisfied.

Chapter 15

DESOLATION OF THE EARTH

"HER SINS HAVE REACHED unto heaven, and God hath remembered her iniquities. In the cup which she hath filled, fill to her double. How much she hath glorified herself, and lived deliciously, so much torment and sorrow give her, for she saith in her heart, I sit a queen, and am no widow, and shall see no sorrow. Therefore shall her plagues come in one day, death, and mourning, and famine; and she shall be utterly burned with fire; for strong is the Lord God who judgeth her. And the kings of the earth, who have committed fornication and lived deliciously with her, shall bewail her, and lament for her, . . . saying, Alas, alas that great city Babylon, that mighty city! for in one hour is thy judgment come." (*Rev.* 18:5-10, 3, 15-17)

"The merchants of the earth," that have "waxed rich through the abundance of her delicacies, shall stand afar off for the fear of her torment, weeping and wailing, and saying, Alas, alas that great city, that was clothed in fine linen, and purple, and scarlet, and decked with gold, and precious stones, and pearls! For in one hour so great riches is come to naught." (*Rev.* 18:5-10, 3, 15-17)

Such are the judgments that fall upon Babylon in the day of the visitation of God's wrath. She has filled up the measure of her iniquity; her time has come; she is ripe for destruction.

When the voice of God turns the captivity of His people, there is a terrible awakening of those who have lost all in the great conflict of life. While probation continued, they were blinded by Satan's deceptions, and they justified their course of sin. The rich prided themselves upon their superiority to those who were less favored; but they had obtained their richcs by violation of the law of God. They had neglected to feed the hungry, to clothe the naked, to deal justly, and to love mercy. They had sought to exalt themselves, and to obtain the homage of their fellow-creatures. Now they are stripped of all that made them great and are left destitute and defenseless. They look with terror upon the destruction of the idols which they preferred before their Maker. They have sold their souls for earthly riches and enjoyments and have not sought to become rich toward God. The result is their lives are a failure; their pleasures are now turned to gall, their treasures to corruption. The gain of a life-time is swept away in a moment. The rich bemoan the destruction of their grand houses, the scattering of their gold and silver. But their lamentations are silenced by the fear that they themselves are to perish with their idols.

The wicked are filled with regret, not because of their sinful neglect of God and their fellow-men, but because God has conquered. They lament that the result is what it is; but they do not repent of their wickedness. They would leave no means untried to conquer if they could.

The world see the very class whom they have mocked and derided and desired to exterminate pass unharmed through pestilence, tempest, and earthquake. He who is to the transgressors of His law a devouring fire, is to His people a safe pavilion.

The minister who has sacrificed truth to gain the favor of men now discerns the character and influence of his teachings. It is apparent that an omniscient eye was following him as he stood in the desk, as he walked the streets, as he mingled with men in the various scenes of life. Every emotion of the soul, every line written, every word uttered, every act that led men to rest in a refuge of falsehood, has been scattering seed; and now in the wretched, lost souls around him he beholds the harvest.

Saith the Lord: "They have healed the hurt of the daughter of My people slightly, saying, Peace, peace;

when there is no peace. With lies ye have made the heart of the righteous sad, whom I have not made sad; and strengthened the hands of the wicked, that he should not return from his wicked way, by promising him life." (*Jer.* 8:11; *Eze.* 13:22)

"Woe be unto the pastors that destroy and scatter the sheep of My pasture! . . . Behold, I will visit upon you the evil of your doings. Howl, ye shepherds, and cry; and wallow yourselves in the ashes, ye principal of the flock; for your days for slaughter and your dispersions are accomplished; . . . and the shepherds shall have no way to flee, nor the principal of the flock to escape." (*Jer.* 23:1, 2; 25:34, 35 (margin).

Ministers and people see that they have not sustained the right relation to God. They see that they have rebelled against the Author of all just and righteous law. The setting aside of the divine precepts gave rise to thousands of springs of evil, discord, hatred, iniquity, until the earth became one vast field of strife, one sink of corruption. This is the view that now appears to those who rejected truth and chose to cherish error. No language can express the longing which the disobedient and disloyal feel for that which they have lost forever—eternal life. Men whom the world has worshiped for their talents and eloquence now see these things in their true light. They realize what they have forfeited by transgression, and they fall at the feet of those whose fidelity they have despised and derided and confess that God has loved them.

The people see that they have been deluded. They accuse one another of having led them to destruction; but all unite in heaping their bitterest condemnation upon the ministers. Unfaithful pastors have prophesied smooth things; they have led their hearers to make void the law of God and to persecute those who would keep it holy. Now in their despair these teachers confess before the world their work of deception. The multitudes are filled with fury. "We are lost!" they cry, "and you are the cause of our ruin," and they turn upon the false shepherds. The very ones that once admired them most will pronounce the most dreadful curses upon them. The very hands that once crowned them with laurels will be raised for their destruction. The swords which were to slay God's people are now employed to destroy their enemies. Everywhere there is strife and bloodshed.

"A noise shall come even to the ends of the earth; for the Lord hath a controversy with the nations; He will plead with all flesh; He will give them that are wicked to the sword." (*Jer.* 25:31) For six thousand years the great controversy has been in progress; the Son of God and His heavenly messengers have been in conflict with the power of the evil one, to warn, enlighten, and save the children of men. Now all have made their decision; the wicked have fully united with Satan in his warfare against God. The time has come for God to vindicate the authority of His downtrodden law. Now the controversy is not alone with Satan but with men. "The Lord hath a controversy with the nations, He will give them that are wicked to the sword."

The mark of deliverance has been set upon those "that sigh and that cry for all the abominations that be done." Now the angel of death goes forth, represented in Ezekiel's vision by the men with the slaughtering weapons, to whom the command is given: "Slay utterly old and young, both maids, and little children, and women; but come not near any man upon whom is the mark; and begin at my sanctuary." (*Jer.* 25:31) Says the prophet, "They began at the ancient men which were before the house." (*Eze.* 9:1-6) The work of destruction begins among those who have professed to be the spiritual guardians of the people. The false watchmen are the first to fall. There are none to pity or to spare. Men, women, maidens, and little children perish together.

"The Lord cometh out of His place to punish the inhabitants of the earth for their iniquity; the earth also shall disclose her blood, and shall no more cover her slain." (*Isa.* 26:21) And this shall be the plague wherewith the Lord will smite all the people that have fought against Jerusalem: Their flesh shall consume away while they stand upon their feet, and their eyes shall consume away in their holes, and their tongue shall consume away in their mouth. And it shall come to pass in that day that a great tumult from the Lord shall be among them; and they shall lay hold every one on the hand of his neighbor, and his hand shall rise up against the hand of his neighbor." (*Zech.* 14:12, 13) In the mad strife of their own fierce passions and by the awful outpouring of God's unmingled wrath fall the wicked inhabitants of the earth—priests, rulers, and people, rich and poor, high and low. "And the slain of the Lord shall be at that day from one end of the earth even unto the other end of the earth; they shall not be lamented, neither gathered, nor buried." (*Jer.* 25:33)

At the coming of Christ the wicked are blotted from the face of the whole earth—consumed with the spirit of His mouth, and destroyed by the brightness of His glory. Christ takes His people to the city of God, and the earth is emptied of its inhabitants. "Behold, the Lord maketh the earth empty, and maketh it waste, and turneth it upside down, and scattereth abroad the inhabitants thereof. The land shall be utterly emptied, and utterly spoiled; for the Lord hath spoken this word. Because they have transgressed the laws, changed the ordinance, broken the everlasting covenant. Therefore hath the curse devoured the earth, and they that dwell therein are desolate; therefore the inhabitants of the earth are burned." (*Isa.* 24:1, 3, 5, 6)

The whole earth appears like a desolate wilderness. The ruins of cities and villages destroyed by the earthquake, uprooted trees, ragged rocks thrown out by the sea or torn out of the earth itself, are scattered over its surface, while vast caverns mark the spot where the mountains have been rent from their foundations.

Now the event takes place, foreshadowed in the last solemn service of the day of atonement. When the ministration in the holy of holies had been completed and the sins of Israel had been removed from the sanctuary by virtue of the blood of the sin-offering, then the scape-goat was presented alive before the Lord; and in presence of the congregation the high priest confessed over him all the iniquities of the children of Israel, and all their transgressions in all their sins, putting them upon the head of the goat." (*Lev.* 16:21) In like manner, when the work of atonement in the heavenly sanctuary has been completed, then in the presence of God and heavenly angels and the host of the redeemed, the sins of God's people will be placed upon Satan; he will be declared guilty of all the evil which he has caused them to commit. And as the scape-goat was sent away into a land not inhabited, so Satan will be banished to the desolate earth, an uninhabited and dreary wilderness.

The Revelator foretells the banishment of Satan, and the condition of chaos and desolation to which the earth is to be reduced; and he declares that this condition will exist for a thousand years. After presenting the scenes of the Lord's second coming and the destruction of the wicked, the prophecy continues: "I saw an angel come down from Heaven, having the key of the bottomless pit and a great chain in his hand. And he laid hold on the dragon, that old serpent, which is the devil, and Satan, and bound him a thousand years, and cast him into the bottomless pit, and shut him up, and set a seal upon him, that he should deceive the nations no more, till the thousand years should be fulfilled; and after that he must be loosed a little season." (*Rev.* 20:1-3)

That the expression, "bottomless pit," represents the earth in a state of confusion and darkness is evident from other scriptures. Concerning the condition of the earth "in the beginning," the Bible record says that it "was without form, and void; and darkness was upon the face of the deep." (*Gen.* 1:2; the word here translated "deep" is the same that in *Rev.* 20:1-3 is rendered "bottomless pit.") Prophecy teaches that it will be brought back, partially, at least, to this condition. Looking forward to the great day of God, the prophet Jeremiah declares: "I beheld the earth, and, lo, it was without form, and void; and the heavens, and they had no light. I beheld the mountains, and, lo, they trembled, and all the hills moved lightly. I beheld, and, lo, there was no man, and all the birds of the heavens were fled. I beheld, and, lo, the fruitful place was a wilderness and all the cities thereof were broken down." (*Jer.* 4:23-27)

Here is to be the home of Satan with his evil angels for a thousand years. Limited to the earth he will not have access to other worlds to tempt and annoy those who have never fallen. It is in this sense that he is bound; there are none remaining upon whom he can exercise his power. He is wholly cut off from the work of deception and ruin which for so many centuries has been his sole delight.

The prophet Isaiah, looking forward to the time of Satan's overthrow, exclaims: "How art thou fallen from Heaven, O Lucifer, son of the morning! how are thou cast down to the ground, which didst weaken the nations. Thou hast said in thine heart, I will ascend into Heaven, I will exalt my throne above the stars of God. I will be like the Most High. Yet thou shalt be brought down to hell, to the sides of the pit. They that see thee shall narrowly look upon thee, and consider thee, saying, Is this the man that made the earth to tremble, that did shake kingdoms; that made the world as a wilderness, and destroyed the cities thereof; that *opened not the house of his prisoners?*" (*Isa.* 14:12-17)

For six thousand years Satan's work of rebellion has "made the earth to tremble." He has "made the world as a wilderness, and destroyed the cities thereof." And "he opened not the house of his prisoners." For six thousand years his prison-house has received God's people, and he would have held them captive forever, but Christ has broken his bonds and set the prisoners free.

Even the wicked are now placed beyond the power of Satan; and alone with his evil angels he remains to realize the effect of the curse which sin has brought. "The kings of the nations, even all of them, lie in glory, every one in his own house [the grave]. But thou art cast out of thy grave like an abominable branch. . . . Thou shall not be

joined with them in burial, because thou hast destroyed
thy land, and slain thy people." (*Isa.* 14:18-20)

For a thousand years Satan will wander to and fro in
the desolate earth to behold the results of his rebellion
against the law of God. During this time his sufferings are
intense. Since his fall his life of unceasing activity has
banished reflection; but he is now deprived of his power
and left to contemplate the part which he has acted since
first he rebelled against the government of Heaven and to
look forward with trembling and terror to the dreadful future, when he must suffer for all the evil that he has done
and be punished for the sins that he has caused to be
committed.

To God's people the captivity of Satan will bring
gladness and rejoicing. Says the prophet: "It shall come
to pass in the day that the Lord shall give thee rest from
thy sorrow, and from thy trouble, and from the hard service wherein thou wast made to serve, that thou shalt take
up this proverb against the king of Babylon [here
representing Satan], and say, How hath the oppressor
ceased! . . . The Lord hath broken the staff of the
wicked, the scepter of the rulers; that smote the peoples
in wrath with a continual stroke, that ruled the nations in
anger, with a persecution that none restrained." (*Isa.*
14:3-6, Revised Version)

During the thousand years between the first and the
second resurrection the judgment of the wicked takes
place. The apostle Paul points to this judgment as an
event that follows the second advent. "Judge nothing before the time, until the Lord come, who both will bring to
light the hidden things of darkness, and will make
manifest the counsels of the hearts." (1 *Cor.* 4:5) Daniel
declares that when the Ancient of days came, "Judgment
was given to the saints of the Most High." (*Dan.* 7:22)
At this time the righteous reign as kings and priests unto
God. John in the Revelation says: "I saw thrones, and
they sat upon them, and judgment was given unto them.
They shall be priests of God and of Christ, and shall
reign with Him a thousand years." (*Rev.* 20:4, 6) It

is at this time that, as foretold by Paul, "the saints shall judge the world." (1 *Cor.* 6:2, 3) In union with Christ they judge the wicked, comparing their acts with the statute book, the Bible, and deciding every case according to the deeds done in the body. Then the portion which the wicked must suffer is meted out according to their works, and it is recorded against their names in the book of death.

Satan also and evil angels are judged by Christ and His people. Says Paul, "Know ye not that we shall judge angels?" (1 *Cor.* 6:2, 3) And Jude declares that "the angels which kept not their first estate, but left their own habitation, He hath reserved in everlasting chains under darkness unto the judgment of the great day." (*Jude* 6)

At the close of the thousand years the second resurrection will take place. Then the wicked will be raised from the dead and appear before God for the execution of "the judgment written." Thus the Revelator after describing the resurrection of the righteous says, "The rest of the dead lived not again until the thousand years were finished," (*Rev.* 20:5) And Isaiah declares, concerning the wicked, "They shall be gathered together, as prisoners are gathered in the pit, and shall be shut up in the prison, and *after many days shall they be visited*." (*Isa.* 24:22)

Chapter 16

END OF THE WAR

AT THE CLOSE OF THE THOUSAND YEARS Christ again returns to the earth. He is accompanied by the host of the redeemed and attended by a retinue of angels. As He descends in terrific majesty He bids the wicked dead arise to receive their doom. They come forth, a mighty host, numberless as the sands of the sea. What a contrast to those who were raised at the first resurrection! The righteous were clothed with immortal youth and beauty. The wicked bear the traces of disease and death.

Every eye in that vast multitude is turned to behold the glory of the Son of God. With one voice the wicked hosts exclaim, "Blessed is He that cometh in the name of the Lord!" It is not love to Jesus that inspires this utterance. The force of truth urges the words from unwilling lips. As the wicked went into their graves, so they come forth, with the same enmity to Christ and the same spirit of rebellion. They are to have no new probation in which to remedy the defects of their past lives. Nothing would be gained by this. A life-time of transgression has not softened their hearts. A second probation, were it given them, would be occupied as was the first, in evading the requirements of God and exciting rebellion against Him.

Christ descends upon the Mount of Olives, whence, after His resurrection, He ascended, and where angels repeated the promise of His return. Says the prophet, "The Lord my God shall come, and all the saints with Thee. And His feet shall stand in that day upon the Mount of Olives, which is before Jerusalem on the east, and the Mount of Olives shall cleave in the midst thereof, . . .

202

and there shall be a very great valley. And the Lord shall be King over all the earth. In that day shall there be one Lord, and His name one." (*Zech.* 14:5, 4, 9) As the New Jerusalem, in its dazzling splendor, comes down out of Heaven, it rests upon the place purified and made ready to receive it, and Christ with His people and the angels, enters the holy city.

Now Satan prepares for a last mighty struggle for the supremacy. While deprived of his power, and cut off from his work of deception, the prince of evil was miserable and dejected; but as the wicked dead are raised and he sees the vast multitudes upon his side, his hopes revive, and he determines not to yield the great controversy. He will marshal all the armies of the lost under his banner and through them endeavor to execute his plans. The wicked are Satan's captives. In rejecting Christ they have accepted the rule of the rebel leader. They are ready to receive his suggestions and to do his bidding. Yet, true to his early cunning he does not acknowledge himself to be Satan. He claims to be the Prince who is the rightful owner of the world and whose inheritance has been unlawfully wrested from him. He represents himself to his deluded subjects as a redeemer, assuring them that his power has brought them forth from their graves and that he is about to rescue them from the most cruel tyranny. The presence of Christ having been removed, Satan works wonders to support his claims. He makes the weak strong and inspires all with his own spirit and energy. He proposes to lead them against the camp of the saints and to take possession of the city of God. With fiendish exultation he points to the unnumbered millions who have been raised from the dead and declares that as their leader he is well able to overthrow the city and regain his throne and his kingdom.

In that vast throng are multitudes of the long-lived race that existed before the flood; men of lofty stature and giant intellect, who, yielding to the control of fallen angels, devoted all their skill and knowledge to the exaltation of themselves; men whose wonderful works of art led the world to idolize their genius, but whose cruelty and evil inventions, defiling the earth and defacing the image of God, caused Him to blot them from the face of His creation. There are kings and generals who conquered nations, valiant men who never lost a battle, proud, ambitious warriors whose approach made kingdoms tremble. In death these experienced no change. As they come up from the grave, they resume the current of their thoughts just where it ceased. They are actuated by the same desire to conquer that ruled them when they fell.

Satan consults with his angels, and then with these kings and conquerors and mighty men. They look upon the strength and numbers on their side, and declare that the army within the city is small in comparison with theirs and that it can be overcome. They lay their plans to take possession of the riches and glory of the New Jerusalem. All immediately begin to prepare for battle. Skillful artisans construct implements of war. Military leaders, famed for their success, marshal the throngs of warlike men into companies and divisions.

At last the order to advance is given, and the countless host moves on—an army such as was never summoned by earthly conquerors, such as the combined forces of all ages since war began on earth could never equal. Satan, the mightiest of warriors, leads the van, and his angels unite their forces for this final struggle. Kings and warriors are in his train, and the multitudes follow in vast companies, each under its appointed leader. With military precision, the serried ranks advance over the earth's broken and uneven surface to the City of God. By command of Jesus the gates of the New Jerusalem are closed, and the armies of Satan surround the city and make ready for the onset.

Now Christ again appears to the view of His enemies. Far above the city upon a foundation of burnished gold is a throne, high and lifted up. Upon this throne sits the Son of God, and around Him are the subjects of His kingdom. The power and majesty of Christ no language can describe, no pen portray. The glory of the Eternal Father is enshrouding His Son. The brightness of His presence fills the city of God and flows out beyond the gates, flooding the whole earth with its radiance.

Nearest the throne are those who were once zealous in the cause of Satan, but who, plucked as brands from the burning, have followed their Saviour with deep, intense devotion. Next are those who perfected Christian characters in the midst of falsehood and infidelity, those who honored the law of God when the Christian world declared it void, and the millions of all ages who were martyred for their faith. And beyond is the "great multitude, which no man could number, of all nations, and kindreds, and people, and tongues . . . before the throne, and before the Lamb, clothed with white robes, and palms in their hands." (*Rev.* 7:9) Their warfare is ended, their victory won. They have run the race and reached the prize. The palm branch in their hands is a symbol of their triumph, the white robe an emblem of the spotless righteousness of Christ which now is theirs.

The redeemed raise a song of praise that echoes and re-echoes through the vaults of heaven, "Salvation to our God which sitteth upon the throne, and unto the Lamb." And angel and seraph unite their voices in adoration. As the redeemed have beheld the power and malignity of Satan, they have seen as never before that no power but that of Christ could have made them conquerors. In all that shining throng there are none to ascribe salvation to themselves, as if they had prevailed by their own power and goodness. Nothing is said of what they have done or suffered; but the burden of every song, the key-note of every anthem is, Salvation to our God and unto the Lamb.

In the presence of the assembled inhabitants of earth and Heaven the final coronation of the Son of God takes place. And now, invested with supreme majesty and power, the King of kings pronounces sentence upon the rebels against His government and executes justice upon those who have transgressed His law and oppressed His people. Says the prophet of God: "I saw a great white

throne, and Him that sat on it, from whose face the earth
and the heaven fled away; and there was found no place
for them. And I saw the dead, small and great, stand before God; and the books were opened; and another book
was opened, which is the book of life; and the dead were
judged out of those things which were written in the
books, according to their works." (*Rev.* 20:11, 12)

As soon as the books of record are opened and the
eyes of Jesus look upon the wicked, they are conscious of
every sin which they have ever committed. They see just
where their feet diverged from the path of purity and
holiness, just how far pride and rebellion have carried
them in the violation of the law of God. The seductive
temptations which they encouraged by indulgence in sin,
the blessings perverted, the messengers of God despised,
the warnings rejected, the waves of mercy beaten back by
the stubborn, unrepentant heart—all appear as if written
in letters of fire.

Above the throne is revealed the cross; and like a pan-
oramic view appear the scenes of Adam's temptation and
fall and the successive steps in the great plan of redemption. The Saviour's lowly birth; His early life of simplicity
and obedience; His baptism in Jordan; the fast and temptation in the wilderness; His public ministry, unfolding to
men Heaven's most precious blessings; the days crowded
with deeds of love and mercy, the nights of prayer and
watching in the solitude of the mountains; the plottings of
envy, hate, and malice which repaid His benefits; the awful, mysterious agony in Gethsamane, beneath the crushing weight of the sins of the whole world; His betrayal
into the hands of the murderous mob; the fearful events
of that night of horror—the unresisting prisoner, forsaken by His best-loved disciples, rudely hurried through
the streets of Jerusalem; the Son of God exultingly displayed before Annas, arraigned in the high priest's palace,
in the judgment hall of Pilate, before the cowardly and
cruel Herod, mocked, insulted, tortured, and condemned
to die—all are vividly portrayed.

And now before the swaying multitude are revealed the

final scenes—the patient Sufferer treading the path to Calvary; the Prince of Heaven hanging upon the cross; the haughty priests and the jeering rabble deriding His expiring agony; the supernatural darkness; the heaving earth, the rent rocks, the open graves, marking the moment when the world's Redeemer yielded up His life.

The awful spectacle appears just as it was. Satan, his angels, and his subjects have no power to turn from the picture of their own work. Each actor recalls the part which he performed. Herod, who slew the innocent children of Bethlehem that he might destroy the King of Israel; the base Herodias, upon whose guilty soul rests the blood of John the Baptist, the weak, time-serving Pilate; the mocking soldiers; the priests and rulers and the maddened throng who cried, "His blood be on us, and our children!"—all behold the enormity of their guilt. They vainly seek to hide from the divine majesty of His countenance, outshining the glory of the sun, while the redeemed cast their crowns at the Saviour's feet, exclaiming, "He died for me!"

Amid the ransomed throng are the apostles of Christ, the heroic Paul, the ardent Peter, the loved and loving John, and their true-hearted brethren, and with them the vast host of martyrs; while outside the walls, with every vile and abominable thing, are those by whom they were persecuted, imprisoned, and slain. There is Nero, that monster of cruelty and vice, beholding the joy and exaltation of those whom he once tortured, and in whose extremest anguish he found Satanic delight. His mother is there to witness the result of her own work; to see how the evil stamp of character transmitted to her son, the passions encouraged and developed by her influence and example, have borne fruit in crimes that caused the world to shudder.

There are papal priests and prelates, who claimed to be Christ's ambassadors, yet employed the rack, the dungeon, and the stake to control the consciences of His people. There are the proud pontiffs who exalted themselves above God, and presumed to change the law of the

Most High. Those pretended fathers of the church have an account to render to God from which they would fain be excused. Too late they are made to see that the Omniscient One is jealous of His law, and that He will in nowise clear the guilty. They learn now that Christ identifies His interest with that of His suffering people; and they feel the force of His own words, "Inasmuch as ye have done it unto one of the least of these my brethren, ye have done it unto me." (*Matt.* 25:40)

The whole wicked world stand arraigned at the bar of God on the charge of high treason against the government of Heaven. They have none to plead their cause; they are without excuse; and the sentence of eternal death is pronounced against them.

It is now evident to all that the wages of sin is not noble independence and eternal life, but slavery, ruin, and death. The wicked see what they have forfeited by their life of rebellion. The far more exceeding and eternal weight of glory was despised when offered them; but how desirable it now appears. "All this," cries the lost soul, "I might have had; but I chose to put these things far from me. Oh, strange infatuation! I have exchanged peace, happiness and honor, for wretchedness, infamy, and despair." All see that their exclusion from Heaven is just. By their lives they have declared, "We will not have this Jesus to reign over us."

As if entranced, the wicked have looked upon the coronation of the Son of God. They see in His hands the tables of the divine law, the statutes which they have despised and transgressed. They witness the outburst of wonder, rapture, and adoration from the saved; and as the wave of melody sweeps over the multitudes without the city, all with one voice exclaim, "Great and marvelous are Thy works, Lord God Almighty; just and true are Thy ways, Thou King of saints;" and falling prostrate, they worship the Prince of life.

Satan seems paralyzed as he beholds the glory and majesty of Christ. He who was once a covering cherub remembers whence he has fallen. A shining seraph, "son of the morning;" how changed, how degraded! From the council where once he was honored, he is forever excluded. He sees another now standing near to the Father, veiling His glory. He has seen the crown placed upon the head of Christ by an angel of lofty stature and majestic presence, and he knows that the exalted position of this angel might have been his.

Memory recalls the home of his innocence and purity, the peace and content that were his until he indulged in murmuring against God and envy of Christ. His accusations, his rebellion, his deceptions to gain the sympathy and support of the angels, his stubborn persistence in making no effort for self-recovery when God would have granted him forgiveness—all come vividly before him. He reviews his work among men and its results—the enmity of man toward his fellow-man, the terrible destruction of life, the rise and fall of kingdoms, the overturning of thrones, the long succession of tumults, conflicts, and revolutions. He recalls his constant efforts to oppose the work of Christ and to sink man lower and lower. He sees that his hellish plots have been powerless to destroy those who have put their trust in Jesus. As Satan looks upon his kingdom, the fruit of this toil, he sees only failure and ruin. He has led the multitudes to believe that the city of God would be an easy prey; but he knows that this is false. Again and again, in the progress of the great controversy, he has been defeated and compelled to yield. He knows too well the power and majesty of the Eternal.

The aim of the great rebel has ever been to justify himself and to prove the divine government responsible for the rebellion. To this end he has bent all the power of his giant intellect. He has worked deliberately and systematically and with marvelous success, leading vast multitudes to accept his version of the great controversy which has been so long in progress. For thousands of years this chief of conspiracy has palmed off falsehood for truth. But the time has now come when the rebellion is to be finally defeated and the history and character of Satan disclosed. In his last great effort to dethrone Christ, destroy

His people, and take possession of the city of God, the arch-deceiver has been fully unmasked. Those who have united with him see the total failure of his cause. Christ's followers and the loyal angels behold the full extent of his machinations against the government of God. He is the object of universal abhorrence.

Satan sees that his voluntary rebellion has unfitted him for Heaven. He has trained his powers to war against God; the purity, peace, and harmony of Heaven would be to him supreme torture. His accusations against the mercy and justice of God are now silenced. The reproach which he has endeavored to cast upon Jehovah rests wholly upon himself. And now Satan bows down and confesses the justice of his sentence.

"Who shall not fear Thee, O Lord, and glorify Thy name? for Thou only art holy: for, all nations shall come and worship before Thee for Thy judgments are made manifest." (*Rev.* 15:4) Every question of truth and error in the long-standing controversy has now been made plain. The results of rebellion, the fruits of setting aside the divine statutes, have been laid open to the view of all created intelligences. The working out of Satan's rule in contrast with the government of God, has been presented to the whole universe. Satan's own works have condemned him. God's wisdom, His justice, and His goodness stand fully vindicated. It is seen that all His dealings in the great controversy have been conducted with respect to the eternal good of His people and the good of all the worlds that He has created. "All Thy works shall praise Thee, O Lord; and Thy saints shall bless Thee." (*Ps.* 145:10) The history of sin will stand to all eternity as a witness that with the existence of God's law is bound up the happiness of all the beings He has created. With all the facts of the great controversy in view the whole universe, both loyal and rebellious, with one accord declare, "Just and true are Thy ways, Thou King of saints."

Before the universe has been clearly presented the great sacrifice made by the Father and the Son in man's behalf. The hour has come when Christ occupies His rightful position, and is glorified above principalities and powers and every name that is named. It was for the joy that was set before Him—that He might bring many sons into glory—that He endured the cross and despised the shame. And inconceivably great as was the sorrow and the shame, yet greater is the joy and the glory. He looks upon the redeemed, renewed in His own image, every heart bearing the perfect impress of the divine, every face reflecting the likeness of their King. He beholds in them the result of the travail of His soul, and He is satisfied. Then, in a voice that reaches the assembled multitudes of the righteous and the wicked, He declares, "Behold the purchase of My blood! For these I suffered; for these I died; that they might dwell in My presence throughout eternal ages." And the song of praise ascends from the white-robed ones about the throne, "Worthy is the Lamb that was slain to receive power, and riches, and wisdom, and strength, and honor, and glory, and blessing." (*Rev.* 5:12)

Notwithstanding that Satan has been constrained to acknowledge God's justice and to bow to the supremacy of Christ, his character remains unchanged. The spirit of rebellion like a mighty torrent again bursts forth. Filled with frenzy, he determines not to yield the great controversy. The time has come for a last desperate struggle against the King of Heaven. He rushes into the midst of his subjects and endeavors to inspire them with his own fury and arose them to instant battle. But of all the countless millions whom he has allured into rebellion, there are none now to acknowledge his supremacy. His power is at an end. The wicked are filled with the same hatred of God that inspires Satan; but they see that their case is hopeless, that they cannot prevail against Jehovah. Their rage is kindled against Satan and those who have been his agents in deception, and with the fury of demons they turn upon them.

Saith the Lord: "Because thou hast set thine heart as the heart of God; behold, therefore I will bring strangers upon thee, the terrible of the nations; and they shall draw their swords against the beauty of thy wisdom, and they shall defile thy brightness. They shall bring thee down to the pit. I will destroy thee, O covering cherub, from the midst of the stones of fire. . . . I will cast thee to the ground. I will lay thee before kings, that they may behold thee. I will bring thee to ashes upon the earth in the sight of all them that behold thee. . . . Thou shalt be a terror, and never shalt thou be any more." (*Eze.* 28:6-8, 16-19)

"Every battle of the warrior is with confused noise, and garments rolled in blood; but this shall be with burning and fuel of fire. The indignation of the Lord is upon all nations, and His fury upon all their armies; He hath utterly destroyed them, He hath delivered them to the slaughter." "Upon the wicked He shall rain quick burning coals, fire and brimstone, and a horrible tempest: this shall be the portion of their cup." (*Isa.* 9:5, 34:2; *Ps.* 11:6, margin) Fire comes down from God out of Heaven. The earth is broken up. The weapons concealed in its depths are drawn forth. Devouring flames burst from every yawning chasm. The very rocks are on fire. "The day has come that shall burn as an oven. The elements melt with fervent heat, the earth also, and the works that are therein are burned up." (*Mal.* 4:1; 2 *Pet.* 3:10) The earth's surface seems one molten mass—a vast, seething lake of fire. It is the time of the judgment and perdition of ungodly men—"the day of the Lord's vengeance, and the year of recompenses for the controversy of Zion." (*Isa.* 34:8; *Prov.* 11:31)

The wicked receive their recompense in the earth. (*Isa.* 34:8; *Prov.* 11:31) They "shall be stubble; and the day that cometh shall burn them up, saith the Lord of hosts." (*Mal.* 4:1) Some are destroyed as in a moment, while others suffer many days. All are punished "according to their deeds." The sins of the righteous having been transferred to Satan, he is made to suffer not only for his own rebellion, but for all the sins which he has caused God's people to commit. His punishment is to be far greater than that of those whom he has deceived. After all have perished who fell by his deceptions, he is still to live and suffer on. In the cleansing flames the wicked are at last destroyed, root and branch—Satan the root, his followers the branches. The full penalty of the law has been visited; the demands of justice have been met; and Heaven and earth, beholding, declare the righteousness of Jehovah.

Satan's work of ruin is forever ended. For six thousand years he has wrought his will, filling the earth with woe and causing grief throughout the universe. The whole creation has groaned and travailed together in pain. Now God's creatures are forever delivered from his presence and temptations. "The whole earth is at rest, and is quiet; they [the righteous] break forth into singing." (*Isa.* 14:7) And a shout of praise and triumph ascends from the whole loyal universe. "The voice of a great multitude, as the voice of many waters, and as the voice of mighty thunderings," is heard, saying, "Alleluia; for the Lord God omnipotent reigneth." (*Rev.* 19:6)

While the earth was wrapped in the fire of destruction, the righteous abode safely in the holy city. Upon those that had part in the first resurrection, the second death has no power. While God is to the wicked a consuming fire, He is to His people both a sun and a shield. (*Rev.* 20:6; *Ps.* 84:11)

"And I saw a new heaven and a new earth; for the first heaven and the first earth were passed away." (*Rev.* 21:1) The fire that consumes the wicked purifies the earth. Every trace of the curse is swept away. No eternally burning hell will keep before the ransomed the fearful consequences of sin.

One reminder alone remains: our Redeemer will ever bear the marks of His crucifixion. Upon His wounded head, upon His side, His hands and feet, are the only traces of the cruel work that sin has wrought. Says the prophet, beholding Christ in His glory, "He had bright beams coming out of His side; and there was the hiding of His power." (*Hab.* 3:4, margin) That pierced side whence flowed the crimson stream that reconciled man to God—there is the Saviour's glory, there "the hiding of

His power." "Mighty to save," through the sacrifice of redemption, He was therefore strong to execute justice upon them that despised God's mercy. And the tokens of His humiliation are His highest honor; through the eternal ages the wounds of Calvary will show forth His praise and declare His power.

"O Tower of the flock, the stronghold of the daughter of Zion, unto thee shall it come, even the first dominion." (*Micah* 4:8) The time has come, to which holy men have looked with longing since the flaming sword barred the first pair from Eden—the time for "the redemption of the purchased possession." (*Eph.* 1:14) The earth originally given to man as his kingdom, betrayed by him into the hands of Satan, and so long held by the mighty foe, has been brought back by the great plan of redemption. All that was lost by sin has been restored. "Thus saith the Lord . . . that formed the earth and made it; he hath established it, he created it not in vain, he formed it to be inhabited." (*Isa.* 45:18) God's original purpose in the creation of the earth is fulfilled as it is made the eternal abode of the redeemed. "The righteous shall inherit the land, and dwell therein forever." (*Ps.* 37:29)

A fear of making the future inheritance seem too material has lead many to spiritualize away the very truths which lead us to look upon it as our home. Christ assured His disciples that He went to prepare mansions for them in the Father's house. Those who accept the teachings of God's Word will not be wholly ignorant concerning the heavenly abode. And yet, "eye hath not seen, nor ear heard, neither have entered into the heart of man, the things which God hath prepared for them that love Him." (1 *Cor.* 2:9) Human language is inadequate to describe the reward of the righteous. It will be known only to those who behold it. No finite mind can comprehend the glory of the Paradise of God.

In the Bible the inheritance of the saved is called a country. (*Heb.* 11:14-16) There the heavenly Shepherd leads His flock to fountains of living waters. The tree of life yields its fruit every month, and the leaves of the tree are for the service of the nations. There are ever-flowing streams, clear as crystal, and beside them waving trees cast their shadows upon the paths prepared for the ransomed of the Lord. There the widespreading plains swell into hills of beauty, and the mountains of God rear their lofty summits. On those peaceful plains beside those living streams God's people, so long pilgrims and wanderers, shall find a home.

"My people shall dwell in a peaceable habitation, and in sure dwellings, and in quiet resting-places. Violence shall no more be heard in thy land, wasting nor destruction within thy borders; but thou shalt call thy walls Salvation, and thy gates Praise. They shall build houses, and inhabit them; and they shall plant vineyards, and eat the fruit of them. They shall not build, and another inhabit; they shall not plant, and another eat: . . . mine elect shall long enjoy the work of their hands." (*Isa.* 32:18; 60:18; 65:21, 22)

There, "the wilderness and the solitary place shall be glad for them; and the desert shall rejoice, and blossom as the rose. Instead of the thorn shall come up the fir-tree, and instead of the brier shall come up the myrtle tree. "The wolf also shall dwell with the lamb, and the leopard shall lie down with the kid; . . . and a little child shall lead them. They shall not hurt nor destroy in all My holy mountain," (*Isa.* 35:1; 55:13; 11:6, 9) saith the Lord.

Pain cannot exist in the atmosphere of Heaven. There will be no more tears, no funeral trains, no badges of mourning. "There shall be no more death, neither sorrow, nor crying, . . . for the former things are passed away." "The inhabitant shall not say, I am sick; the people that dwell therein shall be forgiven their iniquity." (*Rev.* 21:4; *Isa.* 33:24)

There is the New Jerusalem, the metropolis of the glorified new earth, "a crown of glory in the hand of the Lord, and a royal diadem in the hand of thy God." "Her light was like unto a stone most precious, even like a jasper stone, clear as crystal." "The nations of them which are saved shall walk in the light of it; and the kings of the earth do bring their glory and honor into it." Saith the Lord, "I will rejoice in Jerusalem, and joy in My people." "The tabernacle of God is with men, and He will dwell with them, and they shall be His people, and God Himself shall be with them, and be their God." (*Isa.* 62:3; *Rev.* 21:11, 24; *Isa.* 65:19; *Rev.* 21:3)

In the city of God "there shall be no night." None will need or desire repose. There will be no weariness in doing the will of God and offering praise to His name. We shall ever feel the freshness of the morning and shall ever be far from its close. "And they need no candle, neither light of the sun; for the Lord God giveth them light." (*Rev.* 22:5) The light of the sun will be superseded by a radiance which is not painfully dazzling, yet which immeasurably surpasses the brightness of our noontide. The glory of God and the Lamb floods the holy city with unfading light. The redeemed walk in the sunless glory of perpetual day.

"I saw no temple therein; for the Lord God Almighty and the Lamb are the temple of it." (*Rev.* 21:22) The people of God are privileged to hold open communion with the Father and the Son. Now we "see through a glass, darkly." (1 *Cor.* 13:12.) We behold the image of God reflected as in a mirror in the works of nature and in His dealing with men; but then we shall see Him face to face without a dimming veil between. We shall stand in His presence and behold the glory of His countenance.

There the redeemed shall "know, even as also they are known." The loves and sympathies which God Himself has planted in the soul shall there find truest and sweetest exercise. The pure communion with holy beings, the harmonious social life with the blessed angels and with the faithful ones of all ages, who have washed their robes and made them white in the blood of the Lamb, the sacred ties that bind together "the whole family in Heaven and earth" (*Eph.* 3:15)—these help to constitute the happiness of the redeemed.

There, immortal minds will contemplate with never-failing delight the wonders of creative power, the mysteries of redeeming love. There is no cruel, deceiving foe to tempt to forgetfulness of God. Every faculty will be developed, every capacity increased. The acquirement of knowledge will not weary the mind or exhaust the energies. There the grandest enterprises may be carried forward, the loftiest aspirations reached, the highest ambitions realized; and still there will arise new heights to surmount, new wonders to admire, new truths to comprehend, fresh objects to call forth the powers of mind and soul and body.

All the treasures of the universe will be open to the study of God's redeemed. Unfettered by mortality, they wing their tireless flight to worlds afar—worlds that thrilled with sorrow at the spectacle of human woe and rang with songs of gladness at the tidings of a ransomed soul. With unutterable delight the children of earth enter into the joy and the wisdom of unfallen beings. They share the treasures of knowledge and understanding gained through ages upon ages in contemplation of God's handiwork. With undimmed vision they gaze upon the glory of creation—suns and stars and systems, all in their appointed order circling the throne of Deity. Upon all things, from the least to the greatest, the Creator's name is written, and in all are the riches of His power displayed.

And the years of eternity, as they roll, will bring richer and still more glorious revelations of God and of Christ. As knowledge is progressive, so will love, reverence, and happiness increase. The more men learn of God, the greater will be their admiration of His character. As Jesus opens before them the riches of redemption and the amazing achievements in the great controversy with Satan, the hearts of the ransomed thrill with more fervent devotion, and with more rapturous joy they sweep the harps of gold; and ten thousand times ten thousand and thousands of thousands of voices unite to swell the mighty chorus of praise.

"And every creature which is in Heaven, and on the earth, and under the earth, and such as are in the sea, and all that are in them, heard I saying, Blessing, and honor, and glory, and power, be unto Him that sitteth upon the throne, and unto the Lamb forever and ever." (*Rev.* 5:13)

The great controversy is ended. Sin and sinners are no more. The entire universe is clean. One pulse of harmony and gladness beats through the vast creation. From Him who created all, flow life and light and gladness, throughout the realms of illimitable space. From the minutest atom to the greatest world, all things, animate and inanimate, in their unshadowed beauty and perfect joy, declare that God is Love.

This is only part of the larger book—*The Great Controversy.* You will want to send for it in order to make a complete study of these dynamic themes.

Other Paperbacks by the Same Author

THE GREAT CONTROVERSY, 576 pages $3.00 postpaid
This masterful volume reveals the
ultimate plan of God for mankind,
the authoritative answer to the
confusion and despair of this tense age.

HEALTH AND HAPPINESS, 384 pages $2.50 postpaid
Dealing with the physical, the
mental, and the spiritual in our
nature, it describes in a practical
way how to experience the
most in life.

EL CAMINO A CRISTO, 90 pages $1.00 postpaid
(Spanish Steps to Christ)

EL GRAN CONFLICTO, 608 pages $3.00 postpaid
(Spanish Great Controversy)

PATRIARCHS AND PHOPHETS, 656 pages $3.00 postpaid
An authentic history of the beginning
of our world and the conflict between
truth and error through past ages.

DESIRE OF AGES, 735 pages $3.00 postpaid
The best commentary on the life and
teachings of Christ.

THE GREATEST LOVE, 90 pages $1.00 postpaid
Same text as Steps to Christ with a
new title and a beautiful new cover.

IN THE BEGINNING, 90 pages $1.00 postpaid
An inspired account of the beginning
of our world and the first centuries
of its existence.

STEPS TO CHRIST, 90 pages $1.00 postpaid
This little gem tells how you can
enjoy a life of happiness in Christ.

Inspiration Books
P.O. Box 8249
Phoenix, Ariz. 85066